A
WELL-KNOWN
EXCELLENCE

I have always said, although I am an infantryman, that in my opinion the arm of the service which did most to win the last war was the Royal Regiment of Artillery.

Lieutenant-General Sir Brian Horrocks

The British artillery demonstrated once again its well-known excellence. Especially noteworthy was its great mobility and speed of reaction to the requirements of the assault troops.

Field Marshal Erwin Rommel

The artillery fire has been superb and such concentrated use of artillery has not been seen before in N. Africa; we could not have done what we have done without the artillery, and that arm has been wonderful.

Field Marshal Bernard Montgomery

A
WELL-KNOWN
EXCELLENCE

**British Artillery and an Artilleryman
in World War Two**

DENIS FALVEY

BRASSEY'S

To the memory of my former comrades,
alive or dead, of the 64th Medium Regiment,
Royal Artillery

First published in 2002 by Brassey's

A member of **Chrysalis** Books plc

Brassey's
64 Brewery Road, London N7 9NT

North American orders:
Books International, PO Box 960, Herndon, VA 20172, USA

Denis Falvey has asserted his moral right
to be identified as the author of this work.

Library of Congress Cataloging in Publication Data available

British Library cataloguing in Publication Data
A catalogue record for this book is available
from the British Library

ISBN 1 85753 312 7

All photos courtesy Chrysalis Images and Imperial War Museum.

Edited and designed by DAG Publications Ltd
Printed in Great Britain.

CONTENTS

PREFACE

T he excellence of the British artillery in World War Two was acknowledged by friend and foe alike, as both Rommel – whose description is used as this book's title – and Montgomery bear witness. Many believe it was the decisive arm in British land combat, wielding enormous, discriminate power with great flexibility. It was dominated by the superbly designed, ubiquitous 25-pounder field gun. The medium gun, though inferior in numbers, provided much greater range and weight of shell.

The 64th Medium Regiment was the finest and most experienced medium calibre unit in the British Army and exemplified the excellence noted by others. Its eventful odyssey provides the narrative framework for describing the life of the artilleryman in World War Two: the leadership role of the officers, especially in locating and engaging targets; the unique professional function of the surveyor-specialist; the faithful, dedicated and muscular effort of the gunners. The history of the 64th also provides the background for discussion of some fundamental related questions.

The ways of the artillery are mysterious to many so I have given, in Chapters 4 and 9, a description of the art and practice of the British artillery of all field calibres in the mid-twentieth century. This formed the basis of a talk I gave at the Royal Military Academy Sandhurst in September 2000, and the details have not yet, I believe, been available to the public. These principles, of course, apply to all contemporary artilleries.

This book encompasses the complete life-cycle of the 64th Medium Regiment from its birth as a Territorial Army unit, with two hours a week at a London Drill Hall, to its fading away into the mists of demobilisation. The regiment, by extraordinary chance, participated in virtually every campaign in the Mediterranean and Western theatres of the Second World War, as the Contents list shows, and for some time after the fall of

Tobruk was literally indispensable, as it became one of only two remaining medium regiments. This was recognised by the unusual honour of a ceremonial inspection by Winston Churchill in February 1943.

Descriptions are given of the campaigns in Greece and Crete, the struggles in the desert culminating in the battle of Alamein followed by the taking of Tripoli, the breaching of the Gabes gap, and the capture of Tunis, and the Sicilian campaign. The artillery function in the Normandy campaign is described, capped by an account of our unique, and much praised, role in support of the airborne division at Arnhem. Then, in quick succession followed participation in the Ardennes battle, the culminating victory of the Reichswald and the breaching of the formidable, and flooded, Siegfried Line, before crossing the Rhine to final victory. So long and varied was our experience that a record of it amounts virtually to a history of the land war (other than the Far East) from the artillery point of view. The reader may find such a vantage point refreshing. In addition there is discussion of a number of important issues, e.g. the wisdom of using experienced, but resentful, troops for the invasion.

Like many in the Eighth Army, we suffered grievously from the incompetence of Commander-in-Chief Claude Auchinleck, a man in total confusion, holding mutually contradictory strategic ideas, who was unable to handle armour correctly and refused expert advice when it was offered to him. This matter is so critical that I have considered it at some length, so its treatment here differs from that of other matters in the rest of the book. In this connection I have found the recently published *War Diaries* of Field Marshal Lord Alanbrooke (June 2001) most helpful.

Memory is fallible, and for much of the detail in this book I have relied on a troop war diary I was asked to keep from 15 June 1942 until the end of the Sicilian campaign on 9 September 1943.

I am greatly indebted to Jenny Picton for her professional advice and skill in turning my manuscript into a presentable form.

It is difficult to express my deep gratitude to Laurie Milner for his generous help and advice. I can truly say that without his support this book would not have been published; this is a debt I can never repay.

BEGINNINGS

War was looming fast in 1939. The appeasing government of Neville Chamberlain ensured that when the inevitable happened Britain would be pitifully unprepared. Nor could the opposition escape opprobrium; the Lansburyites were convinced pacifists. The position in France was even worse; the Third Republic was socially divided, confused and lacked clear leadership, and the Maginot Line had not been extended to the sea. Thus two palsied governments faced the threat from Hitler, who was not going to be deterred and who had out-trumped them in their feeble and half-hearted diplomatic attempts to involve the USSR. Freed from the nightmare menace of a war on two fronts, Hitler quietly and efficiently prepared to knock out the two 'effete democracies' of Britain and France. With his temporary ally, Stalin, he carved up the corpse of Poland, precipitating the war. Nevertheless, belatedly, some measures of re-armament had been taken in Britain, notably the design and development of fighter aircraft and radar.

By the spring of 1939 realism was beginning to assert itself, and when the British government announced it was doubling the size of the Territorial Army (TA) to some 300,000 men, the response was immediate. Most volunteers were stirred by simple patriotism; they had seen through the deceit of appeasement and knew the country was in mortal peril. Others were attracted by a sense of adventure, or simply by the contagious example of friends. For the more politically minded, voluntary enlistment in this reserve army helped to expunge the shame of the betrayal of Czechoslovakia.

I did not feel destined to be an infantryman. I had, however, heard graphic accounts of the artillery in the 1914–18 war and knew from reading many books that the artillery had been the decisive arm – inflicting far more casualties than any other weapon including the dreaded machine-gun. So a gunner I would be.

In Offord Road, Islington, in north central London, there was a TA drill hall which was the headquarters of the 53rd Medium Regiment, Royal Artillery (RA), a Territorial unit and relic of the 1914–18 war. The doubling of the TA was to be effected very simply by each existing TA regiment throwing off a second-line regiment (in our case the 64th Medium Regiment, RA) for which it would provide a small training cadre of officers and NCOs. The TA man attended his local drill hall for two hours on one night a week, usually followed by a lengthy session in the bar.

We were an ordinary cross-section of people: van-boys, clerks, coster-mongers, lorry drivers and a host of others. We reported at the drill hall in April 1939, filled in a form and saw the recruiting-sergeant. He noticed that I, like many others, had left the space for 'religion' blank. He told me this was unacceptable; you could not join the army without stating a religion. I considered one or two bizarre possibilities but thought the sergeant would not be amused, so I told him, which was true, that I did not have a religion. 'Oh, that's alright,' he said, 'we always call people like you C of E.' Accordingly, with that obstacle so simply removed, I was duly enrolled.

The 64th attended the drill hall on a different night from its parent regiment. We came after work in our ordinary clothes, because naturally no uniforms were available. The officers (many were bankers, stockbrokers, or 'something in the City') had the daunting task of sorting out this mass of some six hundred men according to some sort of coherent principle. They chose educational attainment as the criterion. Most of the recruits had had an elementary school education and had left school at 14 or 15, but there was a seasoning of former secondary or grammar schoolboys. There were some forty of these to be divided mainly between the two batteries (211th and 212th). The educated ones were a mixed, reasonably articulate lot in my battery, including one middle-aged fully qualified practising architect and one graduate (myself).

The division of the rump was not so simple. The bulk of the toughest men were to be gunners because a strong physique was essential for manhandling guns and ammunition. Some of the brighter and more literate were selected as signallers, drivers as drivers, and mechanics as mechanics or artificers. These allocations were inevitably provisional and were modified in the light of experience.

Because Britain had stumbled into war in such a woeful state of preparation, our regiment, like all the other newly formed TA regiments, was totally lacking in equipment. The sixteen guns of the 53rd (6in howitzers of 1914–18 vintage) were available to the gunners for gun drill. (The crew was ten men, including driver, to a gun). Week after week they lugged these great things around, because the whole carriage had to be moved to right or left to engage targets outside the limits of the traversing gear. They were instructed in the loading procedure, and for the brighter ones, gun-laying, which needed the ability to read a simple optical gunsight and range-setting dial. Instruction was also given to everyone in the formalised type of fire orders. The signallers were given lectures and the loan of a few telephone sets and lengths of wire from the 53rd's stores.

The ex-secondary schoolboys became 'specialists', and we soon felt ourselves to be an 'elite', not as a result of intellectual snobbery, but simply because we came to recognise that we were to be the 'professionals', the practitioners of the art of gunnery, and if need be, would have to deputise for an officer. We had a sergeant who had been transferred as part of the training cadre. He was a typical Cockney and had a modest education, but had overcome that disadvantage, was intelligent and knew his subject thoroughly. During our brief training sessions in the short period remaining before the outbreak of war he managed to inculcate in us some sense of what it was we were supposed to be doing, i.e. a knowledge of simple surveying techniques. With two or three borrowed 'directors' (a simplified form of theodolite) we were shown how to align the needle and lay a line on a given bearing from the 'grid north' of the Ordnance Survey maps (requiring a correction for the deviation from magnetic north). On fine evenings we would go to the nearby Highbury Fields, set up our directors on their tripods and practise by reading off the bearings of prominent features such as church steeples. We also did this using the other directors as if they were dummy gunsights, to which we would pass the complementary angle for the back bearing so that all were parallel and pointing to the same direction.

We were also inducted into the mysteries of the 'artillery board' – a metre square of linen-backed paper, with gridded squares on a scale of 1 to 25,000. It was, in effect, a blank map on which gun position and targets could be plotted using map references. A special pivot was used marking the position of the No. 1, or pivot gun, to which an arm, calibrated in yards, and an arc, in degrees and minutes could be attached. Thus the situation on the ground could be precisely mimicked. Obviously, our knowledge from these weekly sessions remained extremely rudimentary for some time.

By early summer some brown dungarees, forage caps, belts and boots had arrived so that our group of miscellaneous civilians looked a bit more uniform for our weekly reunions. In July we were supplied with battledress, just in time for the regiment's first and only TA training camp.

This took place in August at Beaulieu in Hampshire. We were accommodated in bell tents pitched on peaty soil. It had recently rained heavily and we were literally lying in water, so duckboards were issued enabling us to sleep a few inches above the water level. We now had two whole weeks of training, a luxury, indeed, compared with our meagre weekly allowance.

We progressed rapidly. There was adequate loaned equipment, even if some of it was out of date. We went map-reading, improved our use of the director and artillery board and did some plane-tabling (fixing position on a board by aligning on distant objects). We familiarised ourselves with the routines of fire orders and fire control. Meanwhile our colleagues sweated over the guns, or laid telephone wires and sent messages, and were introduced to wireless communication. There were frequent lectures. During the second week we were a little more ambitious and carried out some modest exercises. Positions would be reconnoitred, people had to find their way by map reference, we surveyed-in, guns were moved and we carried out dummy firing. Each group gained familiarity with its own function but it was the first time we had essayed a more comprehensive, co-ordinated operation. Obviously there was a lot to learn before we became a team, and inevitably there were failures and some frustration, which we relieved by evenings spent carousing at the local hostelries.

Our amateur soldiering soon ended and we resumed civilian life – but not for long! The tragic farce of Anglo–Soviet discussions abruptly ended with the announcement of the Nazi–Soviet Pact. To almost everyone, except the editor of the *Daily Express*, who headlined 'There will be No War', it seemed obvious that war was not only inevitable, but imminent. Whitehall buildings were sandbagged, trenches were dug in the London parks and preparations advanced for the evacuation of schoolchildren. We were mobilised and an officer called at the home of every specialist to ensure instant compliance when we returned from work. We were embodied on 1 September and next day the regiment was locked in an elementary school near our drill hall – our only entertainment the banter through the railings with the local girls. On 3 September Chamberlain made the declaration of war in quixotic response to the rape of Poland and our treaty obligations.

The regiment could obviously not remain cooped up in such unsatisfactory conditions and after a few days our group of civilians in uniform was moved to Edgware, the terminus of the Northern Line of the Underground. We were lined up in the road about a mile east of the town in a new suburb and were detailed off in parties of five to a typical three-bedroom semi-detached house of the period. The householders evidently expected us and were presumably being paid a billeting fee. The sitting room had been requisitioned for our use and emptied of furniture. Our bedrolls were placed against the wainscot and only unrolled at night. The owners had no responsibility for providing food – for this a local hall had been requisitioned. Generally the arrangements worked well; the troops treated the property and the women with respect and our hosts felt they were 'doing their bit'.

Life was terribly frustrating for us. Our uniforms were the only military symbol we had. Even the minimal equipment which had been available from our parent regiment was now denied; the 53rd was busy with its preparations for France. All we had were lectures and, for the specialists, the shared use of the invaluable artillery training manual. One activity available to all was the routemarch – invaluable in toughening us up but of no use as artillery training. Being a Cockney regiment most of the men were very near home and could slip away at evenings and weekends, but most people spent their evenings in a local pub or cinema, or wenching.

As an index of our desperation, even Sunday church parade began to seem like a diversion. However, because it was compulsory, the parade was greatly disliked. I remembered that I had been brought up as a nominal Roman Catholic, and made this known, for the dozen or so RCs were permitted to go to mass and so avoided the C of E formal parade. (The fact that I had been enrolled as C of E seemed to have been forgotten.) However, our little group was disrespectful to its faith. Someone usually produced a pack of cards and we sat well back in the empty part of the church for a quiet game. When we emerged afterwards there were admiring glances for those splendid fellows willing to give all for their faith and country. None of my colleagues seemed to feel the slightest embarrassment or pangs of conscience that we were such a disgusting clutch of hypocrites. Perhaps no-one else sensed the incongruity.

That Britain was almost wholly unprepared for war is well known. We – the newly raised regiments – experienced this lack of preparation in the waste, the humiliation and the frustration we felt. Finally, after a month or two some civilian vehicles were requisitioned and my group had the use of a small 15 hundredweight truck with *Jones, the Fishmonger* prominently displayed on its sides. At least we now had some mobility. We went into the countryside around Elstree and Boreham Wood with our Ordnance Survey maps and practised map-reading and fixing our positions. It was not much but it helped keep us sane and give some relief from the interminable routemarches and lectures.

Early in the New Year we bade farewell to our Edgware friends and moved to Berkhamsted, some miles to the north-west. Here one could first begin to sense that our de-civilianisation was beginning to take effect. A corporate identity was being established; we were billeted in empty buildings, not with civilians; there was a properly functioning cookhouse; battery and regimental HQs were set up. Some old 6in howitzers arrived, our very own! We were able to establish a gun park. There were a few rifles; guards could be mounted. The gunners got in plenty of gun drill. Vehicles arrived; we could do small scale exercises. More survey and signal equipment became available. The equipment was old, even obsolescent, but there was enough to begin seriously to improve our professional standards. Yet civilian life went on all around us; we formed friendships and frequented the local pubs, sometimes to excess.

Something seemed very strange, almost sinister, about those early 'phoney' months of the war. We were permitted to proceed with our preparations undisturbed. There was no fighting of any consequence in France, no battle of the Marne. The complacent Chamberlain was so deceived by this lull, solely attributable to Hitler's generals' need to perfect their plans and preparations, that he made the asinine remark at a party conference (2 April 1940) that Hitler 'had missed the bus'. He very soon received a most brusque and unpleasant shock: the storm broke. A blitz attack on Norway, involving a farcical and confused attempt to deny Germany iron ore supplies, was rapidly followed by the blitzkrieg on Holland, Belgium and France. Hitler's 'bus' had arrived at Dunkirk, St. Valéry-en-Caux, Calais.

By this time the regiment had moved to High Wycombe and was accommodated on a large country estate so that at last the whole unit was on one site. The house was taken over as Regimental Headquarters and officers' mess. Army life became more all-embracing, even in sanitation: no longer the civilised WC for us – we dug latrines in the sandy soil.

It was at Wycombe that the terrible news from the Continent broke and it was with profound relief that the nation learned that Winston Churchill was to become prime minister and minister of defence. Almost everyone welcomed the stronger hand at the helm and many remembered his Cassandra-like warnings of earlier years. These stark events added extra zest to our preparations. We acquired some Canadian Ross rifles (of the last war, but nevertheless welcome). Still more important, our complement of vehicles was being brought up to strength and the new AEC gun tractor replaced our old Scammells. The new vehicle was much more comfortable for the crew. Their gear fitted in well, it could carry ammunition for immediate use, and had a powerful winch. Most important of all, the old howitzers were withdrawn in favour of a long-barrelled 60-pounder, which was essentially a naval gun mounted on a carriage. This was also a weapon of 1914–18 vintage but the disadvantage of the lighter shell (the 6in howitzer fired a 100lb shell) was outweighed by longer range.

Our next base was at Tetbury in Gloucestershire, where our training and exercises continued apace. While there we had to look after a few 'bomb-happy' men from the British Expeditionary Force who needed a period of quiet in military surroundings to recuperate. Queen Mary, who was staying at Badminton, came over to talk to them: it was all very informal and she helped to restore their morale.

The Battle of Britain was proceeding fiercely throughout the summer of 1940 and the danger of invasion was always present. The whole of southern England was thought to be vulnerable and the regiment moved to Herringswell, a small village in Norfolk. From there we established a position to bring down fire on Mildenhall aerodrome in the event of German parachute or glider landings. We had an observation post in the tower of a church which commanded a good view of the aerodrome and its surrounding buildings and hangars. At this point we had never fired our guns.

In late summer it became clear there was no immediate danger of invasion and the War Office thought it time we were brought up to fighting pitch by completing our training. We had all fired a few rounds on the butts with Lee-Enfield rifles but we had never fired our guns, the whole reason for our military existence. So, our orders were to go to Otterburn in Redesdale, Northumberland, a lonely and empty stretch of country where the army maintained a firing range, for a two-week course, the peak of an artillery regiment's training. It was also an opportunity to 'calibrate' the guns i.e. ensure they were shooting accurately to range.

The proceedings were controlled by Inspectors of Gunnery (IGs) who acted as examiners, referees and general staff. At first the guns were fired from prepared positions to give the gunners, and everyone else, their first experience of firing live shells. We had to get used to the noise, the shock of the recoil and the smooth recovery to the next firing position which resulted from the work of the buffer-recuperator (an oil-filled hydraulic system). Then things became more ambitious. The IGs issued operation orders. 'Enemy' positions were indicated, gun positions and observation posts (OPs) located by map reference and manned. Communications were established, fire orders were passed and targets engaged. For the first time we had adequate space to deploy all the guns of our two batteries and operate as a fully co-ordinated unit. Moreover, we were living rough, as we would under active service conditions. At last we felt this was something like the real thing. Only later did we come to realise that although good training was crucially important, the only training which ultimately counted was real battle experience. No exercises could simulate the 'feel' of the actual presence of the enemy; enduring his fire and suffering casualties. Our firing camp still left us without experience of being part of a whole much larger than a mere regiment.

At the end of the proceedings the IGs had their usual inquest with the officers, and although there had been a few hiccups we were judged to have passed the test. We were considered fit for service overseas.

The slow return journey south now began. Such a large-scale military movement has a training value. In particular, as the Luftwaffe had been so dominant in the skies of France, it was prudent to get used to good road discipline and the keeping of proper intervals between vehicles. The regiment therefore occupied a great length of road, which was a nuisance to other road users. There were often delays, especially in towns, in spite of the co-operation of the military police and our use of despatch riders.

Our final destination before embarkation was Little Marlow in the Thames valley. We were billeted in the manor house and services were held for us in the adjoining church. Since no-one could play the organ I volunteered, although I was only a modest pianist with no experience of organ pedals, so my deep bass was somewhat tentative and infrequent. This arrangement meant that I had to have time to practise and this involved two of my friends to pump the thing. We nearly had a disaster at one service when I noticed the 'tell-tale' rising ominously, indicating that the air supply was getting low, while clouds of cigarette smoke were emerging from the organ loft. I hissed a warning just in time and the air supply was restored.

The country seemed particularly beautiful that autumn and the thought of leaving home had some poignancy. However, we had volunteered for a job and were anxious to get on with it. Strictly speaking, no-one knew our destination, but the Middle East was the only active theatre of war; we had been issued with 'coal-scuttle' sun helmets and khaki drill, and had received our full quota of injections, so we drew the obvious conclusion. (The 'coal-scuttle' helmet had a small front brim, high peak and sloping rear, protecting the neck. It was heavy and uncomfortable.) After a final leave our guns and vehicles departed and we began what seemed an interminable and uncomfortable journey in a blacked-out train to Glasgow.

In November 1940 we embarked on the P & O liner *Otranto*, c.25,000 grt, which was serving as a troopship. The officers, nurses and women's services had cabins, the men were below decks. I am a good sailor but was not prepared to share the fetor below. Although there was already a touch of winter in the Scottish air I was determined to sleep on deck. I never regretted this decision and after a few days others joined me. By the time we reached warmer climes there were few who did not sleep on deck.

I had never before been to Scotland but as the great convoy assembled off Dunoon the surrounding hills seemed very beautiful with purple and gold blending in the mellow light of late autumn. It was dark when we sailed and each day we viewed the sea empty of everything except the convoy and its escort stretching wide to the horizon. We watched the water creaming in our wake and from the paravanes taut on each quarter, hopefully to deal with any mines. The voyage was uneventful except for one thing: it was enlivened by the presence of the 1st/2nd Australian Machine Gun Battalion, a splendid body of men, none of whom seemed under six feet tall. They played 'two up' interminably and were inveterate gamblers. On one occasion a man dropped his mess-tin and in a flash some wit had betted on which side it would fall. Since those in authority seemed to think the war would be a repeat of the last one, a few Australian troops had already reached the 'Old Country', but after the invasion scare had passed the futility of this was apparent. These men were being re-directed to where they were really needed and would emulate the glorious exploits of their preceding generation.

The voyage was, however, undoubtedly boring and was hardly relieved by boat drill and the ship's library. (It was illuminating to discover the taste in books of liner passengers – primarily romantic novels of the most popular variety.) One break in the monotony was provided by one of our number, quite a gifted pianist. The ship had still retained its grand piano and we enjoyed some excellent concerts of the popular classics, of which our colleague had a goodly repertoire. On arrival in Egypt he was promptly snapped up by Forces Radio and so left the regiment.

It was with relief that we reached Freetown in West Africa, reputed to be hot, steamy and unhealthy. We took on water and fresh vegetables. Many small boats paddled out to sell their wares, mainly melons and there was much good-humoured banter. We were all, including the many nurses aboard, enjoying this animated and novel scene when some wag, probably an Australian, threw a condom into the boat of a strapping fellow in his late teens. He looked at the packet curiously, and with much coarse encouragement, opened it. He gazed at the contents with blank incomprehension but the wags on the ship were not to be disappointed. There ensued a hilarious pantomime to make the purpose of the thing clear. At last the young man appreciated the purpose of his gift and his face wreathed in smiles. The final act, of course, was to persuade him to put the damned thing on, which he duly did with a great grin to roars of applause from his male and female audience. It was good to feel that we were bringing the benefits of Western civilisation to those less fortunate than ourselves!

A further distraction was provided by our medical officer, a grave gentlemanly figure, a specialist paediatrician in civil life, who was greatly liked and respected. He gave a talk to warn us of the dangers of VD (and that it was an offence to contract it). For the benefit of any innocents, although there cannot have been many, he also described some details of the female anatomy.

Our next port of call was Durban, one of the most British of South African cities. During our four-day stay the British element could not do enough for us. We could get a free lunch (or perhaps there was a nominal charge – at this late stage I cannot remember) at the luxury Prince Edward Hotel on the front, near the snake park. There were soldiers' clubs everywhere and free car rides to famous beauty spots like the Valley of the Thousand Hills, notable for its fruit. Yet one could sense that South Africa, although so well endowed, was not a happy country. The gulf between the black 'have nots' and the white 'haves' was immense. I still remember the shock I felt when I saw on a park bench a notice 'For persons of European descent only'.

We had a vivid reminder also of how bitter memories of the Boer War still poisoned relationships. A great gala concert was held for the troops at the Town Hall. It was generally well received by the British and Afrikaaner audience and by the troops themselves. At the end, however, there was a patriotic tableau, complete with Britannia with helmet and shield and music of the 'pomp and circumstance' variety. As if by a secret signal the Afrikaaner audience at once walked out, deliberately causing as much noise and disturbance as possible. Only the British remained for the national anthem. So strong was the feeling of the extremist Boers, the Broederbond, that they hoped for (and expected) an Axis victory. General Smuts certainly had his work cut out.

Our voyage northward continued. We entered the Red Sea; it was hot and hardly an appropriate setting for traditional Christmas fare, but we enjoyed it and were appreciative. So we approached journey's end, the Gulf of Suez and the Canal, fresh, eager and full of expectations for the new world we were to discover and for the tasks which lay ahead.

EGYPT AND CYRENAICA

We disembarked at El Kantara, part way up the canal. The ship seemed trapped and dominated the flat, desert landscape. We were glad to be free of her constricting presence and to be at the threshold of new experiences. Yet we were not ungrateful to the ship and her crew, nor the gallant escort which had brought us safely to our destination.

There is a definite smell about Africa, about Egypt – elusive, mysterious, unforgettable. We stood in groups while men in long galabiyehs sold us leather goods. I bought a wallet of traditional design stamped all over with ancient hieroglyphics. It served me well. Then there were the *gulli-gulli* men producing small chicks from their sleeves and the ears and noses of our bewildered but happy men.

We were going by train to Cairo and we climbed aboard with our light gear – the heavy stuff was going separately. There were huge sliding doors to let in the light (and dust). As there were no sanitary facilities we had to relieve ourselves over the side.

Our camp exceeded our most romantic expectations: it was at the foot of the great pyramids of Cheops and Chephren. Nearby was the Mena House Hotel, at the end of the long tramline to the city centre. We came to know this line well. Occasionally, when we had a late night out, we had to walk all the way back to camp, which was quite a few miles. Everywhere in the camp the presence of India and the Raj seemed to be looming. Our tents were large, bungalow types from Bangalore. There were dhobi-wallahs who would wash khaki drill, dry and iron it in less than three hours and have it ready for you. There were no steam irons, merely great museum pieces, but the dhobi-wallah filled his mouth with water and unerringly directed a stream towards his iron, resulting in clouds of hissing water vapour. There were also native fruit sellers in tiny kiosks, who would dip all purchases in a weak solution of Condy's fluid (permanganate of potash) as a protection against fly-borne diseases. A few wooden huts served for administration, messes and dining halls. The only other structures were ablution benches and latrines.

Raw troops in tropical kit were fit subjects only for music-hall jokes. We looked, and felt, ridiculous. The authorities were terrified their charges would contract heatstroke, so we always had to wear 'coal-scuttle' helmets in the heat of the day, and the buttoned-up portions of our shorts had to be turned down to protect our delicate knees. How it was possible for our authorities to rule a country like Egypt for generations and persist in believing in a myth like that of sunstroke defies explanation. The helmets, which were heavy, were soon replaced by light pith topees, and these, in turn, soon disappeared in favour of the familiar forage cap. The comic shorts were also replaced by more modern ones, with the result that we looked and felt much smarter. On active service in the desert many men went further, particularly those of dark complexion, and were bare to the waist, with perhaps a handkerchief to protect the back of the neck. Hats were rarely worn in action. Winston Churchill commented on the extraordinary longevity of the sunstroke myth and how rapidly it was abandoned without any ill effects

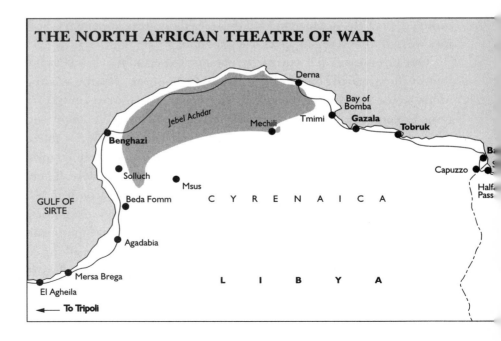

THE NORTH AFRICAN THEATRE OF WAR

whatsoever. (There may, however, be long-term effects such as keratosis and skin cancer from over-exposure to the sun.)

While at Mena we performed a rather pointless exercise by taking a director to the top of the pyramid of Cheops to carry out some survey work. The alabaster casing of the pyramid had long since been removed so that the climb required some energy to mount the stepped blocks to the top. There was, however, a sentimental purpose because the summit of this pyramid had played a classic role as a 'trig' point in army survey history. We gained a rather unusual distinction from this exercise. No-one could say we were not keen.

Many of us developed a decided liking for Cairo. After a long spell in the desert a few days' leave seemed very heaven. Money was plentiful because pay had accumulated. The jangling bells of the trams seemed permanently in action and so had little warning value. Shoe-shine boys were everywhere, even invading the trams. If boots were not as clean as might be many submitted to the blandishments of these delightful but over-persistent urchins. There were also magnificent boot- and shoe-shine emporia where one sat grandly on a raised dais and submitted to the skilled ministrations of what almost seemed to be acolytes carrying

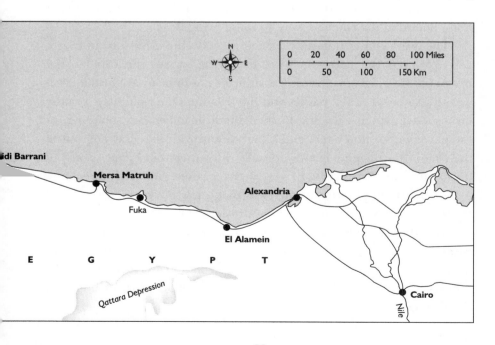

out religious rites. Every other shop seemed to be a barber's and one emerged reeking of scent and brilliantine, unless very strong minded. Bars and cafés abounded, almost invariably run by Greeks. It was *de rigueur* for them to display a picture of King George of the Hellenes and the national flag. We were always welcome, not merely as patrons, but as allies. Mussolini had delivered an insulting ultimatum to Greece on 28 October, which the Greeks had at once contemptuously rejected. The day they said 'No!' is immortalised as Ochi (Greek for No) Day. As a consequence they were at war with the Italians, who were getting the worst of it in Albania after their invasion was repulsed. We also, of course, were at war with Italy, who, hoping to profit from the French collapse, was in a position to invade Egypt without fear of the French in Tunisia.

Many of us had tea or coffee and delicious pastries in Groppi's, which, for some inexplicable reason, was not out of bounds to ordinary soldiers, even though there we would rub shoulders with pashas and their exquisitely dressed women, and with our officers, who commonly escorted British girls, usually from the nursing services. The open-air cinemas were a delight; one could see the fireflies dancing iridescently in the projector beam. It was only later that I realised what a source of noise pollution the cinemas were to those living near.

The army concentrated on having a good time in European Cairo. Few explored the native quarter, the great bazaar, the Citadel, the mosques, the museums. But it was difficult not to be aware of the great wealth gap between the pashas and the fellahin. One would see wealthy tarbushed Egyptians passing in their limousines beggars squatting on the pavements, often blind with bilharzia and with flies crawling out of their mouths. (Begging is now officially discouraged in Egypt.) Some of us, in our quest for diversion, were aware of these underlying realities. A particularly unpleasant feature was that a few of our men displayed racist tendencies and acted boorishly, ordering Egyptians off the pavements with such remarks as 'Get out of my way, you black bastard'. To witness the hatred and resentment in the eyes of those so addressed was a step towards understanding the depth of nationalist feeling and the approach of the dissolution of western, particularly British imperial, dominance.

Prior to our arrival Marshal Graziani had concentrated his forces on the Egyptian–Libyan frontier and had advanced ponderously and cautiously along the coast with a large force, meeting only light harassment on his way to Sidi Barrani. The Italian radio broadcast that there 'the trams were still running'! Intimidated by the presence of the main British defences at Mersa Matruh, his advance ground to a halt in September 1940. Graziani established a number of fortified camps or 'boxes' running south some fifty miles from the coast. This was an enticing situation for a British counterstroke.

The army had had many peacetime years to ponder the defence of Egypt. The desert offered the freedom to manoeuvre, which, to a power with a long naval tradition, naturally suggested an outflanking movement. Since Matruh was not far from GHQ, Lieutenant-General Sir Richard O'Connor, in command of the Western Desert Force, was able to co-ordinate his plans with the Commander-in-Chief of the Middle Eastern Forces, General Sir Archibald Wavell. O'Connor decided to move secretly at night. His small, highly professional force took up advanced positions before attacking points in the enemy defences from the rear. The operation opened on 9 December 1940 and was brilliantly successful. The Italians were routed, two corps were destroyed and much booty taken. The threat to Egypt had been removed and the small desert army had achieved complete moral ascendancy. In spite of supply difficulties O'Connor decided to continue the advance into Libya.

Meanwhile, it was judged that our period of acclimatisation was nearing its end. It was an indication of Wavell's great shortage of resources, particularly of medium guns, that one of our eight-gun batteries (the 212th) was sent to Abyssinia, while my battery (the 211th) was to join O'Connor's westward advance. No more gentle blooding of a 'green' unit could be imagined. To have one's first engagement against a broken and demoralised enemy was good fortune indeed, although at the time we did not fully appreciate it. Later, as the war progressed we saw many times the dreadful results of the first engagements of 'green', albeit well-trained, troops against tough, well-disciplined German opposition.

With our obsolescent 60-pounder guns, we moved rapidly forward along the coast road, soon to become so familiar to us. O'Connor had crossed the frontier and cut the road to the west of Bardia, which soon fell with a further haul of prisoners, vehicles and booty. Meanwhile, the 7th Armoured Division (the 'Desert Rats') advanced towards Tobruk and quickly surrounded it (7 January 1941).

My battery had now reached the scene of operations. From a position on extremely rocky ground south-east of Tobruk we could see black smoke rising from a ship in the harbour, said to be a bombed Italian warship. It was essential to take the port because of our supply problem – our railhead at Mersa Matruh was becoming increasingly distant. Tobruk's defences were formidable, but longer than those at Bardia, and after the Italians' recent heavy losses they could not properly be manned. Early on the morning of 21 January, we and the field artillery opened up and we had the satisfaction of at last engaging the enemy. No more exercises – this was the real thing. We had two OPs well up with the infantry, which very soon penetrated the perimeter and the few remaining 'I' tanks and cruisers broke through. By next day it was all over. The 7th Armoured Division had already had the order to advance further west towards Mechili.

We had joined Western Desert Force, and the experience of working within a formation was invaluable. Units do not normally operate on their own: good co-ordination and full integration were the keys to success. In a short period the group had achieved a string of victories against a far more numerous foe. Our small desert army, largely of regular soldiers, was experienced and exceptionally well trained, with extraordinarily high morale and confidence in its general and his staff. It was a combination not to be seen again until Montgomery took over the Eighth Army. The atmosphere was infectious. It affected us; we felt immense pride in joining this elite force. We had performed our modest task with reasonable competence and efficiency and had suffered no casualties. War seemed a glorious adventure, almost a desirable way of life. But our induction had been very gentle: we were soon to be enlightened!

While still at Tobruk we inspected an Italian encampment. Each man had made a small personal dug-out, with a groundsheet for a roof. The wind was already silting them up. They were littered with small melancholy personal mementoes, family photographs and so on, and in many, particularly those of the officers, there was an overwhelming smell of cheap scent. Nearby was the latrine area which we were astonished and disgusted to find was a small compound with rough rock walls, with piles of faeces drying in the sun and infested with flies. Apparently camp hygiene was not part of the training of the Italian army. One of the fruits of victory was that we received some captured rations to enliven our diet, comprising tins of tunny in olive oil, a great delicacy, and *marmalata solida*, a sort of coarse fruit paste which served as jam for our biscuits.

The whole of Cyrenaica invited our capture, with the port of Benghazi a valuable prize. We were at the gate of the Jebel Achdar, a green and pleasant undulating country, with many colonial settlements such as Giovanni Berta. The Jebel makes a great bulge to the north so that the coastal road is much longer than the rough track across the desert through Mechili and M'sus to the coast south of Benghazi. This formed the chord to the gigantic arc of the Jebel. Logistics dominated everything in the desert and there was a pause while supplies were organised for the tanks and lorried infantry of the 7th Armoured Division and the 6th Australian Division, although matters were helped to some extent by the opening up of Tobruk port. Again, O'Connor showed his grasp of terrain by planning to exploit the open desert flank. He resolved to rush his armour through Mechili across the desert, while the Australians captured Derna and put pressure on the Italian army retreating along the long coast road. Speed was of the essence: the desert force had to cut off the line of the Italian retreat.

We were uneasily aware that the question of which of these two advances we were to support was being considered at group HQ; there were doubts about whether a medium battery would have the necessary speed to keep up with the Mechili force. Eventually it was decided that we could move as fast as any lorried force, so we joined the armoured thrust.

Quite unknown to us, of course, serious differences had arisen on strategy. The War Cabinet, alarmed by German preparations in Rumania – which Germany controlled – was anxious to bring help to threatened Greece (and/or Turkey). It was therefore with some reluctance that permission was granted for us to continue as far as the

Benghazi area. Wavell was in no doubt, however, that sooner or later he would be ordered to send an expeditionary force to Greece. (The consequences would be disastrous, as most informed military opinion at the time prophesied.) Equally unknown to us, was the fact that Hitler had decided to send German troops under Rommel to help his defeated and demoralised ally in North Africa.

The advance began on 4 February. The initial going was appalling and progress was very slow. Indeed, the Italians had assumed that the dreadful conditions precluded any possibility of an outflanking movement. Fortunately for us, the going improved markedly and we were soon bustling along in desert formation at good speed on a dead flat surface. We arrived at M'sus, but since we had started at the back of the 'queue' we were behind our forward elements. We spent the night there but next day advanced to Solluch. We expected to go into action at any moment, but the battle was already moving towards its devastating climax when our leading troops arrived in the nick of time at Beda Fomm, resulting in a short but bloody encounter. It was a complete victory. What was left of the Italian army in Libya was destroyed.

We bivouacked at Solluch and soon witnessed the spectacle of long lines of lugubrious prisoners trudging back towards the prison cages. The sight was pathetic: they seemed overwhelmingly to be peasants, of little more than five feet tall, with some crying piteously for 'mama'. They were a far cry from Rome's legionaries. Even more tragic was the arrival of young Arab girls who had been attracted by the small red Italian hand grenades and as a result had lost one or both hands. Our MO did what he could for them. Such horrible results of war had not been in our expectations.

Also billeted at Solluch was a picturesque group of French legionnaires who had apparently come up from Lake Chad and offered their services. They were a wild lot: I can still visualise one of their number chasing a chicken which he was endeavouring to shoot with a revolver. Their native troops had a penchant for camel meat and it was not long before they purloined one, leaving its severed head as a grisly reminder in the town square. We were not permitted into Benghazi except on duty, but many of us managed to catch a glimpse of the town, because we collected fresh white bread from the *panificio* which the army had requisitioned. It was obviously a place of some substance, with many fine public buildings in the usual ornate Italian colonial style.

In the ensuing pause we naturally hoped that the advance to Tripoli would be on our agenda. We were deployed in open formation south of Solluch, with good intervals as a precaution against air attack. One morning we noticed a single aircraft circling overhead, carefully reconnoitring all our positions. We were intrigued to note it had German markings, the first intimation of a German presence, which certainly gave us something to ponder on. (Rommel had arrived in North Africa on 12 February.) The plane seemed a bird of ill-omen, particularly when it dropped a bomb before turning away, its reconnaissance completed. One man was wounded by this new enemy, a portent of many injuries to come. The symbolism was not lost on anybody.

The implications of this momentous development had hardly sunk in before our first experience of desert warfare was abruptly ended. Despite the looming German menace in Cyrenaica, the 211th Battery and many other units were ordered back to the Nile Delta. This time we went back through the Jebel, relishing the greenness and the little Italian model settlements. These ended in blank white walls, so convenient for Mussolini's bombastic slogans of *Mare Nostrum* and the like, which conjured up incongruously the glories of the Roman Empire. Some of the villas in Giovanni Berta were of high standard, with marbled floors and mosaics, clearly for senior bureaucrats and officers. We left this comparative paradise with regret and retraced our steps along the long coast road – Tobruk, Bardia, Halfaya, Matruh, and so to Cairo and our old base at Mena camp.

A static command had been left in Cyrenaica with a weak brigade of tanks from the newly arrived 2nd Armoured Division. The risk of leaving such a small force was accepted because it was felt Rommel would not be ready to attack for some time. He anticipated the British, however, and attacked on 31 March, apparently before his own command, let alone the British, expected it. He found little to halt his advance.

O'Connor was now in command of all British troops in Egypt, but he was sent post haste to the desert in an attempt to restore the position. On 6 April, returning in an unescorted car to Lieutenant-General

Neame's HQ at Tmimi, O'Connor and Neame were captured. Rommel used O'Connor's strategy in reverse and had soon cut off the 'bulge' of the Jebel Achdar. Wavell asked General Morshead, commander of the 9th Australian Division, whether he could hold Tobruk. Morshead thought he could, and so was laid the foundation of an effective strategy for discouraging any forays of Rommel into Egypt.

Meanwhile, we were in Greece and were concerned with other pressing matters. We could only watch with sadness and dismay the destruction of all the desert army's splendid achievement. Cyrenaica was lost, and with it the string of airfields which controlled the central Mediterranean and the convoy route from Alexandria to beleaguered Malta.

GREECE AND CRETE

The War Cabinet had noted with concern the threat posed to Greece by the German presence in Rumania and Bulgaria. There was great sympathy in Britain for Greece, who was already at war with Italy and was therefore an ally. Before reaching a decision to render help, the War Cabinet sent Anthony Eden, Foreign Secretary, and Sir John Dill, the Chief of the Imperial General Staff (CIGS), to Cairo to discuss with the three Commanders-in-Chief in the Middle East the feasibility of sending an expeditionary force.

After discussion with the Greek government in Athens, the decision to intervene was made. Eden seems to have been the prime mover, but his colleagues shared the responsibility.[1] The decision was taken with full awareness that the expedition would be a gamble: the force was to consist of two infantry divisions plus an armoured brigade, whose tanks were already in poor mechanical condition. This puny force was quite inadequate to hold the German horde, and one can only assume that the German speed of reaction was wholly underestimated, and that wishful thinking had descended into fantasy. According to Churchill, the invasion of southern Yugoslavia and Greece was entrusted to the German Twelfth Army of fifteen divisions, of which four were armoured. The RAF would be outnumbered by ten to one, without even counting the Italian air force. The only charitable explanation is that this information was not available at the time, which means our Intelligence was very remiss. The impression remains that the honourable desire to aid Greece was so strong that an outsize gamble was thought worth the risk.

We were fortunate to be able to snatch a few days' leave in Cairo, which, again, was hugely enjoyed. Then our guns and vehicles disappeared for embarkation and we moved to a camp in the desert to the west of Alexandria. This proved to be remarkably unpleasant because a *khamseen* (sandstorm) blew up which lasted two or three days.

Meanwhile one of our number, a recent arrival named Walker, had developed a rash which the MO could not identify and for which he had prescribed some ointment. To add to his discomfort, Walker discovered a scorpion in his blankets. Walker was a Cambridge graduate, stood well over six feet tall, had some classical Greek and a finely chiselled face. I wondered whether the Greeks would think one of their ancient gods had returned in the unlikely guise of a British solider to aid them in their extremity. For some inexplicable reason he always referred to me as 'le commandant'. Fortunately for him, the *khamseen* blew itself out and with much rejoicing we embarked on a small Greek steamer of some 1,500 grt.

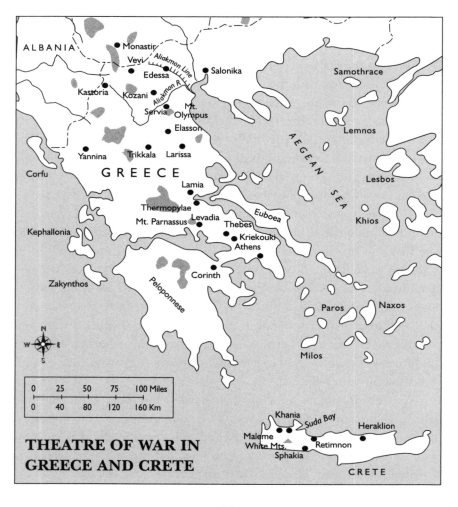

THEATRE OF WAR IN GREECE AND CRETE

The crew welcomed us warmly. There was a small saloon and bar, but the only liquor available was *ouzo*, which, although cheap, was not to many people's taste, whether neat or watered. Our voyage was pleasant and uneventful, the first of our Mediterranean 'cruises' at His Majesty's expense. We were the first combat unit to arrive in Greece, on 6 March 1941, and from Piraeus we were taken a few miles east of Athens.

It was spring, roses were in bloom and the place seemed gloriously attractive after the sandstorm. We were young and high adventure seemed to beckon. I guessed we would have very little opportunity to see anything of Athens. Once the guns and vehicles arrived from Piraeus, I reckoned we would be on our way. Nevertheless, we managed to get into the city for a day and spent the evening at a *taverna*, accompanied by native music. Everyone was effusively friendly and welcoming.

My knowledge of ancient Greece was minimal. I had had a 'modern' education, but at school we had an English master with a taste for the classics, and we had read some Homer in translation. We also had an engaging Cockney maths master who taught us geometry and algebra. In those days the teaching of geometry was based on Euclid and we soon discovered, as boys always will, that our teacher was fascinated by Greek mathematics, astronomy and philosophy. It proved only too easy to tempt him to talk about Pythagoras, who was much more than a geometrician, and to give us an inkling of what Plato and Aristotle had been about. These pleasant memories had been buried in my mind, but now that we were on Greek soil they sprang vividly to life – a vague, inchoate, immature blur, but somehow the authentic spirit of Hellas, or so I felt. I was determined that, as we were so near, I would visit the Acropolis. While my colleagues were enjoying the pleasures of the city, I hailed a taxi and was duly deposited at my destination. I climbed the steps, went through the *propylaea* and, wonder of wonders, the place was entirely deserted. No tourists, no other curious solders, complete emptiness. For two precious hours the Acropolis belonged to *me*. There was then no damage from pollution, the caryatids were still in their ancient positions in the *Erechtheon* and there was no disfiguring steel scaffolding. I had the place entirely to myself, a rare privilege which can now hardly ever be repeated. I was seized with a sort of religious awe, a sense of a numinous presence, a communion with the Beyond, often evoked by old buildings with special associations. I left in a state almost of intoxication. I had had an experience which had been provided only by the vagaries of war. That single experience almost made the war seem worthwhile.

Our route lay through Thebes, Lamia, Larissa, Elasson, Kozani and Vevi. Every town and village showed its delight at our presence. As mentioned, for some reason never fathomed our Battery was the first to be sent to Greece, ahead of the main expeditionary force. Apart from a few reconnaissance vehicles,[2] we were the first British troops that most people had seen. We soon learned that 'Kali mera' meant 'Good-day' and that in the afternoon 'Kali spera' was appropriate. 'Mussolini kaput!' they cried, making bloodthirsty gestures of cutting throats. We decided we liked the Greeks! We bivouacked successively near Mounts Parnassus and Olympus and, since we moved at first light, witnessed the magic spectacle of the top of the mountains catching fire as the rising sun's rays caught the snow on their summits. How appropriate was Homer's immortal phrase 'rosy fingered dawn'.

One day we halted at noon for some hours. Several of us had contracted Walker's 'rash' and the delay offered a welcome opportunity for a little investigation. The truth soon dawned. We had no 'rash', we were lousy! We were both disgusted and amused. I remembered stories of the last war and our louse-ridden troops going over the seams of their uniforms with lighted candles. This remedy was not available to us, but there was a nearby stream. We all shaved our pubic regions, which must have created a diverting spectacle, washed, quixotically abandoned our battledress trousers and donned the khaki drill shorts we had in our packs. There was much good-humoured banter at Walker's expense, and none of us thought to criticise our MO's faulty diagnosis. Presumably as a specialist paediatrician he had not encountered body lice before.

Much of the country was wild and very rugged, the more so as we advanced north. Some of the roads were in poor condition after the winter snows and we saw gangs of old men, women and boys patching up the road, like some medieval corvée. We were obviously headed for the Yugoslav frontier, where the Monastir gap offered a traditional invasion route. At Vevi the road forks, the western branch towards

Monastir, while to the east the road winds its way through high
country to Edessa and Thessalonike (Salonika). We followed this route
and took up position near Lakes Petersko and Vegorritis – both, it was
said, good for trout. We saw no other British troops at any time and
seemed to be in support of Greeks manning the border up in the hills.
Everyone was very cheerful, in spite of our isolation, and totally
trusting in our command and its plans, of which, of course, we had no
inkling. Perhaps it was just as well that we did not know that the staff
planning the arrival of the main expeditionary force was simultaneously planning its withdrawal! We also did not know that we were part
of a forward operation which was meant to delay the expected
German attack while our forces fell back to our main defence, the
'Aliakmon Line', so called after the river which flows through mountain and plain to enter the sea 25 miles west of Salonika and 40 miles
north of Mount Olympus.

The weather was pleasantly warm. We knew from the BBC that the
Germans were in effective control in Rumania, and that Bulgaria was
suspected of offering no opposition to the passage of German troops,
while the attitude of the Yugoslav government was ambivalent and vacil-
lating. One sensed a build-up of tension, but these ominous portents did
not affect our equanimity. Perhaps it was fortunate that we had no real
idea of the relative weakness of our force.

One day we had a welcome but wholly unexpected visitor, in the
shape of Anthony Eden. He was as debonair as ever and offered round
his gold cigarette case to the men standing near. Surely *he* knew of our
perilous position. He told us he had been to Ankara, and was on his way
back to Athens. I have often wondered what thoughts were in his mind
as he conversed so pleasantly with us. Did he know the Germans had
two armies poised to invade southern Yugoslavia and Greece in overwhelming force through the Monastir gap, with a subsidiary attack
through the Strumitsa Pass and the Vardar valley?

Our force was to comprise the New Zealand and 6th Australian Divisions, and the 1st Armoured Brigade Group. Greece had priority over
the desert but a larger force could not have been logistically supported.
The 80-aeroplane RAF contingent consisted of Blenheim bombers and
Gladiator and Hurricane fighters. Against these the Germans had some

eight hundred aircraft, not including the Italian *Regia Aeronautica*. Our puny force therefore faced overwhelming odds. Of all this, of course, we were blissfully unaware. So, perhaps was Anthony Eden.

The German armies invaded Yugoslavia and Greece on 6 April. Resistance in Yugoslavia was ineffective and the whole country was occupied within a week. We were in a state of full alert, but the only sign of enemy activity was huge flights of bombers high overhead on their way to attack strategic targets well to the south. Their prime target was Piraeus, where they hit an ammunition ship, which exploded causing terrible devastation. These activities naturally excited our attention, but they posed no threat to us.

It had been envisaged that our main line of defence would be on the Aliakmon, but this provoked Greek reluctance; they naturally did not wish to give up voluntarily a yard of their soil, least of all to the despised Italians, whom they had so valiantly defeated in Albania. Indeed, it is probable that orders to withdraw to the Aliakmon would not have been obeyed. So, in spite of the powerful strategic case for withdrawal, the Greeks remained in forward positions until too late.

The Monastir gap was obviously threatened, and some attempt had clearly to be made to delay the enemy while our main position was being occupied and prepared for defence. The clapped-out 1st Armoured Brigade, which had been in the Vardar plain to the east of us, was moved near to Vevi, together with the 19th Australian Infantry Brigade. This comprised two battalions; the third was still on its way, so the Rangers supplied the third battalion. We were involved in these dispositions and, since we were already close to the new position, were one of the first units to arrive. We viewed this change in our position with some relief, because we had felt very lonely and exposed in our lakeside residence, which could so easily be outflanked. It was good to know we were again part of a formation and that there were two field regiments also in the line. The critical weakness was in infantry and armour: we had only three battalions to hold a front of nearly twelve miles. This was wholly inadequate and invited penetration.

The German advance was fortunately slower than expected. Snow fell during the night of 9/10 April. This sharp return of Balkan winter was welcome in that it restricted enemy air operations, but the bitter

cold reminded us that there was a price to pay for our unthinking abandonment of our battledress trousers for tropical shorts!

During the morning of 10 April, our OPs reported enemy tanks and
infantry (the Adolf Hitler Division) calmly debussing from special
carriers. We engaged them immediately, and knocked out a tank with
one of our first rounds. Just before dawn the next day, we saw lights in
Vevi, and we promptly shelled the centre of the village. There were brisk
infantry engagements, and towards evening we shelled the road, since
the enemy seemed to be forming up for an attack. There was a risk of a
breakthrough west of the two lakes, which would have threatened our
rear. This was staved off by our tanks, but they had a nasty habit of
breaking down, and there were no repair facilities. At this stage of the
war we had no tank transporters, so tanks had had to advance on their
own tracks all the way from Piraeus, often over very rough terrain. Since
many of them were in poor condition at the start of the campaign, effective strength was always much less than the nominal one.

By now the Greeks had realised that their forces in Albania were
threatened from the flank. However, our armour was too weak to give
any help, and in any case we had been ordered to withdraw on 12 April.
This came not a moment too soon, because our OPs were reporting that
our infantry was thinning out and withdrawing under very heavy pressure. Enemy tanks were also emerging unexpectedly from a railway
tunnel. Our battery command post, of which I was then a member, was
in a small pine wood and consisted of a truck fitted up as an office.
Unfortunately, with the ground sodden by the snow we could not free
the vehicle, which had slithered against a tree. A winch on one of the
gun tractors also failed to extricate it. With the enemy advancing and
our front collapsing, it was urgently necessary to abandon our position.
We hastily collected as much survey equipment as we could carry along
with some of our personal gear and blankets, and staggered along the
track to the road. Here our colonel was glowering at us for the delay.
Our transport proved to be one of our 3-ton ammunition trucks. Sitting
or lying on a pile of shells moving over a rough and pitted road was not
exactly comfortable, and it occurred to us that any other vehicle would
be have been preferable to an ammunition wagon on a road which was
being attacked by aircraft. Progress was very slow: there were many

refugees, and the Greek army units had very primitive transport, including bullock carts.

Meanwhile our rearguards had been doing splendid work against heavy odds. We admired them enormously and were able to observe their tactics as we withdrew. A small group of about twenty men with a few Bren carriers and Bren guns, a mortar or two and their rifles would select a suitable position. Sometimes there was time for the engineers to mine the road or blow a culvert. They would then hold up the enemy briefly, then skilfully disengage and race down the road through a similar position held by their comrades. They would then prepare another position in the rear. They naturally took casualties in this vital and dangerous task. The dedicated work of these skilful groups added up to a significant delay, and their sacrifice aided our withdrawal.

Our line of retreat took us to Kozani and the Servia Pass. The concern was that as we withdrew, the Germans would strike southwards to Kastoria and block the road to Yannina, thereby cutting off the Greek army in Epirus and administering the *coup de grâce*. This was precisely what happened, and the whole of our left flank was exposed.

Our main position was known as the Olympus–Servia Line. It was shorter than the Aliakmon Line, although that river still formed part of the defences. We were to support the Australians at Portas Pass, but found the 7th Medium Regiment, RA already occupying most of the available positions. (This was a regular army unit, lately arrived in Greece, and a friendly rivalry developed between them and us.)

We were on high ground, with a view of the country right down to the river and beyond. In mountain conditions we had to remember the question of 'crest clearance'. If there was intervening high ground between guns and target, it might not be possible to clear the crest. A way round the difficulty was to reduce the propellant charge, which would give the shell a higher, more howitzer-like trajectory. This advantage could, of course, be gained only at the expense of range. It might not be possible to engage certain targets if they were in a 'shadow' area near a crest.

The pass was an excellent defensive position, but our forces were too pitifully weak to hold it. Our force included a 'refugee' Yugoslav 88mm AA troop, but they soon ran out of ammunition. The Luftwaffe was very active. We had the exciting but disconcerting spectacle of Me 109s sweeping over a low saddle to our rear at a height of no more than fifty feet, with the pilot clearly visible. They would then dive and machine-gun our infantry down by the river. From now on air attacks became a major preoccupation, inducing not only fear but also indignation and frustration at our totally defenceless condition. (I do not remember seeing even a Bofors anti-aircraft gun). We never saw anything of the RAF in Greece because it was so hugely outnumbered. It was soon eliminated, being particularly prone to attack while on the ground. So we suffered incessant bombing, especially in passes, and were utterly defenceless.

With our left flank exposed, we were in danger of being out-flanked, but equally we were vulnerable to an overwhelming punch in the centre. If the enemy did break through our mountain crust, there would be no obstacle preventing them gaining the plain of Thessaly, and reaching the vital communications centre of Larissa. Either of these courses would spell disaster. With power and mobility, the Germans had an alarming choice of route. We had a small flank force at Grevena to our west, but there was a poor road leading to Kalambaka, thirty miles to the south. A road from there links with Trikkala, from whence a road runs due east to Larissa. A small group called 'Savige force', to which our battery contributed a small temporary detachment, was therefore assembled to reconnoitre and counter this threat.

It was while we were in the plain of Trikkala that we had the unusual sight of an Me 109 coming down, presumably with engine trouble or lack of fuel. We surrounded it when it taxied to a halt. The pilot was tall, blond and had not recently shaved. He was arrogant and truculent, a typical product of the *Hitlerjugend*. He had the greatest possible contempt for us, and told us in passable English that we faced overwhelming force and that we would certainly be crushed. We were rapidly coming to that view, but certainly hoped he would not escape his just deserts and would reach the POW cage awaiting him in Egypt.

The possibility of envelopment from the direction of Trikkala receded; the danger was now to the east. We accordingly returned to rejoin the battery in support of the 4th NZ Brigade, and engaged the enemy, who was aiming to cross the Aliakmon. On 16 April we withdrew because it had been decided to move back to our next, and as it proved, last main line of defence – the Thermopylae Line. The Luftwaffe was endeavouring to block the streets of villages with rubble to hinder our movements. There was heavy bombing and machine-gunning on the road itself and good space discipline was essential. The column would halt as soon as lookouts saw enemy planes approaching, and everyone ran for cover in the rough ground. When a concrete pipe formed a culvert under the road, it proved a popular, if transient, air raid shelter. Few of our vehicles were hit and casualties were remarkably light, but there was no doubt our nerves became stretched as we watched destruction we were powerless to prevent.

Our route to the south took us from the Portas Pass. We reached Elasson, where the road was heavily blocked by rubble. We continued to the south through the Meneskos Pass, continually harassed by air attacks. There, a spirited rearguard action took place which we and some Anzac field guns also supported. This proved effective for a time, but then we ran out of ammunition, and since there was no possibility of replenishment, there was no point in remaining. We withdrew. The rearguard continued with its task of demolishing bridges and culverts. We passed through Larissa, a vital road junction in the plain of Thessaly. On the coast to the east, the Anzac forces had the difficult task of disengaging from the Olympus position and delaying the enemy as long as possible in the difficult terrain in the Vale of Tempe. Everyone was subject to incessant raids as the Luftwaffe pounded all roads.

We had cleared Larissa without mishap, but were caught in the Lamia Pass. Our commanding officer, Lieutenant-Colonel R. L. Syer, was killed by a bomb splinter in the head. This was our first fatal casualty, a rare and unwelcome distinction to befall a commanding officer, and it was felt by us to be a cruel blow of fate. The distressing news soon spread. Battered, but still in relatively good order and spirits, we came into our position in the Thermopylae Line, being in the coastal sector near the village of Molos.

I realised we were very near the site of the classic encounter between Leonidas and his band of 'immortals' and the Persians. It was an unfavourable omen. I hoped we would emulate the Spartans, but not too literally!

To our immediate north the coast was heavily indented by the Gulf of Lamia (or Malia). There was concern that the Germans would cross the water to the large island of Euboea, which they could quickly over-run. At Khalkis, (Halkida) in the south of Euboea, there was a bridge linking the island with the mainland well to our rear. Some modest precautions were taken against this possibility. We were in a good posi-tion to block the coast road from Lamia, as it crossed the bridge near Thermopylae. We could also cover the north-south road over the Brallos Pass. Our infantry was weak in number, but fortunately there were plenty of 25-pounder batteries and the artillery would have a crucial part to play.

It was while we were at Molos that I witnessed a sight that epito-mised the splendid fighting spirit of the Anzac forces, and at the same time illustrated graphically the dreadful consequences of our country's lack of preparation for the war. Exasperated by the continuing air raids, a New Zealand sergeant had tied a Boys anti-tank rifle (firing solid shot) to the springy branch of a tree in a desperate attempt to rig up some sort of reply to low-flying aircraft. I was filled with admiration for his indomitable spirit, even though it was a vain endeavour, but filled with bitterness for those who had landed us in this appalling mess.

We were frequently in action on 22 and 23 April. It was on the latter day that our battery commander, Major E. B. Eason, broke the grave news that all British forces were to be withdrawn from Greece very shortly, but that we were not to worry: the Royal Navy would get us off and we could trust them absolutely. Such was our faith in the Navy that we accepted this assurance as a matter of course. In the event, this trust was not misplaced. But this was not the worst news. After the present engagement we were to destroy our guns and incapacitate all vehicles, except for those needed for the evacuation. To be ordered to destroy our guns was to negate our very purpose. It was the most terrible news an artillery regiment could possibly receive: it numbed us. We would no longer have any military function, for we lacked even small arms: in those days these were in such short supply that gunner regiments had only enough for guard duties. That day, 23 April, was therefore for us the black day of the war, quite unforgettable: it was already marked as St. George's Day, Shakespeare's birthday and the day of the heroic raid

41

on Zeebrugge by the Royal Navy in 1918. We were very distressed at the prospect of another, smaller Dunkirk. It was agonising even to contemplate the deliberate destruction of equipment which was so scarce and was so desperately needed in the Middle East. We were filled with a deep resolve to make every round count before we ceased to be artillery, if only transiently.

On 24 April the Germans were repairing the bridge over the Sperkhios river, and this provided some good targets for all our artillery. Several enemy tanks were knocked out. We also took on an enemy battery which was located on the other side of the Gulf of Lamia.

During the night, we had the melancholy task of carrying out our orders. In the old days before the invention of breech-loading, a gun was put out of action quite simply by driving a spike into the touch-hole. With modern weapons 'spiking' is more complex. The gun was loaded in the normal way, but another round was rammed nose-first, blocking the muzzle. The procedure was hazardous and everyone took cover while, in a slit trench, the 'Number One' (a sergeant), fired the gun with an extended lanyard. The resultant explosion split open the piece at the muzzle end, like the petals of a flower opening. No-one who has seen a gun destroyed in this way can possibly mistake the signs. After this terrible deed, all our surplus vehicles were dealt with by leaving the engines running with the sump oil drained. We left this tragic scene able to muster little cheerfulness. All the Navy would permit us to carry was a haversack crammed with our few personal possessions.

The only exception we made were the gunsights, one of which I carried. There was nothing more we could do, so we silently withdrew, leaving the New Zealanders to form a rearguard covering Levadia, Thebes and Kriekouki on the route back to Athens. They had also to do what they could to cover the isthmus of Corinth and to destroy the bridge over the canal. Piraeus was thought to be too badly damaged for evacuation, so we were directed to the open beaches east and south-east of Athens. (Others were to be picked up from various places in the Peleponnese.) We halted briefly in a pleasant suburb where I spoke to a charming middle-aged lady who commanded excellent English. I found myself stammering an apology for leaving them in the lurch. 'Don't worry,' she said, 'I am sure you did your best, but what can you do in the face of *that*–?' and she shrugged her shoulders as she gazed to the north. The Germans would reach her house in a few hours. I have often wondered how, indeed whether, this indomitable lady survived the occupation, starvation and finally, civil war.

We made our way after dark towards Marathon. No lights were permitted and all was silent as a grave. We abandoned our vehicles in a wood and marched to Porto Rafti where we were under orders of the naval beachmaster. Gradually our column reached the water's edge and we split up into parties, wading out to the oared boats which came for us. The sides were quite high and the crew hauled us up and over. A burly chief petty officer saw the leather case I was carrying which held a gunsight. 'Our orders are nothing but haversacks', he said. I remonstrated, saying it was precious optical equipment and I was under orders to get it away. 'We're in charge here', he grunted, and he grabbed the case and threw it into the bay. I was naturally annoyed, but he was bigger than I was and an altercation with our 'saviours' hardly seemed appropriate, so I accepted the inevitable.

We climbed aboard the destroyer *Kandahar* in inky darkness. (She was one of the famous destroyer flotilla commanded by Lord Mountbatten in the *Kelly*.) We were understandably dazzled by the lights below. The crew were welcoming and bustled about with hot tea, bully beef and biscuits for which we were most grateful: it had been a long time since we last had food. We sailed with other ships at about 02.00 hours, making full speed so as to be well clear of the coast before dawn, when air attacks could be expected.

As the distance from Greece increased, the risk of attack diminished somewhat, although we were still well within enemy range, and we felt we could relax. Already we were envisaging our joyful arrival at Alexandria and the pleasant things we would do on leave. Somehow, however, a sense of unease developed, and when we asked the crew what our destination was, we were informed that it was Crete! This was intensely disappointing, yet, with hindsight, it can be seen to have been inevitable. The Navy had an enormous task. Our total strength in Greece had been 58,000, and eventually 42,000 were successfully evacuated. (In addition there were some independent escapes, e.g. by *caiques*.) This remarkable achievement was only possible by using Crete, the short sea passage from the mainland permitting a rapid turn-round of ships to bring away further evacuees. The use of Crete in the evacuation was, in other words, dictated by logistics. In consequence, the defence of the island was predominantly in the hands of the evacuees, not the small existing garrison. Some of the flotsam and jetsam was quite unsuitable for battle purposes, being more of a hindrance than otherwise. Fortunately the force disembarked included the magnificent Anzac infantry. Some of the New Zealanders had actually experienced the parachute attack at Corinth which was, in effect, a small scale rehearsal for the battle of Crete.

* * * * * * * * * * *

We sailed into Suda Bay having long noticed the plumes of black smoke from earlier raids. The cruiser *York* had been sunk in the shallow waters of the bay. She was sitting grounded, with only her superstructure above the water. We disembarked at a tiny quay, forming single file and passing a small team which handed each of us a rifle and fifty rounds of ammunition. 'You're infantry now,' they said. Someone with a sadistic sense of humour sent this 'crack' infantry unit straight towards Maleme, which was to be the focus of the German attack, and where the issue was to be decided. We hardly had time to digest this news before we formed a column and marched for Khania (which everyone then spelled in the Italian fashion, Canea), the capital of the western province. At a road junction, however, we left the Khania road and marched steadily westward before turning off the road near a village.

Our position was a mile or two from Maleme. We were in an olive grove and were detailed off, two men to a tree, which was to be our 'home'. None of us had the slightest notion of infantry tactics, although we had done rifle drill, of course, and had fired a few rounds at the butts in England. Against well-armed and trained airborne troops, we would naturally be at some disadvantage. We were entirely without equipment of any sort other than our rifles: we did not even have a field telephone. The period of waiting for we knew not what was tense. All we knew was that if fighting erupted, we were immediately to man a dried-up ditch which ran through our position, and to hold it.

The general feeling was that there would be a seaborne invasion (we were near the coast). The idea of an airborne attack never occurred to us. Some optimists thought Crete was merely a staging post and that we would soon be on our way to Egypt! The New Zealanders holding Maleme airfield, however, were fully informed, were well positioned and dug-in. The atmosphere was tense but they were quietly confident.

After a few days our 'A' Troop was detached and equipped with four Italian 75s captured during O'Connor's successful campaign. Their function was to cover the Australian-held Heraklion airfield, roughly half way along the east-west road which hugs the coast and runs the length of the island. We envied them: at least they had a clearly defined role and were gunners once more, albeit with unfamiliar and inferior equipment.

We were bored, had nothing to do, and nothing to do it with. There was underlying concern about whatever lay in store for us. To aid morale, we were able to have a few hours' leave in Khania. We much enjoyed the scene at the little fishing harbour, with remnants of the old Venetian fortifications. There was an excellent fish restaurant near the quayside and cafés selling sticky honey cakes, like *baklavas*. The place was essentially a fishing port, very picturesque with a maze of narrow alleys, which were soon to be obliterated in the bombing.

We seemed to be becalmed in a quiet backwater, helpless spectators of the continuing destruction of our dumps and oil stores at Suda Bay, which the enemy air force attacked relentlessly every day. (Our puny air force had long since been withdrawn.) We noticed that the intensity of our anti-aircraft fire slackened progressively, until all the guns were knocked out and there was no opposition of any sort. Tension rose dramatically.

At dawn on 20 May the volume of enemy air activity reached a crescendo: clearly something unusual and significant was happening. We took an early breakfast and noticed a large number of aircraft a little to the west over the airfield at Maleme. We were so badly informed that we did not then know there *was* an airfield there. We had a clear view (without binoculars) and were astonished to note that these low-flying aircraft were towing gliders. The word sprang simultaneously from everyone's lips. So now, at last, we knew the nature of the threat to the island. Soon after the gliders landed came waves of parachutists. A few drifted off-course and we took a few pot shots, but not very effectively, since the range was too great. We then manned our ditch. We sent out a patrol, as did other units, to look for parachutist stragglers and deal with them. Our patrol saw the bodies of about six parachutists, but it was not clear whether they were already dead or if our party was responsible. Each corpse was well equipped with benzedrene (energy) tablets and contraceptives.

We remained in the ditch, but towards midday one of my friends suggested a cup of tea. We were under cover of a tree about twenty yards away when we heard the approach of a Messerschmitt, which had obviously spotted the manned ditch. We threw ourselves to the ground. I saw a string of bullets knocking up the dust only about a foot away, and then I was hit in the back of the thigh. Several thoughts went through my mind: I did not wish to be incapacitated in a strife-torn island. I put my hand down, found no blood and realised I had been hit by a stone ricochet. Relieved, I headed back to our ditch, to find four of our comrades lying face down with neat holes in their backs. All dead, killed by the same burst that had nearly accounted for me. We remained a little dazed and shocked for a time. I reflected that one could describe the occurrence in histrionic terms as being 'brushed by the wings of the angel of death', or, more prosaically, as a damned narrow escape. (On a gun position there would, of course, be others). I thought more and more of the wisdom of the 1914–18 soldiers, who comforted themselves with the fatalistic 'They'll only get you if it's got your number on it'. This is a self-protective, if irrational, attitude, but it was good for morale. It seemed the most natural example to follow, and very comforting. (Although we would seldom deliberately expose ourselves to risk, we developed a certain nonchalance which enabled one to give of one's best and get on with the job.)

The next day was similar: we had another unwelcome visitor. Presumably our location had been reported. The Germans are very adaptable (witness their use of the 88mm anti-aircraft gun in an anti-tank role). Realising that the enemy might be dug-in and therefore fairly well protected from low-flying fighter aircraft, they hastily improvised. A slow-flying Fieseler Storch (a reconnaissance and spotter plane) came over. We were astonished to see a man standing near the tail, protected by a guard rail, who had stood there all the way from the Greek airfield. He was manning a machine-gun, firing almost vertically down and so negating the value of any slit trench. Fortunately they had not got our location quite right, and gave a place about 100 yards away very effective treatment. This placed us in a quandary: with such a slow-moving target it was tempting to open fire and hit the plane or the gunner. However, if we did this we would expose our position and invite retaliation. Everyone made this calculation spontaneously and not a shot was fired at the intruder.

Things were obviously not going well at Maleme, because we were withdrawn during the night of 21/22 May and took up position some three miles further east. There we were delighted to be issued with picks and shovels so that we could dig ourselves in. Many enemy planes were seen; we kept movement to a minimum and we spent the day unheroically in our slit trenches. This, sadly, was the pattern at each withdrawal towards Suda Bay.

Our nerves were beginning to get rather frayed: we were of marginal fighting value (and not yet engaged) and yet, like everyone, were exposed to risk. Nor was morale encouraged when we heard that on 24 May, HMS *Hood* had been sunk in an encounter with the *Bismarck* in the Denmark Strait, with the loss of almost all her crew.

As we fell back, slit trenches were dug by night and most of each day was spent in them. It was hazardous to move outside the trenches – it attracted unwelcome attention – so our excursions were infrequent. There were no Germans on land with whom we were in contact.

Someone had 'found' some pipe tobacco and 'cigarettes' of a sort were made from thin Bible pages, which were also found useful for sanitary purposes. The men can hardly be blamed for being practical in such circumstances. Since nearly all the soldiers I came across during the war were unashamedly pagan, or at least indifferent, although cheerfully nominally Christian, their attitude to the scriptures was not reverential. No doubt such attitudes were encouraged by our unfortunate experience of army chaplains; with one possible exception, they were parasites and did *nothing* to bring comfort to the men. We had not yet met our first padre, who remained at RHQ, but we came across him in Crete when our RHQ personnel were mixed up with us. He was thoroughly defeatist and was unsurpassed at spreading gloom and despondency. (There were plenty of grounds for this without his advertising the fact.) He supposed there was no hope and that we should all finish up as prisoners, or worse. He did, in fact, become a prisoner, it was thought voluntarily, which aroused no feelings of regret or loss on our part.

By 27 May, in spite of the gallantry of the Australian and British forces at Heraklion and Retimnon, as well as the dogged rearguard of the New Zealanders, it was clear that the island could not be held. Preparations began for our second evacuation. We marched at night towards Suda Bay, under the glare of parachute flares, so the enemy probably had an inkling of what was happening. Each man drew a tin of bully beef and some biscuits. Casualties were still being inflicted next day and several men, including some Australians, would never see home again. Beyond Suda the road forks, and at Vrisses we were to strike south and make our way by the White Mountains, which rise to some 8,000 feet, to the little fishing village of Sphakia, on the very rugged south coast, where it was hoped we would be taken off. The track was rough, but mercifully the air attacks dwindled markedly and the retreating column was able to march in daylight. Our rations soon gave out and there was no food to be found in the occasional abandoned hamlets. Water was available, but, as events were to show, was probably of poor quality. We eventually arrived on some high ground overlooking the little port, and had to settle down while the officers negotiated with the naval representatives. It seemed that the Navy would not be able to take off everybody; some would be left behind. As an 'infantry' unit we could hardly expect a high priority, and our best hope was to emphasise that we were trained artillerymen, who were crucially scarce in the Middle East. Meanwhile, we suffered pangs of hunger. This did not diminish my curiosity and I visited a charming little whitewashed church, but found my first glimpse of Byzantine style, with its ikons and gaudy brass, not to my taste.

At dusk we marched down to the quay. A high proportion of the Anzac rearguard was being embarked, deservedly so, but at the last gasp we were lucky, and room was found for us on a destroyer, HMS *Kimberley*, the last to leave on the night of 1 June, as we were soon to discover. We noted at once the difference in our reception compared with that on leaving Greece. In the interim the Navy had suffered grievously: many ships had been sunk or damaged and casualties had been high. The crew had obviously been at full stretch and, understandably, had no time for courtesies. Our feelings were of profound relief, with gratitude to the Navy, and some quiet rejoicing that we had been selected for embarkation. We were abundantly to justify that decision.

We left before first light and soon a message came over the ship's loudspeaker system to the effect that General Wavell had signalled Admiral Cunningham thanking him for all the Navy's efforts and sacrifices on the army's behalf, and stating that in view of the heavy losses sustained by the Navy, the evacuation was at an end.

Our return voyage was uneventful. As the destroyers came into Alexandria harbour, with their decks crammed with khaki-clad figures, we were impressed and a little touched because the French battleship *Lorraine*, which (like the rest of the French fleet) was disarmed and interned due to the tense situation regarding the Vichy authorities in Syria, nevertheless had its men line the rails, standing rigidly to attention with pipes shrilling, as we sailed by. I felt the infantry fully deserved this honour: in Greece we had done a workman-like job, but in Crete, through no fault of our own, we hardly justified heroic status.

There was a moment of bathos when we disembarked. The British ladies of Alexandria welcomed us and gave each man a bun, a bar of chocolate and an orange, as if we were attending the vicarage fête! However, although it seemed incongruous, we appreciated the spirit in which the gesture had been made.

At Suda Bay the Imperial War Graves Commission has provided a beautiful setting for those of our comrades who rest permanently on the island. In a tiny chapel near the entrance is a book of remembrance enabling the visitor to locate a particular grave. At the German cemetery at Maleme the graves are on the notorious hill 107, topped by a large wooden cross, overlooking the airfield for which they died. So confined is the space, and so numerous the dead, that they have had to be accommodated two to a grave. There are no headstones; the commemorative tablets are flush with the ground, with purple mesembryanthemums growing between, as if blood was seeping from the ground. The inscriptions show that the vast majority were killed on the first or second day of fighting. The price was horrendous: 4,500 lie buried in the German cemetery, while some 1,500 British and Dominion dead rest at Suda. Never again did the Germans essay an airborne operation.

* * * * * * * * * * *

The defence of Crete had been extemporised and our infantry had displayed great courage against the cream of the Nazi airborne forces. As most commentators are agreed, it very nearly came off – defeat was by the narrowest of margins. Yet in a wider context the outcome was fortunate. Had the attack been repulsed it would not have been long before another invasion was mounted, predominantly seaborne but with heavy air support. After its already very serious losses, the Royal Navy would almost certainly have been unable to prevent a seaborne invasion, nor would it have been able to sustain the already gravely weakened garrison in narrow waters totally dominated by the Luftwaffe. The Germans could have island-hopped from Kithera and Milos, as well as coming directly from Piraeus. Our losses would have been far higher because few of the garrison would have escaped. And, the island would not have been of any strategic value to us. So much for speculation.

Military historians have analysed the reasons for the failure in Crete, and an expert consensus has emerged. Yet the wider public is puzzled to understand how it happened when 'Ultra' intelligence had provided such detailed and precise information about the enemy intentions. Major-General Bernard Freyberg, who was made commander of the island as soon as he arrived from Greece, knew from 'Ultra' (made specially available to him) that the main focus of attack would fall on the airfield at Maleme, some fifteen miles west of Khania. As well as holding Maleme, he had to hold the main road to it from our supply base at Suda Bay, and the villages along the road. These places, like beads on a string, had to be held if contact was not to be lost with Maleme. If the whole of the NZ Division had been available, he would have had sufficient forces for both objectives. He landed at Suda Bay with his 4th and 5th Brigades, but, unfortunately, owing to some administrative confusion, the convoy left for Egypt without disembarking his HQ and 6th Brigade. (These arrived safely in Egypt after completing the hazardous eastern voyage, during which they were exposed to attack from the Italian-held Dodecanese.) Freyberg had, therefore, to extemporise his HQ and was short of three battalions. He now faced a cruel dilemma. To hold Maleme strongly risked isolation there if the crucial road was cut. Alternatively, if the line of communication was kept intact, he risked losing the airfield, allowing the enemy to become established. With the limited resources available in this desperate situation, Freyberg's efforts were doomed, although in the event by the narrowest of margins.

His general dispositions were excellent, but there was a fatal flaw. There was insufficient strength at the airfield itself. In particular, the dried-up bed of the Tavronitis River, which formed the western perimeter of the airfield, was lightly held and there were none of our troops in the riverbed itself. Those three battalions were sorely missed.

The German parachute attack was a disastrous and costly failure and the glider troops did little better. General Student in Athens was appalled, but kept his nerve and summoned an experienced Ju 52 pilot. General Student ordered the pilot to take his plane and land briefly at Maleme, with his engines running, and quickly assess the situation. The mission was entirely successful: the pilot reported that the Tavronitis offered dead ground and was not defended. This was decisive: Student ordered a mountain division to land by glider, whatever the cost, in the river bed. The tide of battle turned. Gradually the gallant defenders, heavily bombed, were overwhelmed and had to withdraw.[3]

NOTES

1. W. S. Churchill, *The Second World War*, Vol. III, pp. 63–68.
2. Base and Lines of Communication troops had been in Greece since the previous autumn.
3. A major contributory factor was the desperate shortage of wireless sets so that commanders lost contact with their forward troops.

INTERLUDE

The balance sheet at June 1941 made grim reading. There had been victories in Abyssinia and Cyrenaica (the latter now lost), severe defeats in Greece and Crete, serious trouble in Iraq, unrest in Palestine (fomented by the Mufti of Jerusalem) and conflict with recalcitrant Vichy French in Syria. All these problems occupied the thoughts and energies of General Wavell, Commander-in-Chief, Middle East, who as Britain's senior representative also had political and diplomatic responsibilities. The burden was too much even for a man of Wavell's ability and capacity. To make matters worse, Churchill was pressing for an offensive against Rommel, who was glaring at us on the Egyptian frontier. An attack, Operation 'Battle-axe', was therefore launched and was a dismal failure. It was clear Wavell had been bearing too heavy a burden, and was over-strained and tired. He would have to be replaced, and the choice fell on General Auchinleck. Wavell was made viceroy of India. There was great sympathy for him from the ordinary soldier, who did not blame Wavell for the disasters: presumably politicians were responsible. Foremost in memory was the dash to Benghazi, and his placing a strong garrison in Tobruk, which effectively restricted Rommel's ambitions.

The new commander-in-chief was exceedingly fortunate. The slate had been wiped clean. All the triumphs and disasters (mainly the latter) had been resolved in one way or another. The only outstanding military problem was the looming presence of Rommel and this demanded decisive action. Auchinleck could concentrate on this without distraction. To sustain his efforts, substantial reinforcements were on their way and the Western Desert Force was to become the Eighth Army. Moreover, he had been freed from political and diplomatic responsibilities. These would now be assumed by a Cabinet minister resident in Cairo, initially Oliver Lyttelton. The contrast with the situation with which Wavell had to cope could not be more striking. Sadly, this wonderful opportunity was to be squandered in defective strategy and incompetence.

* * * * * * * * * * *

Soon after our escape from Crete, we were back at base near Cairo, somewhat the 'worse for wear' after two evacuations! For some reason, all the marquee tents had been removed, leaving their outline marked by a low sand parapet, presumably the remains of anti-aircraft protection. We therefore slept in the open and were awakened early, either by the sun, or by comrades still in their dreams reliving the weeks in Greece and Crete and crying 'Look out', 'Take cover!' and so on. Fortunately, with daily visits to Cairo, we had all regained our equilibrium within a few weeks.

Meanwhile, after Abyssinia, the 212th battery was engaged against the Vichy French in Syria. After our mauling our battery was in a disorganised state, lacking guns and vehicles. It was an appropriate moment to contract malaria. I was sent to a hospital in Alexandria. During my recovery I was gratified and impressed by being prescribed a daily small bottle of Guinness – the doctor had evidently read all those advertisements! I could not help reflecting on the real cost of this luxury, the long and hazardous voyage round the Cape. There followed two weeks' convalescence at El Arish, whose wadi, the ancient 'brook of Egypt', lies on the frontier with Palestine. Life was extremely pleasant, with a beautiful sandy beach among date palms. I noticed that some of the natives had blue eyes and fair complexions. On enquiry I was gravely told that Napoleon's army had passed that way! (I did not know whether to take this as a slur on Allenby's army, or not!) We were also given a talk by a tarbushed British pasha in the Egyptian police (one of the many signs of the imperial presence) about their desert adventures and the difficulties in attempting to extirpate the drug trafficking by Arab gangs infiltrating from Iraq and Saudi Arabia.

I was also fortunate to be given a few days' leave in Jerusalem. With the lack of tourists there, even the rude soldiery was welcome. The Greek archimandrite at the Church of the Holy Sepulchre tried to sell us certificates (ten piastres, please) showing we had come to the city as devout pilgrims. As we hadn't, we didn't! The church was, however, well worth a visit, a fourth century basilica originally built by Helena, mother of the emperor Constantine who had made the minority religion, Christianity, the official religion of the Roman Empire. Then there were the swarms of Arabs at the Church of the Nativity in Bethlehem striving to sell small Eyre & Spottiswood bibles covered in 'real' cedar of Lebanon. The rivalry for precedence in the basilica between Catholics, Orthodox and Copts was obvious, and I was reminded of the tensions which Sir Ronald Storrs had to deal with when Governor of Jerusalem, which he describes so graphically in *Orientations*. Shortly afterwards, and much refreshed, I returned, via El Arish, to my regiment.

On 22 June came the dramatic news that Hitler, now that he was no longer haunted by the fear of a war on two fronts (or so he thought), had invaded Russia. Churchill, although strongly anti-communist, was a supreme realist and promptly secured an alliance with Russia. We all recognised the immensity of this transformation: we were no longer alone. Meanwhile, we were re-united with the 212th Battery, but our deficiencies persisted. We were still condemned to non-combatancy, when I again reported sick.

I was diagnosed with impetigo, which was then very prevalent. This is a most unpleasant and highly infectious condition of facial running sores. It prevents shaving, so that one looks a frightful mess. I was admitted to No. 9 General Hospital at Heliopolis. The treatment consisted of a bright purple ointment, so that the appearance of the victims was even more bizarre. One day, those interested were able to attend a concert of Schubert lieder given by a very Germanic lady with a heavenly voice. At night we would lie awake with all the windows open listening to the soundtrack of the film being shown at the nearby open-air cinema. This left each of us to visualise the scene, but after a few nights we became very irritable and longed for the change of programme. I began to pity those living nearby who had to endure this nuisance. My sores soon cleared up. I could shave again and was due for discharge. When I told the nurse I had a temperature she looked at me very sceptically; malingerers were not popular. Her thermometer restored her faith in me, however, and the doctor diagnosed sandfly fever, which I had contracted in the hospital (I remembered having been bitten by an insect a few days before). This is not serious and I was soon fit for discharge.

I rejoined my battery and soon we were equipped with 6in howitzers, our familiar friends of First World War vintage, so we were still haunted by Britain's lack of preparation. It was at this time that I ceased to be a member of the command post team and was posted to 'A' troop as GPO Ack. (Gun Position Officer's Assistant) and given a single stripe – the first step to my field marshal's baton! I rather relished the change, because while I missed the conversation with my specialist colleagues, I realised that as the only specialist in the troop (apart from the OP Ack.) I would be able, within limits, to 'do my own thing' – the nearest I could get to independence in the circumstances. I also felt that being with the guns made me more of a genuine artilleryman than was the case as an 'office-wallah'. In addition, the gun position rivalled the OP in potential danger. The battery command post was relatively safe: RHQ we regarded as non-combatant!

In August or September 1941, I and two of my fellow 'specialists' were nominated for the Officer Cadet Training Unit (OCTU). We were the first nominees from the 211th Battery, and possibly from the regiment. There was no residential selection board in the Middle East as there was in the UK, and the procedure was for nominees to be interviewed by their divisional commander, or Commander Royal Artillery (CRA) in the case of the artillery. Our CRA, Brigadier Dimerline, was well known and liked by the men because he was a frequent visitor and always had a smile and a cheerful wave of the hand, so we were quite looking forward to our interviews. When we arrived we were disconcerted to hear that he had been summoned to an important conference, and we were to be seen by a brigadier unknown to us. We took this information philosophically; there was nothing we could do about it.

My interview seemed to be proceeding fairly well when the brigadier said: 'I see that you have a degree in economics. Where were you trained?' I at once felt unease. The London School of Economics had a reputation of being a 'hotbed of communism', a phrase coined by the *Morning Post* (which perhaps the brigadier read). I told him that the LSE was, indeed, my college. There was a pause and the interview soon terminated. Both my friends were accepted: I was rejected. I do not, of course, know the reason for this, but suspected my association with the LSE may have had something to do with it. I was naturally chagrined, but took it stoically enough and concentrated on my new job as the sole 'specialist' on the 'A' troop gun position. This was in fact rather lonely, since I now had less opportunity for serious discussion with other specialists.

Our gunners were thoroughly familiar with the 6in howitzer, but since it was short-range and obsolescent, we could not be risked in the mobile operations of the large-scale offensive Auchinleck was planning for the autumn. We were condemned to the sidelines. We spent much of the autumn in the barracks at Mersa Matruh, thoroughly bored and somewhat dispirited. The only thing of interest was the titanic struggle on the eastern front.

* * * * * * * * * * *

We are now very familiar with the pattern of a prime minister pressing his generals to attack before they considered themselves ready. Auchinleck experienced this remorseless pressure himself, but being a new man it was possible to withstand the Churchillian demand: he could hardly be dismissed so soon after his appointment. He insisted he would not be ready to attack until November. The desert force was now officially designated the Eighth Army and Auchinleck was urged to appoint General Wilson to command it. Unfortunately, Auchinleck insisted on his own choice, Lieutenant-General Alan Cunningham, (the brother of the redoubtable commander of the Mediterranean fleet), who had successfully completed the Abyssinian campaign. This soon proved a disastrous choice. One of Auchinleck's most conspicuous failings was that he was a poor judge of men; a weakness of which he seemed unaware. This contributed to his downfall.

The offensive, code-named 'Crusader', was designed to relieve Tobruk and regain Cyrenaica. It opened on 18 November. A critical situation soon developed with some very heavy fighting, notably at Sidi Rezegh and El Gubi. General Cunningham, who had never been engaged in tank warfare and was meeting the Germans for the first time, lost his nerve and wanted to order a retreat. The BGS Eighth Army, Brigadier Galloway, urgently requested Auchinleck's presence. He flew up to Cunningham's HQ and ascertained that both corps commanders favoured continuing the attack. Auchinleck concurred. On 25 November Cunningham was sacked and replaced by Major-General Neil Ritchie, the deputy Chief of Staff in Cairo. Ritchie was another unfortunate choice, although for rather different reasons. Auchinleck then returned to Cairo.

Operation 'Crusader' swayed dramatically, but Rommel was eventually forced to withdraw, abandoning his garrisons at Bardia and Halfaya. Tobruk was relieved (after a siege of nine months), Cyrenaica cleared once more and Benghazi captured. We were back in the position of a year before, but at much greater cost.

We had been following these events while in reserve at Matruh when the dramatic news came through of the Japanese attack on Pearl Harbor on 7 December. The two Axis powers, with overweening self-confidence, promptly declared war on the USA, and so our prospects, now with two major allies, were revolutionised.

The isolated enemy garrisons at last provided us with the opportunity of being actively engaged, because our antiquated equipment was perfectly suitable for a static siege. We therefore were ordered to move in December to the rather bleak plateau overlooking Bardia. The weather was cold and we had Christmas dinner in this inhospitable place.

The garrison, having been besieged for some weeks, capitulated on 2 January 1942, and some 8,000 prisoners were taken. Attention was now concentrated on the last remaining pocket of resistance at Halfaya, and this surrendered shortly afterwards, with a further haul of about 5,000 prisoners.

* * * * * * * * * * *

With Cyrenaica freed and Rommel back in his long-stop position at Agheila, it was judged that, given our disabilities in armament, our regiment could not further be usefully employed. We would be better employed against the threat of a German breakthrough in the Caucasus, an obsession of Auchinleck's, so we were directed to Syria. The early part of 1942 we spent near Damascus. Since Wavell's suppression of the Vichy authorities, relations with the French had eased, but were not really cordial. French influence was very apparent, but their troops, having no active role to play, kept a low profile. A few American officers and NCOs arrived as 'observers' and were later in attendance at Alamein. Presumably they were intended to get the 'feel' of the Middle East and to gain some insight into German and British tactics and methods.

There was a large white house, near the main road into Damascus, which was the local brothel. The troops naturally referred to the place as the 'White House', which incensed some of the Americans. They retaliated by calling it 'Downing Street'. This was getting childish and it was in vain that I remonstrated, pointing out that the name was a literal description, nothing more. It was not meant as a slight. The Americans remained unconvinced.

As a precaution, we were to prepare defensive anti-tank positions in the hill country to the north of Damascus and in the Barada Gorge. We had to select suitable positions, survey them in and site each anti-tank gun indicating its field of fire. An officer of the Royal Engineers then arranged with a local contractor for four concrete-filled oil drums to be placed at each corner of a 6in reinforced concrete roof, under which the gun would be sited. All this effort seemed to me at the time to be of very doubtful value. That the roof might come crashing down on the unfortunate gun crew seemed only too likely. I hoped that the positions would be quickly camouflaged, because the glaring white of the roofs made the positions very obvious to air reconnaissance. The only beneficiaries of this misguided zeal were the Syrian contractors, who were greatly enriched.

About this time our 6in howitzers were withdrawn and replaced with 155mm howitzers, which bore the name-plate 'Rock Island Arsenal, N.Y. 1916'. We had therefore not made the exchange in the direction of modernity. The change seemed pointless, but my guess was that the 6in howitzer had been withdrawn as ammunition was no longer available. The Americans had ample stocks for their equally antiquated guns. It was decided we should go to a firing camp to calibrate and to get used to the new equipment. They had a very low muzzle velocity, and it was diverting to stand behind the gun and watch the shell as a tiny blob at the top of its trajectory before it disappeared on its downward plunge. The breech mechanism attracted some undeserved derision: it was so simple. One pulled a 'lavatory chain' and a small hammer came up and hit the percussion cap a sharp blow to fire the weapon. Yet the system was undoubtedly trouble-free and effective, whereas the finely engineered British breech sometimes caused problems.

EIGHTH ARMY'S GUNS

Soon after our return from firing camp (April or May 1942) we were to our great joy re-equipped, at last, with modern guns – 4.5in for the 211th Battery and 5.5in for the 212th Battery. For almost a year and a half of active war we had perforce been condemned to obsolescent pieces. We felt forgotten and abandoned, always handicapped. We were entranced, intoxicated, by the new guns. We felt we had never seen guns so beautiful. The effect on morale was dramatic: we were eager to bring them into action as soon as possible and settle some old scores.

The new guns had identical carriages, which suggests that the designers had standardisation in mind from the outset. They weighed about six tons (one ton equals 2,240 pounds), which called for considerable muscular effort by the gunners. The 4.5in had a long, slender barrel, that of the 5.5in was stubbier, and naturally the breech mechanisms were not identical. The split trail ensured stability and enabled the detachment to serve the breech without encumbrance. There was a spade on each leg which was always bedded-in to the soil. For wide deflections the gun had to be manhandled, the crew being helped by hand-spikes. The designers had, however, been considerate, and quick traversing gear enabled the piece to be moved rapidly 30 degrees either side of the centre-line, so that a substantial zone (60 degrees) could be covered without the need to move the gun. The detachment numbered ten, including the tractor driver, commanded by a sergeant. Each member had a specific task, although was capable of switching tasks to ensure flexibility in case of casualties, or to provide some variety. The ideal gunner was stocky and strong, not only to serve the gun in action but to carry ammunition and dig gun pits when necessary.

As mentioned above, the common carriage of the 4.5in and 5.5in guns suggested the designers had standardisation in mind: it would simplify the supply of spare parts and ammunition.

Unlike the field regiments, we were very well served by our gun tractor. It had good accommodation for the gun crew. There was room for 60 rounds of ammunition, hand-spikes, picks and shovels, camouflage netting, a tarpaulin, rifles and personal kit. The AEC engine was similar to that used on London buses, and there was a powerful winch. The side brailings could be rolled up to improve ventilation, a useful feature in the desert. The only disadvantage was the high vehicle profile, which perhaps was unavoidable.

Since the field artillery outnumbered the medium guns by some 16:1, it will be appropriate to say something about our colleagues and their invaluable contribution to our success. If excellence is the hallmark, some description of the superbly designed 25-pounder gun is necessary.

In 1933 the field artillery consisted of 13-pounder and 18-pounder guns, and 4.5in howitzers. These compared badly in range and explosive power with foreign artilleries. The need for flexibility of direct fire to engage moving targets in armoured warfare was foreseen. By 1937 an 18-pounder had been converted to the Mk. I 25-pounder. The Mk. II version was introduced in 1940 for British and Commonwealth armies, but only in very small quantities. The position much improved in 1941 when Australian and Canadian production became available. (Britain alone produced 12,000 of these guns by the end of the war.) This successful outcome followed a most imaginative collaboration: tests at Larkhill with the artillery, who commented on the various versions.

The 25-pounder had a box trail; a split trail, with both spades dug-in, would have restricted flexibility, which was a primary consideration. Flexibility was achieved by mounting the gun on a circular platform, enabling rapid changes in deflection. There were variable charges placed in a brass cartridge case. Shells were loaded separately. The gunshield was partially hinged at the top, permitting the layer to engage tanks over open sights. The maximum range was 13,400 yards, the calibre of the shell, 3.45in. The gun was quick-firing, accurate and flexible. It was a joy to operate and was dubbed 'the gunners' favourite'. By 1943, the gun, in its anti-tank role with armour-piercing shot and supercharge, was fitted with a double bafffle muzzle brake to control the violence of the recoil. The detachment was six men. The gun was a triumph of design and contributed greatly to the excellence of the British artillery.

Sadly, its tractor – the 'Quad' – had many design faults, unlike the medium artillery equivalent. Its fuel tanks were at the sides, which made them vulnerable to tracer fire, and there was no armour. The short wheel base and high clearance made for a rough ride. When fully loaded (96 rounds), and with the trailer (limber) holding 32 rounds and towing the gun, the vehicle was slow and a liability in mobile desert warfare. Finally, the all-metal body of the 'Quad' made it like an oven in the desert for the unfortunate crew, though such was the quality of these men that they triumphed over all adversity. The various defects of the 'Quad' were, of course, recognised but in the stress of war they remained uncorrected.

The Eighth Army had an advantage over the enemy in numbers of guns, but its establishment included only four medium regiments, of which two were lost in Tobruk in June 1942. There was no heavy artillery at all, whereas both the Germans and Italians had a full range of calibres, including 170 and 210mm heavy guns. The enemy had therefore an advantage in range and weight of shell.

GUNS OF THE FIRST AND SECOND WORLD WARS

Since we had experience of the guns of both wars, the reader may be interested in a comparison of their characteristics. Clearly many changes in design objectives had been incorporated. Great strides in design concept were being made as war loomed near.

The most striking difference was the increase in range of the Second World War guns as a result of higher muzzle velocities. Reference has already been made to the very low muzzle velocity of our US 155mm howitzers, and this was typical of First World War artillery. During the Second World War, the 4.5in gun threw a shell of 56lbs a maximum of 20,500 yards (about 12 miles) on Charge III, with a muzzle velocity of 2,250ft/sec, some three times the speed of sound. If one was forward of this supersonic artillery, one first heard a sharp crack overhead as the shell broke the sound barrier, followed appreciably later by the boom of the gun. As a result, in sharp contrast to the First World War, the enemy received no warning of the approach of the shell and thus incurred casualties before they could get to ground. Supersonic muzzle velocity caused enormous stress on the recoil mechanism, leading sometimes to breakdown and indicating the limits of this advanced design.

The introduction of an 86lb shell, replacing the earlier 100lb shell of the 5.5in gun (also supersonic) increased its range from some 16,200 to 18,000 yards. This meant that the 4.5in gun, which with its lighter shell had previously had a better range, now had only a marginal advantage over the 5.5in. So, the larger calibre gun became standard for the still unengaged forces in the UK. But, the 4.5in persisted in the Eighth Army, which has confused many commentators.

In the First World War in France, artillery of both sides suffered heavy casualties from counter-battery fire, the result of poor internal communications. One needed a stentorian voice, even with the help of a megaphone, to make fire orders audible against a huge background of noise. Guns were therefore bunched, even wheel-to-wheel, with the command post very close. In the Second World War, the position was transformed by the development of the Tannoy loudspeaker. Each gun had one of these connected by wire to the command post microphone control box. Orders could now be heard clearly and without difficulty, permitting the guns to be dispersed some 50 yards apart, invariably in a diamond formation. This dispersion naturally reduced the risk of casualties not only from counter-battery fire but also from air attack. At the same time it gave the most effective deployment in the unlikely event of a tank incursion. That this diamond pattern was reproduced in the target area was considered an advantage, giving a good spread of shot. Pinpoint targets were rare, and if encountered, could be dealt with easily.

Trench warfare was dominant in France during the First World War, and great use was made of howitzers, with their high trajectory and steep descent angle. They had, however, limited range. They could be regarded as heavy mortars. In the Second World War, as we have seen, the designers gave much more emphasis to range, but they did not wish to lose the advantages of the howitzer. The result was a very happy compromise, already foreshadowed by the old 60-pounder, incorporating the benefits of both by the introduction of varying propellant (cordite) charges for both medium guns and for the ubiquitous 25-pounder field gun, which were all, strictly speaking, gun-howitzers.

Artillery had been controlled by direct fire since the 14th century, but the First World War, with the dominance of indirect fire, saw the apparent demise of direct fire. The development of armoured warfare, however, caused the revival of direct fire with a variety of anti-tank guns. The 25-pounder field gun was specifically designed with an anti-tank function as a valuable secondary role.

For a substantial spell the Eighth Army was reduced to two medium regiments, of which the 64th was one. The demand for range and weight of shell meant we were never out of action, and much of our fire was on Charge III, which increased wear on the barrel rifling and increased the risk of buffer-recuperator and other problems, requiring the attention of the troop artificers.

In the First World War, the lighter calibre guns fired a great deal of shrapnel. In the Second World War, High Explosive (HE) only was used because of its devastating destructive power. One could pick up a shell splinter (after it had cooled!) and note its irregular shape and jagged edges, and realise the terrible nature of the wounds, often fatal, it could inflict.

* * * * * * * * * * *

Our artillery was well directed, intelligent and imaginative. Guns could be used to great effect in isolation, or a troop could have a roving or specific task. Used in a co-ordinated, fully integrated manner, its mass effect was devastating and often decisive. This was particularly the case after Montgomery arrived. (See Chapter 9.) The British artillery was thoroughly professional and compared well with its German and Italian counterparts. Criticism is often made of other arms, notably the armour, but I have yet to come across adverse comment of the artillery's role. Indeed, our contribution is often taken for granted and receives scant mention.

FIASCO AT MATRUH

I n the previous chapter, reference was made to our relatively minor role in the concluding stages of the 'Crusader' battle, and to our belated re-equipment in Syria with modern guns. It will be helpful to relate briefly the dramatic events demanding our urgent return.

History seldom repeats itself exactly. Rommel attacked unexpectedly in January 1942, utilising the well-known desert route to Mechili. We lost Benghazi, but halted at Gazala, at the eastern end of the 'bulge', not at the Egyptian frontier. At this point, both sides took a defensive posture until ready to launch a major offensive.

Rommel's strategy was simple and practical. The long siege of Tobruk had convinced him that this town must be his overriding priority. He had been trying to take Tobruk at the precise moment the Eighth Army was attempting to relieve it. Hence the confused nature of the 'Crusader' battle. Tobruk still remained Rommel's objective and Gazala was conveniently near.

Auchinleck's ambitions were much grander. There was a funda-mental contradiction in his strategic ideas of which he seemed completely unaware. He seemed to simultaneously hold the views that (1) Tobruk was essential to provide logistical support for his advance to Benghazi and, hopefully, Tripoli and (2) Tobruk was of no value; it could be abandoned and troops should not be invested in it. Events were to show that it was this latter view which came to predominate. Defeat was fore-doomed against a ruthless and single-minded opponent.

From his distant desk, Auchinleck exercised a strong influence on his newly-appointed protégé, Ritchie. This was most unfortunate because of Auchinleck's confused views on strategy. For him, the hypo-thetical was more important than the actual. With a greatly exagger-ated fear of a German breakthrough in the Caucasus, he was obsessed with the idea of 'keeping the army in being'. He completely failed to appreciate the crucial importance of holding Tobruk and the vital need to supply Malta. He told Ritchie early in January that if the Eighth Army had to retreat he had no intention of holding Tobruk permanently or any place west of the frontier.[1] For good measure, a month later, he told Ritchie that troops were not to be invested in Tobruk,[2] in spite of the spectacular proof only a year before of the strategic value of the place. Still more strange was Auchinleck's apparent willingness to abandon the huge supply base he had established just east of Tobruk (at Belhamed) to sustain our next offensive, and for which he had authorised and constructed an extension of the railway line from Matruh to Belhamed, as well as a water pipeline. These measures had been taken to reduce dependence on the little port of Tobruk and lessen naval escort casualties. Thus his policy was riddled with contradiction and invited disaster.

Poor Ritchie must have found this rather puzzling. To add to his difficulties, on appointment he had been promoted Lieutenant-General, but as General Brooke points out, he had not even commanded a division, so not only his two corps commanders, but also his divisional commanders were senior to him. Moreover, they were experienced in desert ways and regarded Ritchie as a novice and unduly subservient to the C-in-C. Ritchie sometimes had difficulty in enforcing his orders. Quite inadvertently, Auchinleck had weakened the army's command structure. No wonder Churchill said the army had been reduced 'to bits and pieces', no doubt a reference to Auchinleck's preference for the brigade group, rather than the division, as the basic unit, as well as his poor sense of the need for co-ordination between the various arms.[3]

The British defensive line consisted of a series of 'boxes' running south at increasing intervals from the coast at Gazala. If the line had a purpose, it was to defend Tobruk. Unless our armour controlled the intervening spaces, a particular box could be overrun and a breach made in the line. Three of the boxes were at brigade strength and so were liable to be overrun. Auchinleck had a hunch the attack would come in the centre. Ritchie loyally passed this opinion to his subordinate commanders, who accepted it, naturally assumed it was based on good intelligence. But, Ritchie himself thought (correctly) that the attack would be in the form of a southern enveloping movement. As a result, a compromise was reached leading to divided counsels and confusion when battle was joined. If ever a battle was lost before it began, Gazala was it!

Rommel launched his attack on the night of 26/27 May, his southern outflanking move biting deeply into the British position. He was, however, himself in an exposed and vulnerable position, and withdrew westwards to the eastern side of our minefield, where he attacked the 150th Brigade box from both sides, overrunning it with a haul of 4,000 prisoners. By the end of May he now had a much shorter line of supply, and was protected from attack by a ring of anti-tank guns and tanks, 'the Cauldron'. The crisis of the battle occurred on 12 June when the British armour suffered a heavy defeat just south of the 'Knightsbridge' box. After further hard fighting Rommel captured Tobruk on 20 June, taking 33,000 prisoners, much artillery, equipment, vehicles and large quantities of petrol and stores. It was one of the blackest days in the history of the British army.

The grave crisis of 12 June caused alarm bells to ring in Cairo. The decision was taken to denude Syria of troops and accept the risk of a Russian collapse in the Caucasus. The 64th Medium Regiment must have been one of the first alerted, because on 15 June we were in the Delta area drawing stores to bring us to full efficiency. (The NZ and 9th Australian Divisions left Syria and Palestine respectively soon after.) Our command post vehicle had developed a wireless fault and I had to take it into the repair shops in Alexandria, but we caught up with the regiment at Daba. We by-passed Matruh and were at Sidi Barrani on 17 June. Next day we were on the plateau overlooking Halfaya Pass with a number of OPs in position. Our sudden move told its own story, but the BBC news underlined the gravity of the situation. On 19 June a troop of Gurkhas with six 2-pounder anti-tank guns was attached to provide local defence, but there was no other sign of our forces. The enemy appeared on 20 June, and we engaged targets towards Sidi Azeiz and transport near Capuzzo. It was a great thrill to fire our new guns for the first time: they behaved splendidly. Our morale was very high. The guns were uncalibrated, but that did not matter in observed shooting. The next day was spent in a similar fashion, then we heard the shocking and incomprehensible news of the surrender of Tobruk. Like everyone else, based on the previous experience, we had expected a long siege. This news spelled disintegration. Our faith in the high command was deeply suspect. Yet we remained confident. With our new guns we could face anything.

Our part of the desert was very empty, but we were aware that the broken remnants of the Eighth Army were streaming back in disarray on the coastal road. Incongruously, we were delighted to welcome a small NAAFI van which had recently left Tobruk and was loaded with cigarettes. The driver very sensibly had decided that there was little point in taking his precious cargo all the way to the Delta when there was a fully organised group of customers so readily to hand. We each received a carton of 200 *Wings* cigarettes. In the cartons was a small slip of paper reading something like: 'From the people of the USA to the front-line defenders of democracy'. We were to earn those cigarettes over the next few days.

On 22 June we engaged enemy transport and in the evening fired on tanks in the Capuzzo area. After dark, we withdrew on orders through the minefield, but as there was no means of lifting all the ammunition, arrangements were made for the Indian army engineers to detonate it. We were not engaged in the Bagush area but there was plenty of welcome RAF activity overhead. Three days later, the two troops of our battery were reunited at Mersa Matruh.

Ritchie had decided to fight a delaying action at Matruh, rather than on the frontier, and Auchinleck concurred, intending to use the delay to strengthen and organise the Alamein defences. (XXX Corps had been sent back for this purpose.) On 25 June Auchinleck belatedly accepted responsibility for the mess and sacked Ritchie, taking over the army command himself. He made another of his extraordinary misjudgements and appointed Dorman-Smith his personal chief of staff in the field, as an *éminence grise*. Still more serious was the fact that he intended the emphasis to be on mobility and fluidity. Unfortunately, this was widely interpreted as an order to withdraw, and this impression dominated the action. It was the dominating influence on the ensuing confused action. Too many formations found a reason for precipitate withdrawal. Command and control disintegrated. Beyond question, this was the most incompetently directed operation in which we were ever engaged.

On entering the perimeter of Mersa Matruh we noticed that the anti-tank ditch was silted-up and there was a general air of unpreparedness. We were already critical of being cooped up in defences (which were less formidable than those of Tobruk) with a wide open flank to the south. A garrison of a scratch character, mainly the 10th Indian Division under the newly formed X Corps, spent a few precious days in limbo before any orders were issued to organise and deploy. Some enemy aircraft flew over and dropped a few bombs, but their main purpose was clearly reconnaissance. On 26 June we were in action at night at 'Charing Cross', a track junction south-west of Matruh, but the next day we returned and reconnoitred a position in the perimeter near the coast road. During the day we learned the main road east towards Alexandria had been cut. We were not surprised: we had seen tracer fire to the east. No-one seemed very disconcerted at this news.

Freyberg had arrived with the NZ Division fresh from Syria and placed it on a bluff at Minqar Qaim, south-east of Matruh, with the 50th Division close by. The 1st Armoured Division, comprising 159 tanks, including 60 of the new Grants with 75mm guns, covered the south-west of the minefield. We outnumbered the enemy in all departments. But, our centre was held by only two small groups, of the 5th Indian Division. Rommel was aware of this weakness from his aerial sorties.

The Deutsche Afrika Korps (DAK) was weak, with only 60 tanks and 2,500 infantry. (The Italians following on had 70 tanks and 4,000 men.) The German armour and the 90th Light Division, already alerted, soon located our weak spot. Although vulnerable to a British counterattack, this never materialised. Rommel saw his chance and cut the coastal road east of Matruh. He then turned to deal with the NZ Division. During the night a fierce and wild battle ensued, with the Germans getting the worst of it after a bayonet charge by the 4th Brigade. The New Zealanders, cramming every man they could on vehicles, charged through the confusion. Freyberg himself was wounded yet again. They escaped, not badly mauled. Meanwhile, the corps commander, Lieutenant-General 'Strafer' Gott, seeing the attack developing had assumed the New Zealanders had been overrun, and gave the order for the armour to withdraw, ignominiously. X Corps, inside the box, was abandoned to its fate when the order for them to withdraw was delayed by a signals failure.

We were blissfully unaware of the pending withdrawal. All we knew for certain was that the road to the east had been cut. The next day, 28 June, gave little time for quiet reflection because we were in action all day, my troop firing 500–600 rounds, which was probably typical of the rest of the regiment. Our OPs were very active, and we were firing mainly on enemy batteries and transport. Our gun position was open, with no cover and our flashes must have been very conspicuous. In due course we were shelled fairly heavily and accurately, but only suffered one minor casualty. Towards evening, no-one seemed to know what was happening and there was great confusion. One of our reconnaissance vehicles had attempted unsuccessfully to discover a route out of the German ring. (We had forgotten about the minefield!)

Enemy infantry were infiltrating between the road and the sea. 'C' troop of our sister battery was engaging enemy tanks of the 21st Panzer Division with its 5.5in guns over open sights and with small arms fire, the only such action by a medium artillery regiment in the whole of the war, although there were several such instances with field batteries. The enemy clearly did not relish this treatment, but was closing in on our sector, and at night fired many success rockets to inform command of their location.

We were cut off, surrounded; but the fruit of experience had ripened. Danger was met with coolness, almost indifference. It would be better that way.

After dark, we were told that we were to break out that night. We were to make for Fuka on the coastal road to the east. This was made clear to everyone, in case we were dispersed. I vividly recall that the idea of being 'surrounded' did not greatly worry me. It seemed absurd that there could be a continuous ring of steel around us; there must be some gaps and, with luck, we should find one. I do not know whether my comrades shared this view, but there seemed a remarkable lack of concern about our predicament. It does not seem to have occurred to us that in an *organised* breakout there was a risk the enemy would locate the critical point, which is precisely what he did. We were to move single file through a cleared path in the minefield and follow a line of telegraph poles stretching indefinitely to the south-west. Actually it was the track to Siwa oasis, the one followed by Alexander the Great when he went to consult the oracle of Ammon. No orders were given as to how far we were to follow this line. We had, of course, no maps. We were dismayed on entering the minefield gap to find it brightly lit by some burning lorries which had evidently strayed from the markings and blown themselves up, or had been ambushed. This was not a happy augury for a supposedly secret move. Obviously, other units had used the same route, so surprise was lacking. Gratefully, we were soon swallowed up again by the darkness. As the guns were leaving in sequence, 'A' troop was leading, with only an OP armoured car ahead. As a precaution we all had rifles at the ready. Suddenly the silence was broken: we had run into an ambush, apparently by tanks, armoured cars and infantry, across our line of advance, which was the most obvious one. There was heavy firing at close range and I noticed how slowly the tracer seemed to loop its way towards us. My vehicle was not hit, but a man was killed and others wounded in the following vehicle. In the chaos which followed, *sauve qui peut* was inevitable. We swung sharply to our right, i.e. to the west, and hoped the guns would follow. The confusion was indescribable: one man, who was mentally weak, jumped off to ask the way and was promptly taken prisoner! Our guns seemed to be following us, but in the darkness we lost contact. As we were subsequently to find out, perhaps not surprisingly, the rear of the column suffered more than its head, as the enemy reacted more strongly. The 212th Battery ran into great difficulty and came under heavy fire. Three guns and crews were lost. Every patch of scrub seemed to our taut nerves to be a tank. We passed through several enemy wagon lines with sleeping men, and may have run over some of them. We took a few pot shots; there was little reply – they were too astonished.

Gradually we turned south and later swung east. We were delighted to find one of our guns and some other vehicles, but before dawn a heavy mist descended and we again lost contact. At first light on 29 June we perceived we were alone, the regiment had disappeared, like the mist. We must have been some forty miles south of the coast. The going was firm and from tyre marks we could see that others had passed that way. During the morning we came across an abandoned British truck and were pleased to find a case of pineapple chunks: luxury indeed! In the afternoon we regained contact with our lone gun. The scenery now was quite dramatic. The weather had eroded the softer stone so that huge crenellated columns of rock in fantastic shapes stood proud from the desert floor, with the track winding its way between. We were almost sorry to leave this remarkable landscape. We judged we must be very near the point where we should turn north for Fuka when, at a track junction, and no doubt by design, we came upon a motorised NZ patrol. They informed us that the Germans were already in Fuka and we were directed further east to a place called Alamein. As far as I recall this was the first time we had heard that historic name: it was so far back it had never featured in anyone's thoughts except for the engineers and others who had the job of fortifying it. That we had been directed to Fuka was one of the many signs of incompetence and confusion at the top. It was hardly surprising the Germans were already there because they started from east of Matruh straight along the coastal road, whereas we had had to make a long detour across the desert.

We followed the track without further incident along the escarpment of the Qattara Depression to enjoy the invigorating spectacle of the whole NZ Division sorting itself out and obviously in high spirits, apparently not the least disturbed by their sharp and bloody encounter at Minqar Qaim. The last day of June we spent sorting out and collecting stragglers after the confusion of the retreat. Many other units had suffered in the breakout, sustaining damage and casualties. It still remained for us to draw up a balance sheet and discover our losses. Only individual skill, desert craft and determination – and a dash of luck – meant that we had not shared the fate of the two medium regiments captured at Tobruk.

The affair at Mersa Matruh exhibited grave weaknesses and a missed opportunity for which Auchinleck must bear most of the blame. 'Once more, with greatly inferior force, under frequent air attack and operating on a logistic shoe-string, Rommel had routed a force, superior in number of tanks, artillery and infantry. Command in the Eighth Army had been totally ineffective and practically broke down as, inter-

mingled with Rommel's advancing troops, Auchinleck's divisions strag-
gled back to the El Alamein line. Rommel had in fact been in a very critical and dangerous situation. If, instead of a precipitate and ill-organised
withdrawal, the Eighth Army had delivered a resolute and properly
organised counterattack either on 27 or 28 June, the subsequent battles
on the El Alamein line might never have been necessary. Both Auchinleck and Gott must bear a heavy load of blame ...'[4]

NOTES

1. M. Carver, *Dilemmas of the Desert War*, p. 55. (Field Marshal Lord Carver is the
outstanding historian of the desert war.)
2. Carver, p. 60.
3. *The Battle of France and Flanders: Sixty Years On*. Eds. Professor Brian Bond, M.D. Taylor,
p.173
4. Carver, p. 131.

JULY 1942

THE SCENE

The enormous strategic importance of the Alamein position is that it could not be turned. Appreciating this, General Marshall Cornwall, commanding British troops in Egypt, instituted a careful survey in June 1940, and recommended that the modest natural defences should be reinforced by fortifications and minefields. The logic was clear: this was a 'last ditch' which had to be held to the death. When Auchinleck took up his appointment in July 1941, he implemented these recommendations, without appreciating this crucial strategic imperative.

The terrain at Alamein has been described by many authors.[1] It is a forty-mile gap between the sea and the impassable Qattara Depression. Modest natural defences were provided by small ridges and depressions and patches of bad going, but it was essential that art should reinforce nature, with fortifications and minefields. It is easy to see that with huge distances, logistics dominated everything: every mile either side advanced from its base made it more difficult to maintain the forward striking force, while the defending force, falling back, would be nearer its base. The line of communication itself helped to consume an army's substance. These disadvantages roughly balanced at the eastern and western frontiers of Cyrenaica, which was thus an area of rough logistic equilibrium. This is why the battle swayed typically to and fro within the borders of Cyrenaica.

A dramatic exaggeration of this feature appeared when Rommel advanced beyond the Egyptian frontier to Alamein, an area not previously fought over by the Germans. His logistic problem was exceptionally difficult and precarious, and aggravated by shipping losses. Intercepted messages show his great concern about his supply position, which was often critical. To add to his difficulties, he faced a defensive position which could only be pierced by a full-scale, properly mounted offensive.

The Eighth Army had long been infatuated with the 'box' concept. A box would normally be held in brigade strength, the perimeter consisting of barbed-wire and mines. Their only supplies of ammunition, food and water were what was already stored within the perimeter. In principle, the boxes formed part of a system, offering mutual support and *points d'appuis* for our mobile forces, and for success, the intervening spaces had to be controlled by our armour: otherwise, the brigade boxes were vulnerable. If the essential condition could not be fulfilled, they became exposed, hostages to fortune. These weaknesses were recognised before the disaster which overcame the 150th Brigade box at Gazala. The new concept was more formidable, with storage facilities and capacity to withstand at any rate a short siege: they were known as 'fortresses'.

None of the descriptions of the Alamein campaign I have seen pay any attention to this change in policy. Since we twice occupied the central box at Bab el Qattara ('Fortress A'), it will be helpful to describe the new type of box. The perimeter consisted of a really dense barbed-wire apron, surrounded by mines. Inside, we were surprised to find a water point, supplied by a 15-mile pipeline laid and buried, as well as underground concrete bunkers, with electric light, for use as HQ, medical centre or storage. There was also a trig. point (Qaret el Abd) – very useful to an artillery unit. On each occasion we were there, we were the only occupants; we saw no stores, from which it could be deduced that Auchinleck had decided not to hold the place very early in July. It was in fact abandoned without a fight on 9 July, and Rommel spent that night in 'Fortress A', duly impressed by it. Only the box at Alamein itself was retained, with the box at Naqb abu Dweis also given up. Rommel concluded that the Eighth Army was 'finished'! We were told that these surrenders were to shorten our line, giving a more north-south orientation. It was a pity this was not foreseen and the waste of a great deal of money and effort avoided.

Lieutenant-General Willoughby Norrie, commanding XXX Corps, had had just over a week to instil some sort of order into the confused mass of stragglers which came streaming back nose to tail, under the protective shield of the RAF, after the fall of Tobruk on 20 June. The bungled affair at Matruh had at least provided him with a little more breathing space. Gradually order was established, units sorted out and allotted positions.

The 1st South African Division was in the Alamein box on the coast with some mobile forces to the south. The 50th Division was to the south of the South Africans. Both divisions comprised only two brigades, but were reasonably cohesive after their escape from Gazala and had longer to recover. Norrie intended they should form the anchor of the position.

To the western end of Ruweisat Ridge at Deir el Shein was a hastily prepared box established by the newly arrived scratch 18th Indian Brigade, with a miscellaneous collection of guns and a few Matilda tanks. To the south-west, including Bab el Qattara, was the 2nd New Zealand Division. All the armour was collected in the 1st Armoured Division, which was straggling back from Fuka. Further back in the Delta was the newly arrived 44th Division, in reserve.

Rommel appreciated that speed was vital to achieve a decisive penetration before the main body of the Eighth Army could organise itself after the Matruh débâcle. He personally reconnoitred the Alamein position on 29 June and ordered a forced march of his pursuing troops in order to attack on 30 June. After their victories, morale was justifiably high, but following their long and arduous advance, they were thrown into action piecemeal as they arrived, when what they most desperately needed was sleep. So, a precious day was lost and the attack was deferred to 1 July.

THE ACTION

'Rommel's now exhausted and attenuated forces made contact with the northern end of the so-called Alamein line ... on 30 June'.[2] He intended to repeat the manoeuvre which had been so successful at Matruh, and cut the coastal road east of the Alamein box. The two armoured divisions were, however, in only token strength. The 21st Panzer Division had only 37 tanks, and the 15th Panzer Division had 17 runners. This total of 54 tanks was not exceeded during July.

Rommel delivered a concentrated attack with his small tank force on 1 July. His target, at Deir el Shein, was the unfortunate 18th Indian

Brigade, which was virtually wiped out. Their sacrifice had, however, blunted the German armour, which lost 18 tanks they could ill afford. Their scope for offensive action with the residue was clearly limited.

The crucial day was unquestionably 1 July, when there was a possibility that the Eighth Army could be caught not fully organised and off balance. This was thwarted primarily by the gallant sacrifice of the 18th Indian Brigade, and, on the coast, of XXX Corps. The first day, therefore, laid the foundations for the fierce and often bloody ding-dong struggle for the rest of July.

Meanwhile, the German 90th Light Division was attempting to repeat its success at Matruh by advancing to cut off the coastal box. This crack formation was, like the armour, suffering severely from attrition and exhaustion, and could only muster 1,500 men. At Matruh, XIII Corps, with the armour, had withdrawn, abandoning X Corps. Thus the 90th Light Division had been able to cut the road without much opposition from the south. The situation at Alamein was totally different, because on their right flank was XXX Corps, with the 50th Division. The weak German thrust therefore collapsed under heavy artillery fire coming from both north and south. Thus the northern door to the Alamein position was closed to the Germans. On 2 July the 9th Australian Division, at full strength and absolutely fresh, took over the Alamein box, enabling the 1st South African Division to sidestep to the south and thicken up the defences.

With his puny force, Rommel lacked the strength to break through, although further exhausted troops dribbled in. All he was able to do subsequently was desperately to try his luck with fierce, but essentially small-scale, local attacks. This set the pattern for the July encounters. 'By 4 July Rommel realised he had failed, his exhausted troops reduced to a total strength of 26 tanks fit for battle'[3].

Events were showing all too clearly that Rommel, who was heavily outnumbered, had no chance of a breakthrough after 1 July until he had had an opportunity of recuperating and adding to his strength.

Eighth Army had suffered some terrible reverses, was in some bewilderment, and not surprisingly, had completely lost confidence in the high command. We had not shared those experiences, but the appalling muddle and ineptitude at Matruh meant we shared the general distrust of the high command. Yet the army knew from long experience of desert fighting that it enjoyed a huge logistical advantage at Alamein. So the mood was dour and determined: *'Ils ne passeront pas!'* What the army craved above all else was competent leadership.

Morale was hardly a problem with recent arrivals, like the Anzac divisions who were fresh and full of fight. They were crack formations; the Germans were particularly fearful of the Australians. Morale in my own regiment was high, stimulated by our new guns. Indeed, it had increased after our recent mauling. We felt we had an account to settle after the loss of our battery's guns in Greece, and our resolve was further strengthened by our recent losses.

On 1 July, with the few guns then available, we occupied 'Fortress A'. We supported the NZ Division, and also shelled the panzers attacking Deir el Shein. Significantly, as already mentioned, we were the only occupants of the box, the New Zealanders preferring not to shut themselves up. The next day we heard three more guns had arrived from the débâcle at Matruh. Again we supported our friends who were attacking west of Ruweisat, but little came of it. There was some shelling and desultory bombing of the box, the tyres of two of our A.E.C. tractors being damaged. This clearly underlined the dilemma of troops within these so-called fortresses. If we established wagon-lines to our rear to protect our vehicles, they would be outside the perimeter and so vulnerable to an armoured foray. Thus we risked being immobilised and running out of ammunition. Although air attacks were frequent, the RAF was much in evidence, with many flights of Boston light bombers seeking targets to the west. They were no doubt helped by the proximity of our airfields. After Greece and Crete we found this most welcome and encouraging.

After two days in 'Fortress A', we moved back to the Munassib area, where we were delighted to be reunited with our other guns. My battery was now complete but, sadly, the regiment had lost three of the 212th Battery's 5.5in guns, with a corresponding number of men missing. This was very painful because we had had the new weapons for only about two months, and had lost them through no fault of our own. (We were soon brought up to strength with replacements.)

On 4 July there was a considerable concentration of vehicles in our area, offering a good bombing target. A powerful attack was delivered and the 212th Battery sustained heavy casualties, with two guns damaged. Fate seemed to bear them a grudge. Our battery was luckier: damage was slight and soon repaired. The NZ Bofors crews were very effective, and shot down a Ju 87. On another occasion they shot down three within half an hour! With so many Hurricanes and Spitfires now in evidence, the dive bomber was becoming obsolescent. The RAF was establishing air superiority.

In France and Greece, the Ju 87s had caused fear and pain with their screaming 'organ pipes'. Now we were quite *blasé*: we knew they were more bark than bite.

We remained attached to NZ Division and on 5 July re-occupied 'our' box. We now had more guns, and these were dispersed along a section of the perimeter. Again we were the sole occupants. There was some shelling of our wagon-lines, which were more conspicuous than the gun position, and on 7 July we finally vacated the fortress, moving back to divisional HQ.

The next day my vehicle was detached, and we set up an OP at Alam Nayl, or Bare Ridge as it was appropriately known. I always felt happy and at home in the desert, but there was something sinister about this wholly desolate ridge. For one thing it was very rocky and quite impossible to dig. Our only protection was a 'sangar', a 'slit trench' *above* ground, formed by piling up a protective wall of rocks. In such a place, rock splinters could be as lethal as bomb fragments. We kept a steady watch to the north-west in case the enemy should slip through where the New Zealanders had been operating, but there was no sign of activity of any sort. The next day was very quiet, and we gratefully rejoined our guns. We had officially abandoned the box at Bab el Qattara. Rommel now switched his attention to the central sector, by-passing the evacuated box.

On 10 July, the Australians attacked in the direction of Sidi Abd el Rahman, capturing ground at Tel el Eisa. Rommel reacted vigorously with every man he could scrape together, and the attack was held. It was a reminder of the Australian presence in a most sensitive area. A breakthrough here would have unhinged the whole Axis position. Any pressure on the Italians in the north could be relied on to disrupt Rommel's plans: he would have to come to the assistance of his ally. We took no part in this operation and things remained quiet. Five days later, the New Zealanders attacked a strongpoint on Ruweisat, but it was frustrated by lack of co-ordination between infantry and armour, a fault which persisted.[4]

We had noticed that every evening a flight of some twenty Ju 88s flew over and bombed a mile or so to the north quite heavily. The troops christened it 'Stuka Valley'. On 15 July, about 17.00 hours, we were ordered to prepare to move. Without even looking at the map I sensed that our destination was 'Stuka Valley' – and so it proved. There were already many vehicles in the area when we arrived, at just about the bombing hour. We deployed, and the guns were just coming into position as I left the command post vehicle with the director to give the line to the guns. (See Chapters 1 and 9). I heard the noise of aircraft and looked up to see some twenty Ju 88s overhead, with their bomb doors open and the clusters of bombs already on their way to ground. I flung myself into a shallow slit trench, the only one available, with a muttered apology to its Australian occupant. 'That's all right, cobber. Come right in!' he said. I was probably a quite welcome guest, because I gave him protection from above. When the raid had passed and the smoke and dust had cleared, I saw that our command post vehicle was on fire. Remarkably, it was the only casualty. We rushed over and threw off all the survey equipment we could, including a percussion tube box in which I kept my books.[5] The heat was intense. The GPO and all the command post staff were injured, and we did what we could for them pending the arrival of the MO. Only the wireless signaller seemed seriously wounded. He had remained at his post at the set with his headphones on, normal practice on a move, and had heard the bombers too late. He had been hit in the back of the neck as he clambered out of the truck, and died some days later. Not only was he a pleasant person, good at his job, but he had passed his Inter B.Sc. in mathematics through evening classes, a much more widespread practice in those days than these pampered times, when almost anyone can get a university place. There was nothing more I could do. I went back to the director and completed the alignment of the guns. A replacement officer quickly took over as GPO, and another vehicle assumed the command post function. We were ready for action within an hour. Then the quartermaster-sergeant arrived and rapidly re-equipped me – all my kit had been destroyed with the vehicle.

At 02.00 hours on 16 July we abandoned this ill-omened place and moved back 2,000 yards whence we came. We were in action at dawn because the enemy had counterattacked and regained some ground on Ruweisat Ridge. Strong pressure continued and we were heavily in action all day, but by evening the attack had been frustrated by our armour, and the New Zealanders, having inflicted severe casualties, held much of the ridge. The next few days were very quiet.

By 21 July, the Germans had only 42 fit tanks, and the Italians had 50. The 1st Armoured Division had 172 tanks[6]. The balance had therefore tipped still more decisively in our favour. An attack was to go in that evening, and we fired a supporting programme. The attack was three-pronged, the 5th Indian Division attacking westward along Ruweisat Ridge while the NZ Division struck north-west, hoping to form a junction at El Mreir where the panzers were concentrated. XXX Corps was to attack in the coastal sector. All these thrusts were supported by armour. In every case the co-ordination was poor and muddled and the attacks petered out after substantial tank losses, particularly from newly laid mines.

Three of our guns had been giving breech trouble and by the day of the attack there was virtually only one gun in action. Four new guns soon arrived, and we spent most of two days calibrating the new guns. This is normally carried out unhurriedly and carefully at firing camp. Thus a quiet spell in the line was very welcome, and we could inflict damage at the same time. Gunners set great store on careful calibration because accuracy in range is essential, and this naturally declines as the guns get worn in periods of intense activity. Each gun is therefore carefully ranged by observation on to a target, and the mean range, as recorded by the gun, is compared with the physical distance as revealed by the map. After an allowance for meteorological conditions, an appropriate correction can be made for each gun to ensure it is firing accurately to range. (See Chapter 9.) This accuracy could be of critical importance, e.g. in supporting the infantry with a creeping barrage.

On 27 July, we supported an Australian attack on Miteiriya Ridge. This involved a busy programme, and we fired an average of 138 rounds per gun, probably the highest expenditure rate of all the July fighting. Unfortunately, the attack was inconclusive and casualties were heavy. Apparently there was confusion at the minefield exits, and the infantry advanced beyond the armoured support. So 'yet another attempt to defeat Rommel's inferior forces petered out.' [7]

Two days later, the enemy carried out airburst ranging (involving the use of time, rather than impact, fuses) over our position. It is always a tense moment being ranged upon and waiting for the main weight of shelling to fall. The bombardment was quite heavy and accurate, but surprisingly we sustained no casualties. We were helped by the fact that about one third of the rounds were duds. Having been accurately located, we moved to a nearby position, previously occupied by a field battery, where we had the benefit of a bulldozer in digging the gun pits. Moving when located is quite normal, and is part of the deadly game of 'hide-and-seek' which the opposing batteries play. On the last day of July we were lightly shelled – we guessed by the same battery that had recently attacked us.

Our experience of the July encounter with Rommel was that he delivered a number of generally fierce, but very local, small-scale attacks, and that these were interspersed with counterthrusts by the Eighth Army, not usually well planned or co-ordinated. There were tranquil troughs between these peaks; indeed, we had been able to calibrate. This pattern was reflected by spells of brisk action on our part, because enemy attacks were frequently broken up by artillery fire, and gun support was invariably given for our own attacks. Moreover, as a battery with 4.5in guns, we commanded a vital half of the forty-mile front from positions south-east of Ruweisat. Consequently, we were unlikely to miss any really significant action. Ammunition was plentiful, and our expenditure of it mirrored these activities fairly closely, and so provided an index of what was happening.[8]

THE CONTROVERSY

Some military historians have attempted to restore Auchinleck's reputation by alleging that the July fighting represented a great victory – 'it saved Egypt' – and so is entitled to the same distinction as the October–November battle at Alamein. This is a ludicrously silly assertion to anyone who was there, but has had remarkable success, converting many to this view. It has, however, serious defects: 1) the spasmodic and disconnected nature of the July encounter discloses no overall pattern or design. Never do we feel the presence of a British commander imposing his will on events. Indeed, what we encounter is reactive, rather than proactive. 'Battle' is a misnomer. 2) The result was inconclusive, with the decision deferred until Rommel had recruited his strength for a more substantial attack. Auchinleck himself recognised this, and correctly inferred that the blow would fall at Alam Halfa. So, July did not result in victory, but merely a reprieve. Auchinleck had little confidence in the outcome, and this was reflected by panic in Cairo, the burning of official files, and contingency plans for retreat.

The impression of mainly small-scale activity is confirmed by the weakness of the German armour, a maximum of 54 tanks on the first day. To compare the July encounter with the titanic struggle at Stalingrad, as Corelli Barnett does, is to display defective judgement. That 'First Alamein' was a rather muddled series of fierce, small-scale, ding-dong actions is undoubtedly true, and it ended inconclusively through mutual exhaustion. With the issue still to be decided, it was hardly a victory. There was no epic quality, no plan being imposed on events. We did not feel we had participated in a 'battle', and when this term first began to come into use in the early 1960s, I remember being distinctly surprised and puzzled that a tough job of work was so described. We suffered more severely from enemy action in July than in any other month of the war: our judgement is unlikely to be ill-founded.

General Charles Richardson catches the mood entirely: 'I can state from my continuous presence as GSO 1 (Plans) throughout those weeks that no battle entitled to that name 'First Alamein' ever took place.'[9] He also stressed that in the period of stabilisation 'many small-scale attacks were mounted, often without adequate preparation' and these 'were the negation of that careful "stage management of the battle", that was to be the hallmark of our next manager: Montgomery.'[10]

The nature of signals intelligence (Sigint) itself tended to impose haste and short-termism rather than strategic planning. Time elapsed from receipt of signal in the UK, decoding, intelligence interpretation, coding, transmission to Egypt and decoding. There was thus little time before the pending enemy attack. Auchinleck was well informed about Rommel's intentions and his critical supply position through 'Ultra' intelligence. 'It is not surprising therefore that his own general intentions were sound in concept. The problem lay in execution.'[11] Because much of the information was based on wireless intercepts, Auchinleck's orders often 'demanded action at very short notice ... This tendency to demand instant action, which was strongly encouraged by his mercurial chief of staff in the field, Dorman-Smith, was ... in the opinion of the Brigadier General Staff, de Guingand, ... an error.'[12] Thus, paradoxically, because of the priceless asset of foreknowledge, the July fighting was a series of hasty, ill-planned counterstrokes which petered out in mutual exhaustion. So the ding-dong nature of the contest is explained: the demand for instant response. The resultant stalemate meant the decision was deferred until Alam Halfa. Both Auchinleck and Dorman-Smith knew perfectly well that 'First Alamein' had not resulted in victory, but in temporary reprieve. They were expecting the decisive battle to be fought at Alam Halfa, and were planning on that basis.

The critics have gained a supporter in a most distinguished and authoritative source. The appearance of *British Intelligence in the Second World War*, general editor Professor H. Hinsley, (first volume, 1979) meant that much of the military history which had been previously published needed revision. Here was an absolutely authoritative account based on signals intelligence derived from 'Ultra' and Army 'Y' intercepts. The impression of authority and impartiality holds for all analysis based on Sigint, but unfortunately, the editors sometimes express personal opinions, which are quite out of place in such a work. They sometimes display bias or misjudgement.

A good example is the account of the July 1942 events. There is frequent reference to the 'Panzer Army', whereas the same source shows that the German tank strength never exceeded its opening tally of 54, as we have seen. (There were some 200 German tanks at Alam Halfa.) This exaggerated term is surely misleading. The vast amount of Sigint led Auchinleck 'to his last and greatest victory, the first battle of Alamein'.[13] This is pure fantasy, a total distortion of history, because it implies that this was the culmination of a long series of victories. In fact, Auchinleck had never commanded an army in the field until Matruh, which was a disaster and a disgrace. 'Crusader' had been a hard fought and bloody victory, but, except for a few days, Auchinleck's influence had been exercised from his desk in Cairo. Then had come the loss of Cyrenaica, the severe defeat at Gazala–Tobruk and the débâcle at Matruh, until the position stabilised at Alamein, pending the real trial of strength at Alam Halfa. The July struggle was therefore not the crowning glory of a sequence of victories, but stalemate at the end of a series of disasters.

THE PANIC

It seems that as a result of the double disaster at Gazala–Tobruk, Auchinleck lost his nerve. Rommel gave him an inferiority complex. He offered his resignation on 23 June (see next chapter) and when this was refused, sacked Ritchie on 25 June and assumed command of the Eighth Army himself at Matruh (under the malign influence of Dorman-Smith), with the results already described. He regarded the prospective fighting at Alamein in July and later with foreboding, and issued contingency orders for withdrawal from that position should it prove necessary, believing 'that but for the Sigint Rommel would certainly have got through to Cairo'.[14] Surely this shows lack of confidence in the outcome, and explains his bizarre and unrealistic contingency plan for withdrawal, which should never have been even contemplated.

There were confused and contradictory plans for withdrawal of GHQ and the army. There was concern for such vital matters as the officers' baggage allowance in case of a move. De Guingand says the plan was to move GHQ sixty miles south of Cairo.[15] General Richardson is more sensational. He was instructed to draw up plans to withdraw the Eighth Army to Khartoum, some thousand miles upstream![16] A more detailed account draws attention to Auchinleck's strategic obsession: 'Auchinleck was determined to keep his army in being and give up ground rather than see it outmanoeuvred in the field. He gave orders for defences to be prepared on the edge of the Nile delta and for plans to be made for a move of GHQ to Palestine and for a step-by-step withdrawal through Egypt, part of his remaining force defending the Suez Canal, while the rest withdrew up the Nile. The Mediterranean Fleet had already left Alexandria and moved through the canal into the Red Sea.'[17] With such leadership it was hardly surprising there was chaos in Cairo.

'On 1st July Cairo had been in panic with the railway stations thronged with refugees, and smoke rising from the gardens of GHQ and the British Embassy as their staffs burnt their files'.[18] GHQ clearly had no confidence in its commander-in-chief.

The troops at Alamein were completely unaware of these disgraceful events and were in a dour and determined mood. Senior commanders did, however, know of these fantastic arrangements, and XXX Corps, anchoring itself on the coastal box, ignored them.

* * * * * * * * * * *

The War Cabinet had viewed the series of disasters with grave concern, as did the CIGS, as we shall see. The army had fallen back to its 'last ditch', almost at the gates of Alexandria. However, in view of the strength of the prepared position, and the overwhelming advantages in Intelligence, logistics and numbers we enjoyed, it was felt early in July that the slogging match was likely to peter out by the end of the month without a decision, so there would be a lull before Rommel had rested his men and recuperated his strength for a more serious and organised effort to break through. This pause would provide an opportunity for a thorough investigation on the spot to ascertain precisely what was wrong, for there was no doubt that something was seriously amiss. These worries were increased by the current news from Egypt.

Winston Churchill gives a description of the Matruh affair[19] but has virtually nothing to say about the events of July. 'Both sides fought themselves to a standstill ... Egypt was still safe'.[20] There is no suggestion that he considered the July events to have any great significance. The CIGS, General Brooke, who was preoccupied with the 'Torch' operation, showed a similar lack of concern in his diary entries.

So, the two men chiefly responsible for the direction of Britain's war effort displayed little interest in the apparently aimless and disconnected local struggles currently taking place at El Alamein, and most certainly did not see them in the apocalyptic terms of some military historians. Their overwhelming purpose in July was their forthcoming visit to the Middle East to ascertain the causes of the loss of Cyrenaica and, in particular, the recent disasters of Gazala–Tobruk and Matruh, and to identify those responsible. (This is the subject of the next chapter.) Is it not remarkable that the two men with the heaviest responsibility did not notice the great 'victory' of 'First Alamein', which they saw merely as a slugging match leading inexorably to indecision?

APPENDIX

Sergeant Keith Elliott, VC
Ruweisat Ridge, 15 July, 1942
[As related this was a tragic and eventful day for us. More dramatic was the savage fighting on Ruweisat Ridge by the New Zealanders, whom we were supporting. Absolutely outstanding was the bravery of Sergeant Keith Elliott of the NZ 22nd Battalion.]

At dawn the battalion was attacked on three flanks by enemy tanks. Under heavy tank, machine-gun and shellfire, Elliott led the platoon he was commanding to the cover of a ridge 300 yards away, receiving a chest wound. He regrouped his men and led them to a dominating ridge a further 500 yards away where they came under heavy machine-gun and mortar fire. The citation to the award of his VC, according to the obituary notice in *The Times* on 10 October 1989, says:

'He located enemy machine-gun posts on his front and right flank and, while one section attacked on the right flank, Sergeant Elliott led seven men in a bayonet charge across 500 yards of open ground in the face of heavy fire and captured four enemy machine-gun posts and an anti-tank gun, killing a number of the enemy and taking 50 prisoners. His section then came under fire from a machine-gun post on his left flank. He immediately charged this post single handed and succeeded in capturing it, killing several of the enemy and taking fifteen prisoners. Although badly wounded in four places Sergeant Elliott refused to leave his men until he had reformed them, handed over his prisoners, which were now increased to 130, and arranged for his men to rejoin their battalion.

'Owing to Sergeant Elliott's quick grasp of the situation, great personal courage and leadership, nineteen men who were the only survivors of B Company of his battalion captured and destroyed five machine-guns, one anti-tank gun, killed a great number of the enemy and captured 130 prisoners. Sergeant Elliott sustained only one casualty among his men and brought him back to the nearest advanced dressing station.'

NOTES

1. An excellent topographical description is given by M. Carver in *El Alamein*, pp. 16–18.
2. M. Carver, *Dilemmas of the Desert War*, p.132.
3. Carver, p. 133.
4. See Appendix at end of this chapter.
5. H. A. L. Fisher's *History of Europe*, F. A. Mignet's *French Revolution* and Sir Arthur Eddington's *Nature of the Physical World*. (There was a splendid English–French bookshop in Cairo.)
6. Carver, p. 134.
7. Carver, p. 135.
8. Unfortunately, we were not ordered to keep these records from the beginning of the campaign but only commenced on 21 July. Thereafter a continuous record was kept until the end of the campaign in Sicily. (These records were useful as part of the gun history and were used by the ordnance people to correlate usage with wear data.) The peak rate of 138 (27 July) compares with 125–150 at Matruh. Interestingly, the rates at Alam Halfa do not exceed this level. With the obvious exception of the very heavy rates at Alamein in October–November, much higher rates were recorded in the Tunisian battles, which may surprise many readers.
9. C. Richardson, *Flashback*, p.105.
10. Richardson, p. 104.
11. Carver, *Dilemmas of the Desert War*, p. 132.
12. Carver, p. 132.
13. Professor H. Hinsley, *British Intelligence in the Second World War*, Vol. II, p. 380.
14. Hinsley, Vol II, p. 380.
15. De Guingand, *Operation Victory*, p. 132.
16. Richardson, p. 104.
17. Carver, *Dilemmas of the Desert War*, p. 133.
18. A. Bryant, *The Turn of the Tide*, p. 419.
19. Churchill, Vol. IV, pp. 381–3.
20. Churchill, Vol. IV, p. 389.

THE INQUEST

In the summer of 1942 the Eighth Army had lost confidence in its
commanders. It was confused and bewildered, but it knew for
certain that something was seriously wrong in the higher reaches
of the command, a view shared by the War Cabinet. The record was
dreadful. After the costly victory ('Crusader'), we had been jostled out of
Benghazi in early 1942 without the excuse of the previous year, when
the competing claims of the Greek campaign had diverted attention and
resources. At Gazala, Auchinleck had the advantage in infantry and
artillery and the superiority in tanks he had specified, (three for every
two enemy tanks, but four to one against the Germans alone, who,
nevertheless, defeated our armour decisively). He was directly responsible for the strategic misjudgement which led to the loss of Tobruk.
Then had followed the muddled scramble to the Alamein gap, and the
ensuing blocking action. The War Cabinet had some confidence that the
position could be held in spite of the panic in Cairo. This is clearly
shown by the activities of the CIGS (General Brooke).

In July his energies were principally concerned to divert American
pressure from an early 'second front' into a more fruitful channel, and
this led to agreement about 'Torch', the invasion of French North Africa,
which was to be dovetailed with the Eighth Army's activities in the
desert. So, it was envisaged that Rommel's thrust into Egypt would not
only be held, but that subsequently the Eighth Army would be able to
advance westwards in concert with the 'Torch' operation.

Brooke determined to visit the Middle East as soon as he could
persuade Churchill to release him. He had been longing to go to see
for himself what was wrong: 'It was quite clear that something was
radically wrong but not easy from a distance to judge what this something was ...'[1] Meanwhile, the situation was not improving, and 'the
Auk' was suggesting giving the Eighth Army to Corbett (Chief of Staff
in Cairo). This increased the CIGS's concern: he was very doubtful

about Auchinleck's choice of subordinates. Many shared this view, including the influential Field Marshal Smuts.

Brooke appreciated that Ritchie's appointment weakened the army's command structure. Ritchie was Auchinleck's protégé, and would no doubt be turning to Auchinleck for advice. Auchinleck was very ready to interfere, even in a fluid, mobile battle, from his office in Cairo, where distance, time-lags, and signals problems could make such advice wholly inappropriate at desert HQ.

In fact, Brooke had a pretty good idea of what was wrong. We are no longer dependent on the brief extracts from Brooke's War Diaries provided by Bryant, because these have now been published unexpurgated and in full (under the title of Lord Alanbrooke, in June 2001). Brooke places full responsibility for the débâcle in Cyrenaica from December 1941 to January 1942 on Auchinleck. On 30 January he writes: 'News bad on all sides. Benghazi has been lost again ... The Benghazi business is bad and nothing less than bad generalship on the part of Auchinleck. He has been overconfident and has believed everything his overoptimistic (DMI) Shearer has told him. As a result he was not in a position to meet a counter blow.' Then follows a detailed criticism of Shearer's methods, involving far too heavy estimates of enemy casualties.[2] Only the day before, there had been serious criticism of Dorman-Smith, a continuing theme. 'I was at that time beginning to be upset by many messages that emanated from Auchinleck's office. I was beginning to be suspicious that "Chink" Dorman-Smith ... was beginning to exercise far too much influence on him. Dorman-Smith had a most fertile brain, continually producing new ideas, some of which (not many) were good and the rest useless. Archie Wavell had made use of him but was wise enough to discard all the bad and only retain the good. Auchinleck was incapable of doing so and allowed himself to fall far too deeply under "Chink"'s influence. This became one and possibly the major cause of his downfall'.[3] Similarly, on Corbett: 'I am not happy from all that I hear of the situation at Middle East Headquarters. Auchinleck's chief of staff (Corbett) is nothing like good enough for the job, and yet he insisted on selecting him. On the other hand I do not feel that Neil Ritchie is a big enough man to command the Eighth Army with an offensive impending'.[4] Brooke's diary entry for 3 August 1942, the day of his arrival in Cairo, was that Corbett 'was a very, very small man unfit for his job of CGS and totally unfitted for the command of Eighth Army, an appointment which the Auk had suggested. Consequently Corbett's selection reflected very unfavourably on the Auk's ability to select men and confirmed my fears in that respect'.[5] The inference must surely be that if a man selects second-raters as his most trusted and intimate advisers, he must be second-rate himself. Auchinleck was also extremely obstinate.

On 5 February 1942 Brooke wrote to Auchinleck about his proposed reorganisation 'and on the very indifferent handling of his armoured forces'.[6] Brooke's concern continued as the entry in his diary for 3 March shows: 'I had been worried for some time by Auchinleck's handling of armoured formations, mainly due to his listening to the advice of "Chink" Dorman-Smith. I had therefore informed him that I was sending him out one of our best armoured divisional commanders to act as his adviser at headquarters on the use of armoured forces. I knew that Dick McCreery might have a difficult time with the Auk and I warned him frankly that he might have a difficult furrow to plough. I must say that I had not expected that he would be practically ignored and never referred to by the Auk on the employment and use of armoured forces'.[7] This shows not only Auchinleck's obstinacy, but his blind faith in those who would actually destroy him and themselves. Brooke was prescient: on 12 June we suffered a crushing tank defeat. It was all of a piece that Auchinleck had refused to come home for consultation, so infuriating Churchill. This had obviously rankled, and on 24 March Churchill was talking of replacing the Auk. Brooke comments: 'I have already ridden him off trying to replace him by Gott! It is very exhausting this continual protecting of Auchinleck, especially as I have not got the highest opinion of him'.[8] This is typical of other entries, where Brooke feels he must defend a brother officer from criticism which lacks local knowledge of conditions and difficulties, while agreeing privately that the criticism is justified.

A further source of friction was the Auk continually deferring the date of his offensive. The diary entry for 8 May about this delay says, 'I do not like his message – it is a bad one based purely on number of tanks and not on the strategical situation. He never takes into account the danger Malta is exposed to through his proposed delays'.[9] On 10 May, Brooke again refers to Auchinleck digging his toes in and refusing to attack: '... he entirely failed to realise the importance of Malta and over-estimated the danger to Egypt in the event of his being defeated.' [i.e. at Gazala.][10] All talk of a British attack disappeared with Rommel's onslaught at Gazala on 26/27 May, followed by a string of disasters. When the position stabilised at Alamein, attention was concentrated on the forthcoming visit to Cairo.

There is virtually no comment by Brooke on this dreadful episode. It is odd that there is no reference to the panic at GHQ in Cairo, the burning of files, the crowds besieging the railway stations, the foolish and impractical plans for withdrawal by the army, and the proposed evacuation of GHQ. The panic was too graphic and recent a condemnation of the conduct of the war so near to Egypt's heartland to be ignored. Then there is the eloquent silence in the diary about Willoughby Norrie's visit, immediately after his resignation (dismissal?) following his successful organisation of XXX Corps' defence of the Alamein box and the sorting out of the troops retreating from the Tobruk catastrophe. The entry for 21 July could not be more bald and uninformative: 'In the afternoon Norrie, back from ME came to see me and I had an hour with him.'[11] Twice in July Brooke saw Ritchie, but still there was no reference to the current fighting. This reticence surely conceals a damning verdict on Auchinleck's competence as army commander, Brooke must have had final confirmation of all the doubts which had caused him so much anxiety since January. Sadly, the nettle was not grasped earlier, when, perhaps, some of the disasters could have been avoided.

* * * * * * * * * * * *

Churchill, of course, shared these concerns. Brooke awaited a favourable opportunity to raise the subject of his projected visit, and received permission for his fact-finding mission. He was soon discon-certed to find that the prime minister also intended to make the trip, Cairo being a convenient stop-over for the visit to Stalin in Moscow, which had just been arranged. The North African mission was thus transformed from an investigative to also an executive function.

Churchill arrived in Cairo on 3 August, Brooke having just preceded him. Churchill, too, had felt unease about the conduct of the desert war, and this was dramatically increased by the events of June. It was a dreadful shock for him to learn at the height of the Gazala battle that Auchinleck was planning to abandon Tobruk. The War Cabinet believed there was 'no doubt it should be held at all costs.'[12] As soon as he became aware of Auchinleck's plans, on 14 June, Churchill signalled Auchinleck: 'To what position does Ritchie want to withdraw the Gazala troops [1st South African Division and 50th Division]? Presume there is no question in any case of giving up Tobruk. As long as Tobruk is held no serious advance into Egypt is possible. We went into all this in April, 1941.' This was embarrassing to Auchinleck who, as we have seen, had no intention of holding Tobruk if this implied investment. Churchill found his reply equivocal, and determined to put the issue beyond doubt: 'We were glad to have your assurance that you have no intention of giving up Tobruk. War Cabinet interprets your telegram to mean that, if the need arises, General Ritchie would leave as many troops in Tobruk as are necessary to hold the place for certain.'[13] Auchinleck replied that this interpretation was correct. Sadly, the issue had already been decided because of Auchinleck's failure to understand that Tobruk must be held, even if this did involve investment. Hence his willingness to evacuate Tobruk. Later, Churchill wrote: 'In consequence of these orders the defences had not been maintained in good shape. Many mines had been lifted for use elsewhere, gaps had been driven through the wire for the passage of vehicles, and the sand had silted up much of the anti-tank ditch so that in places it was hardly an obstacle.'[14] This was especially true of the eastern perimeter. More than 30,000 troops were in Tobruk, but these included 10,000 administrative staff, and much of the rest had taken refuge there from the battlefield. It was not a determined, coherent, and resolute garrison. Inevitably, sensing the weak point on the east of the defences, Rommel attacked there on 20 June and completed the capture of the port that day. Auchinleck's grave strategic blunder explains why Tobruk was captured so quickly, a point which so puzzled public opinion after the earlier, long siege. It can have hardly improved Auchinleck's standing with the prime minister.

'The doubts I had about the High Command in the Middle East were fed continually by the reports I received from many quarters. It became urgently necessary for me to go there and settle the decisive questions on the spot.'[15]

Churchill saw the fundamental issue with great clarity. 'Had General Auchinleck or his staff lost the confidence of the Desert Army? If so, should he be relieved, and who should succeed him?'[16] Many factors played their part. Auchinleck seemed to have lost confidence in himself. He had offered to resign on 23 June, in the immediate wake of the Gazala–Tobruk disasters.[17] This offer had been rejected: with the situation in so dangerous and fluid a state it was no time to sack the commander-in-chief. So two days later, Ritchie was sacked by Auchinleck as a convenient scapegoat! The bungled affair at Matruh followed, with the scramble back to Alamein. The bloody, blocking interlude of July provided plenty of opportunity for reflection on recent gruesome events.

Churchill appeared to have had doubts about Auchinleck after the reverse in Cyrenaica. What really alarmed him was his sudden discovery that Auchinleck was preparing to evacuate Tobruk. This was utterly incomprehensible to him, as we have seen, because he thought the absolute necessity of holding the place at all cost was blindingly obvious on general strategic grounds and, in any case, had been amply demonstrated only the year before. Then there was the extension from Matruh of the broad-gauge railway, and the huge supply dump at Belhamed, which were quite pointless if Tobruk was not to be held.[18] This extraordinary contradiction must have played a major part in the decision to sack Auchinleck.

Then, presumably, had come Churchill's exposure, through the many discussions with senior officers, to the recent panic in Cairo. He had also visited several units at the front to gauge the opinion of the troops. These contacts revealed a marked lack of confidence in the high command, accompanied by a sense of bafflement. Brooke's experience of the army gave a similar impression: determination, but bewilderment. Churchill had come to the Middle East precisely to ascertain whether Auchinleck retained the confidence of the army. He clearly did not. It was, therefore, obvious that Auchinleck would have to give up at least the command of the army. Whether he should remain as commander-in-chief had still to be determined.

Initially Churchill seems to have been willing to keep Auchinleck in the Middle East, but he was to relinquish command of the army in favour of 'Strafer' Gott, commander of XIII Corps, although Brooke stressed that Gott was tired and needed rest. Then the Prime Minister offered the theatre command to Brooke himself, who was sorely tempted, but refused, reflecting that he now had some small influence on Churchill, which it would take a successor some time to establish. This is the first hint that Churchill was ready to drop Auchinleck as theatre commander, no doubt encouraged by the latter's non-committal replies about the date of his planned offensive. This clearly annoyed the Prime Minister. Meanwhile, of course, all sorts of informal opinions were ventilated, with gloom and despondency very apparent.

With the benefit of briefing from Norrie, Ritchie and many others, Brooke had arrived in the Middle East already convinced that Auchinleck should at least relinquish command of the Eighth Army, and should be replaced by Montgomery. As early as 4 August, Brooke had 'a long discussion with the Auk. A most useful one. I fortunately found that he was in agreement as to the necessary changes, i.e. a) new commander for the Eighth Army – Montgomery b) new CGS to be selected vice Corbett ...'[19]

Brooke had no doubt that Montgomery was the man for the Eighth Army, and was surprised when Auchinleck indicated that this would be acceptable to him. Brooke knew, however, of Auchinleck's tendency to interfere, and doubted whether these two could establish a working relationship. He, too, therefore, contemplated Auchinleck's removal to another command.[20] Things took a decisive turn when Churchill decided to split the command and move Auchinleck to Persia–Iraq, as he had lost confidence in him.[21] Brooke concurred. It was eventually decided that Churchill should recommend to the War Cabinet that Auchinleck should go and be replaced by Alexander, with Gott in command of the army. Brooke accepted Gott's appointment with misgivings, but was not prepared to make an issue of it. Then Fate intervened and Gott was killed in an aircrash after being shot down,[22] and Brooke fortuitously achieved his objective with Alexander as commander-in-chief, Middle East and Montgomery as commander of the Eighth Army. Both men had served with Brooke as divisional commanders in France, and he was delighted with the outcome, although he made it clear to Alexander that Montgomery was to have a remarkable degree of freedom.

Auchinleck received his dismissal as C-in-C, Middle East with ill-grace and refused the Persia–Iraq appointment. The main reasons for his downfall were the clear evidence that he had lost the confidence of the army, and, indeed, as shown by the July panic, of his own GHQ; the extraordinary contradictions in his strategic policy, notably as regards Tobruk; and his reluctance to accept advice, for example about his poor handling of armour. Crucially, he accepted uncritically poor and unsound advice, which reflected badly on his own competence. Finally, his ill-judged appointment of Ritchie to command the Eighth Army was bound to cause grave problems and was foolish, reckless and irresponsible. [23]

* * * * * * * * * * *

General Alexander arrived in Cairo on 9 August, providing opportunity for good discussion before the prime minister and his party left for Moscow. When they returned, some days after Montgomery, who had arrived on 12 August, there were further useful talks. Again, Churchill visited the forward area to assess the attitude of officers and men. He was obviously pleased with what he saw, as he reported to the War Cabinet on 21 August about his two-day tour: 'I am sure we were heading for disaster under the former regime. The army was reduced to bits and pieces and oppressed by a sense of bafflement and uncertainty. Apparently it was intended in face of heavy attack to retire eastwards to the Delta ... So serious did this appear that General Montgomery insisted on taking command of the Eighth Army as soon as he had visited the front, and by Alexander's decision the whole command in the Middle East was transferred on the 13th. Since then from what I could see myself of the troops and hear from their commanders, a complete change of atmosphere has taken place...'[24] Churchill had judged the change of mood exactly. Every man serving with the Eighth Army would cordially endorse that judgement. This remarkable transformation was achieved in a few days.

Auchinleck had a major strategic deficiency. He accepted the recommendation to fortify the Alamein 'gap' without appreciating its vital significance as the 'last ditch' which must be held at all cost. Retreat was not an option, as Montgomery realised immediately. Similarly, Auchinleck could not see the strategic value of holding Tobruk securely, in spite of the spectacular demonstration of its crucial importance only a year before. Moreover, this attitude was schizophrenic because he contemplated abandonment, while simultaneously building a huge supply dump, sustained by an extension of the railway from Matruh. He seemed unaware of this glaring contradiction. Finally, and fatally, there was his dependence on poor quality advice, e.g. on the handling of armour, which reflected on his own competence, the main cause of his downfall in the opinion of General Brooke. Auchinleck was totally unfitted for high command: his ceiling was as head of the 'imperial gendarmery'.

It is quite incomprehensible that some writers have attempted to portray Auchinleck as a competent and victorious commander. He was neither: that was the judgement at Cairo in August 1942 after diligent enquiry.

NOTES

1. Bryant, quoting Brooke, p. 431.
2. Field Marshal Lord Alanbrooke, *War Diaries*, Eds. Danchev and Todman, p. 225.
3. Alanbrooke, p. 224.
4. Alanbrooke, p. 259.
5. Alanbrooke, p. 289.
6. Alanbrooke, p. 227.
7. Alanbrooke, p. 235.
8. Alanbrooke, p. 241.
9. Alanbrooke, p. 255.
10. Alanbrooke, p. 256.
11. Alanbrooke, p. 283.
12. Churchill, Vol. IV, pp. 331–2.
13. Churchill, Vol. IV, pp. 331–2.
14. Churchill, Vol. IV, p. 371.
15. Churchill, Vol. IV, p. 408.
16. Churchill, Vol. IV, p. 412.
17. Churchill, Vol. IV, p. 421.
18. Churchill, Vol. IV, p. 333.
19. Alanbrooke, p 291.
20. Bryant, pp. 441–2.
21. Bryant, p. 444.
22. Hinsley, Vol. II. p. 380.
23. As a result of these dramatic events, in future all senior appointments had to be confirmed by London.
24. Churchill, Vol. IV, pp. 465–6.

ALAM HALFA

The July fighting ended indecisively, with the fate of Egypt still in the balance and the Eighth Army in a determined mood. It had successfully blocked the crucial gap between the sea and the impassable Qattara Depression, and felt it could do so again if necessary. The idea of withdrawal had never occurred to the rank and file. Montgomery was entirely misinformed when he told Churchill: 'Many were looking over their shoulders to make sure of their seat in the lorry.'[1] This was quite untrue. The disgraceful and confused plans for withdrawal were certainly known to senior commanders, but they had the good sense to ensure that no hint of this leaked out.

Auchinleck had correctly anticipated that Rommel's forthcoming attack would come as an enveloping movement in the south (as at Gazala, where the Auk's judgement had been at fault). Whatever 'Ultra' may have disclosed, a glance at the map would show the vital importance of the Alam Halfa ridge as a possible block to such a movement. (His appreciation of 27 July). Because all Auchinleck's attention had been concentrated on the concluding stages of the July conflict, and almost at once thereafter he was preoccupied with Churchill's visit and its disastrous – for him – outcome, no changes in disposition or defensive work had been undertaken at Alam Halfa.

The Eighth Army remained relatively serene during the early part of August 1942. Things were fairly quiet. So relaxed was the atmosphere that five percent leave rosters to Cairo were opened on 8 August, but I have no recollection if this was actually implemented. On 25 August, we moved to the 'empty quarter' in the south for the day, firing 40 rounds per gun as part of the deception programme described later.

As already related, Montgomery arrived on 12 August (at dawn) and went immediately to see Auchinleck, still nominally C-in-C. Montgomery was shocked and horrified to hear of the contingency plans for retreat, which was totally unacceptable to him, since it was obvious that

Alamein was the 'last ditch' and must be held at all costs. He had a very busy day and received abundant impressions of the recent panic at GHQ and the continuing confusion and lack of confidence. He resolved that urgent action was imperative, and left at 05.00 hours the next morning for the front, being met on the way by de Guingand, (BGS Eighth Army), who gave him, en route, a brief, lucid and comprehensive situation report. Arrived at the Eighth Army HQ, Montgomery immediately announced he was taking over command (two days early). With a serious enemy attack pending, this was no time for the niceties of protocol. He did not know how long he would have before Rommel attacked, and could not afford to lose two precious days 'kicking his heels'. (Churchill, as we have seen, approved this prompt and decisive action.) That evening Montgomery addressed the staff. The effect was electric, and many accounts have been given. Fortunately, a shorthand writer was present, so the address has been preserved.[2] Montgomery told them that the plan for withdrawal had been cancelled, they should purge their minds of the very idea. The Eighth Army would stand and fight, and if necessary, die where it stood. There would be no withdrawal. There was to be no 'bellyaching', no querying of *his* orders, which must be obeyed. The gist of his address formed an order of the day for all troops.

Montgomery had only two to three weeks to prepare for the Battle of Alam Halfa. Necessarily, he fought it with the men and resources which had been available to his predecessor. What is sad is that so august and authoritative a source as one of the Hinsley editors again lets his personal opinions intrude, showing a marked bias. He makes the ridiculous claim that 'no basic change was made to Eighth Army's plans following the change of commanders ... His [Auchinleck's] successors retained his general plan for holding the main Alam Halfa feature ... General Montgomery's appointment did, however, produce a change in style.'[3] This is quite grotesque: the claim that Montgomery merely fought the Auchinleck–Dorman-Smith plan is untenable. Montgomery fortified the feature, summoned the 44th Division from the Delta to man it, organised extensive artillery preparation, and kept everyone fully informed. The earlier plan, as has been shown, involved 'a collection of brigade "boxes" based primarily on artillery, from which surplus infantry would be sent back to the Delta ... between which mobile forces would operate against Rommel's incursion. In case that plan failed – as a good many people including notably Freyberg thought it would – troops were being held back in the Delta to defend it directly.'[4]

Montgomery tore up this plan: it no longer existed. Instead, the Eighth Army would fight where it stood. 'Montgomery's decisive contribution was to realise immediately that, if the 44th Division, held back for that purpose in the Delta, were sent up to reinforce the Eighth Army, he would have enough troops to hold a continuous line of defence as far south as Alam Halfa.'[5] Thus he was 'to refuse his flank'. Tanks and anti-tank guns were to be dug-in on the southern flank. Moreover, Montgomery, knowing the tactical inferiority of our armour and its tendency to be enticed on to a gun-line and destroyed, made it very clear that the tanks were to remain in their hull-down positions and not to be tempted. He also directed that all artillery should be capable of firing in any direction from its existing positions. Finally, he made sure that every man understood the enemy's plan and his role in defeating it.

The Eighth Army viewed the arrival of a new commander with some scepticism. We did not have much faith in generals in the summer of 1942. Montgomery was on trial, and he knew it. He was a brilliant exponent of the art of leadership, and understood soldiers' psychology. So, his showmanship was a means to an end. Hitherto, the army commander had been a remote figure; some might not even know his name, but all had heard of Rommel! Montgomery intended not only to win the battle, but to win over his army. Nothing succeeds like success.

Much has been written about the remarkable effect Montgomery had on the troops, his appearance in peculiar hats, and so on. This was superficial. We judged him on results and his manner of achievement. Many of the troops never saw him: our first encounter was months later at Tripoli. Yet the signs of a new grip on affairs was palpable, as Churchill noticed. There was the first of those special messages to the troops. These were printed on sheets, some 11 inches by 8 inches, and were widely circulated. The first gave the gist of the famous address to the staff. We were going to fight where we stood. There would be no withdrawal, no surrender. We had to do our duty so long as we had breath in our bodies. There was an invocation to the deity. (This was to become a standard feature: Montgomery was not a bishop's son for nothing.) At least the message was clear and unambiguous, and we welcomed it as a firm statement of intent, even though none of us had envisaged any withdrawal. Adjustment of position, possibly, but retreat had never crossed our minds. (We knew nothing of the scrapped plans or of the panic at GHQ in Cairo.) I read the message very carefully. Was it bombast, mere rhetoric? Who was this new general who told us to stand and fight, and if need be, die? We soon discovered he meant business and could deliver. The signs were there before battle was joined. Dumps were moved forward, so improving morale.

Montgomery's great emphasis on the need to keep the troops informed inspired emulation. Each gun position, as we have seen, had a loudspeaker system for the transmission of fire orders, replacing the old, unsatisfactory megaphone. The metal diaphragm of the loudspeaker also served as a microphone, so we had two-way communication with each gun. Naturally, the Army Commander's special message was read to all gun crews, and it was not long before we were disseminating Intelligence information and news of wider import, via the BBC. This simple method ensured good communication and promoted morale.

The incident which most convinced us that Montgomery meant precisely what he said was conveyed graphically by the appearance on our gun position one morning of a bulldozer. Our gun pits were of the normal fan-shape with their axes coincident with our zero-line, which was roughly north-west over Ruweisat Ridge, where 'the front' lay. The purpose of the bulldozer was to help us make our gun pits completely circular, so that we could fire in any direction. We had never before received such an order – nor would we ever again. Then three hundred rounds per gun were dumped. The combined import of these events was unmistakable and unambiguous. Our new general's order to stand and fight where we were was to be taken literally. We were to continue to fire even if surrounded, and preparations had been made for just this contingency. The message rapidly sank in. I am certain that the effect was to stiffen resolve.

Then there was the remarkable business of the Intelligence reports based on 'Ultra', particularly one report on Rommel's plans. Brigadier Edgar Williams has stated that the priceless 'Ultra' information had not previously been properly used, but now we had a commander who was going to use it to good purpose.[6] The effect of this change was to filter right down through the army. Details of Rommel's plan of attack were circulated down to troop command posts, Montgomery taking the risk of men being captured who were privy to this remarkable information. (This happened again in the October and other battles.) I remember clearly the report giving Rommel's plan of attack precisely and with absolute assurance. There was to be a feint attack on Ruweisat, but the real threat would come from the rear, as the enemy worked through the southern minefields, advancing east, and endeavouring to sweep round our southern flank anchored on the Alam Halfa feature.

The detail and the air of absolute assurance stimulated a lively discussion with my fellow specialists. How could we be so certain? The report was attributed to Italian POWs, but we immediately and unhesitatingly rejected this 'cover story' as totally unconvincing. We wondered whether the LRDG (Long Range Desert Group) could have been the source. We thought probably not. I had the most imaginative explanation. There were German-speaking Palestine Jews serving with the Eighth Army: perhaps some of these in captured uniforms and identity papers had infiltrated German positions? This, too, was dismissed as far-fetched. So we remained puzzled, but quite sure of the reliability of the information.

Montgomery inaugurated a revolution with his policy of 'putting the troops in the picture'. It was eminently sensible, and paid off handsomely. But there were obvious security risks. The Germans, of course, realised there had been a security leak and set up a formal enquiry. Interrogation of British POWs disclosed that we did, indeed, have foreknowledge, but, fortunately, they had all accepted the official cover story and attributed the leak to Italian prisoners. So, the Germans thought they had identified the source. We had obviously been sailing in dangerous waters and our security people would have to be more circumspect in future.[7]

With the knowledge of Rommel's plans, our prepared facility for firing to our rear became readily comprehensible, and acted as a warning of what to expect.

The battle opened at 01.30 hours on 31 August – exactly as forecast. The attack on Ruweisat was soon dealt with. The main thrust came from the two Panzer divisions, now with some 200 tanks, the 90th Light Division and the 164th Division, a recent arrival from Crete, as well as some Italian divisions also with 200 tanks. Before long, we were receiving SOS calls to bring down heavy concentrations on previously determined locations. Co-operation with the RAF had much improved now that the Eighth Army HQ was alongside the desert air force command. So, the sky was lit with flares as the bombers added to the enemy's discomfiture. These bombing attacks continued round the clock.

Our targets now called for us to swing round 180 degrees, firing towards what had previously been our rear, i.e. to the south-east. I am sure that had we not had prior warning, the sudden calls for heavy fire to our rear would have been at least somewhat disconcerting. As it was, it seemed like some drama unfolding of which we knew the script. 'Ah! Yes,' we said, 'Act I, Scene II.' Everyone was calm, phlegmatic and in good spirits. A master hand was at work – and it was not that of Rommel. This pattern continued during the day with every field and medium battery pouring in fire both on observed and predicted targets. Our hull-down tanks and dug-in anti-tank guns were heavily engaged in repelling the attacks on the ridge.

Our OPs were having a busy time in daylight, but observation was difficult because of the clouds of dust thrown up by enemy tanks and vehicles as they milled around, desperately looking for a weak point to exploit. The murk was intensified by dust and smoke from bombs, shells and the many burning vehicles. Targets were generally given as 'transport': I can only remember one target identified as a possible HQ. The battle continued nominally until 7 September, but the peak was reached on 3 to 4 September, when the enemy felt he had had enough and began to withdraw westwards. There seemed an obvious opportunity of cutting off the enemy retreat, and the NZ Division and 132nd Brigade did attack to the south. This was, however, more of a hopeful gesture, though costly, for Rommel reacted vigorously with his armour. It would have been most unwise to move our own armour from its prepared defensive position: the risks were too great. Montgomery was satisfied to have repelled the attack, and to prepare methodically for the blow he contemplated in October.

Our highest ammunition expenditure rate was 125 rounds per gun on 4 September, which was nearly equalled on the first day of the Alam

Halfa fighting. It seems surprising that the rates were not higher, but our forward troops had all the predicted fire they required. As regards observed shooting, the poor visibility restricted our potential. Yet no-one doubted that Alam Halfa was a battle.

Given the vigour and promptness of our response, Rommel realised from the outset that he had failed to achieve surprise. This was a grave disappointment, and allied to his desperate supply position, especially fuel – aggravated by the sinking of tankers whose supplies were so crucial – he decided quite early that he would have to withdraw. The Germans had managed to scrape up 54 tanks for the 'Panzer Army' for its initial attack on 1 July. By dint of great effort, he had managed to collect 234 tanks for Alam Halfa, of which 41 were total losses. The Italians lost eleven tanks from a total of 242,[8] and there were heavy losses of guns and vehicles from the sustained attacks by the RAF and artillery fire. Rommel therefore withdrew west of the minefield. He was aware that he now encountered a more formidable and professionally competent opponent, and that the next attack would be by the Eighth Army. The future emphasis of the Axis forces would therefore be on defence. So Rommel began a programme of constructing formidable strongpoints and extensive minefields.

Montgomery had certainly conducted a masterly defensive battle, giving an immense impression of professionalism. The unfolding of the drama according to plan seemed inevitably to imply total control of events. Our general had passed the test triumphantly. He had won the battle for the hearts and minds of his army. We craved leadership: he supplied it. I have considerable doubt that the outcome would have been so satisfactory under the previous management, which we now know was Churchill's view also.

NOTES

1. Churchill, Vol. IV, p. 466.
2. Nigel Hamilton, *Monty*, Vol. I, pp. 622–5.
3. Hinsley, Vol. II, p. 409.
4. Carver, *Dilemmas of the Desert War,* pp. 135–7.
5. Carver, p. 137.
6. Hamilton, Vol. I, p. 626.
7. Hinsley, Vol. II, pp. 413–14.
8. Hinsley, Vol. II, p. 417.

THE ART AND PRACTICE OF BRITISH ARTILLERY IN THE SECOND WORLD WAR

The Royal Artillery and the Royal Engineers were the most intellectual arms of the British army. In the opinion of friend and foe alike, our artillery was of a high standard of excellence. Members of it believed they were part of an elite force. There is little doubt it was the decisive arm of the Army. Although highly regarded by other arms, its methods were something of a mystery. It may therefore be of interest to readers to have some description of its organisation and methods in the Second World War, particularly, as far as I am aware, this is not available elsewhere. What follows applies equally well to the ubiquitous field artillery as regards observed and predicted fire.

A medium regiment comprised two batteries, each of eight guns (there were three batteries in a field regiment). Each battery consisted of two troops of four guns. The regiment was the administrative centre, responsible for rearward signals, medical services and supply organisation. Tactically, it normally prescribed the general area each battery was to occupy and specified the 'zero-line' intended to cover its section of the front.

Yet, in a very real sense, the individual troop of four medium guns was the essential workhorse, with a high degree of autonomy within this general framework. It usually knew the whereabouts of its sister troop, but the other battery and its activities seemed remote. The troop had its own observation post (OP) from which it received its fire orders during observed shooting, its own first-line ammunition column of four three-tonners, its own water bowser of 250 gallons, and, at Alamein, its own cookhouse.

The troop commander, a captain, used an open-top armoured car, with a specialist surveyor (OP Ack.) as his technical assistant and deputy, a signaller and a driver. The OP could operate from the vehicle, but normally this would be parked behind any small desert ridge to protect it. The OP would be established on the ground with a short telephone line laid by the signaller who would transmit fire orders by wireless to the troop. (In static positions a line might be laid all the way to the guns.) The disposition of our own and the enemy forces would be carefully noted.

OBSERVED FIRE

In unmapped country all fire perforce was by observation, which means most of the desert fighting. One found one's way by compass bearing and distance (the vehicle milometer) and such features which were known, e.g. track junctions or the small coastal settlements, because otherwise the desert was featureless. If the OP spotted a target justifying the ammunition expenditure, it could engage, but after a move it would not know where its guns were, except they were somewhere to the rear. As a preliminary operation, on first occupying the OP, the area would be 'registered'. Full registration would consist of putting two rounds on the ground at different ranges on the zero-line. It would be essential to spot these shell-bursts, and it was a help that when the ranging gun (normally the 'pivot', right hand or No. 1 gun) was fired, the gun position signaller would say 'Shot' into his microphone. Since the OP knew the time of flight for those ranges (from range tables) they knew precisely when to expect the shell-bursts. Assuming these were spotted, an imaginary junction line on the ground would indicate the zero-line and, if projected back, would, of course, lead to the gun position. The process would then be repeated with the same two ranges, at more than, and less than, 20 degrees (i.e. six shots in all). These imaginary lines if projected back would intersect at the gun position. An experienced OP might, however, dispense with these additional four rounds. Once a 'frame of reference' had been established in this way in this featureless terrain, it became easier to ascertain the line and range to the target by trial and error ('ranging'), correcting line and 'bracketing' the target progressively. The fire orders would have indicated 'troop target', so the other three guns would have been following the fire orders, mimicking the ranging gun, so that they would be ready immediately to fire the specified number of rounds. The more familiar the OP became with the terrain, the shorter the ranging process. If there was a man-made object visible, e.g. a burnt-out tank, an experienced OP might dispense with registration and range on the tank as a reference point.

The OP Ack. would help in identifying the fall of shot and would prepare a panorama, exaggerating the vertical distance since the ground was normally fairly flat, and noting such features as there were. He would also indicate the registration lines and keep a record of all targets engaged. If the officer was a casualty or was absent for any reason, the OP Ack., although perhaps only a junior NCO, would assume control and had full authority to engage the troop, or even the battery. No-one thought this odd, although unless the officer was a casualty, no-one might know, since the gun position would be receiving its orders via the OP signaller, as usual.

If, in the opinion of the OP, a target was sufficiently important, a 'Battery Target' might be ordered bringing down the fire of all eight guns. Having already engaged the target with its own troop, the OP would range the sister troop on to the target. This would be fairly simple, because of the proximity of the two troops. In principle, the process could be extended to the whole regiment, but it was clumsy and time-consuming. Moreover, since most targets were potentially mobile, they could hardly be expected to remain obligingly static while they were ranged upon.

A very important conclusion must be drawn with observed fire. Because the organisation rested essentially on troop autonomy, observed fire was fragmentary: concentrated mass fire was not possible. Regimental targets, by observed fire, were therefore extremely rare.

The principles outlined above for observed shooting relate to mobile warfare in the open desert, i.e. in unmapped country. In mapped country, as at El Alamein, some modification occurred, because one unknown, the map reference of the gun position, was eliminated. Since we occupied the area for some four and a half months, the terrain became very familiar to OPs. Although the desert itself remained relatively featureless, the presence of so much battle debris provided reference points and ranging could be simplified to zero-line registration or even eliminated. In western Europe, where the theatre of operations was extensively mapped, the map references of guns and targets were generally known. Observers, therefore, concentrated on their essential function of anticipating the needs of the assault troops for supporting fire. Arnhem was unique, with observers and gunners complete strangers but able to co-operate effectively by adherence to standard procedures, with the airborne's observers using whole troops for ranging, and engaging targets which were virtually identical with their own positions. In the Ardennes most of our fire was as described above. These examples show principles always had to be interpreted in terms of local circumstances.

The GPO Ack., besides fixing the position of his guns in mapped country, had to perform a vital task, applicable to both observed and predicted shooting. He had to ensure his guns were pointing in the right direction, i.e. the 'zero-line' prescribed by RHQ. For this purpose, on first occupying a position he would place four markers on the ground, in diamond formation, pointing roughly in the right direction to assist the guns when they came into position. He would then set up the director (a theodolite) using the compass needle to set the zero-line grid bearing. Since the instrument was responding to magnetic North, he had to apply the appropriate magnetic variation. When the guns arrived and the tractors had cleared the site, he would order 'Aiming Point – Director'. He would then read the angle from zero-line to each gunsight in turn and give each layer the reciprocal, or complementary angle, i.e. plus or minus 180 degrees. (If I am north of you, you must be south of me.) With the violence of the recoil, it was continually necessary to re-align the gun, so the layer would then record the angle on an ivorene plate on the gun, so that if he were a casualty, or for any other reason, soneone else could serve as layer and keep the gun accurately on line. The training manual recommended that the angle to other notable features, e.g. church steeples, should be noted. In the absence of these, or indeed any other feature, the angle 'Aiming Point – Director' was of crucial importance, and at night, when it was necessary to illuminate it, the director position was essential, because without it the troop would become 'blind' and would be out of action. Since most set-piece battles were fought at night, the maintenance of this light was an absolute necessity.

The importance of the director is obvious: it was a delicate instrument and once the line had been given to the guns, it and its tripod were removed to avoid damage. The director position would be marked by a 'banderolle' (a black and white survey pole some six feet in length) and this served as aiming point for the layers. The director was kept in a stout leather case, and a spare was always carried.

The procedures laid down were beyond criticism and had been proved on innumerable occasions. Our new guns were of excellent design and we loved them. But there was one small detail which had not received sufficient attention, and that was the night illumination of the aiming point. There was only the ubiquitous hurricane lamp available. If this was used unmasked, it would reveal the position to marauding aircraft. Given the paucity of resources in the desert, we improvised a mask for the lamp from a 4-gallon petrol tin: cutting out the bottom and making a slit in the side. It proved eminently satisfactory. But why were we not provided with a proper screen for the light?

PREDICTED FIRE

When, in July 1941, it was decided to fortify the Alamein position, some imaginative person thought it would be a wise step to survey the area thoroughly. This was done, and the existing Egyptian survey data were brought forward, the 4th Survey Regiment, Royal Artillery, establishing a number of beacons and reinforcing the natural 'trig.' points. As a consequence, the whole Alamein area was extensively mapped. The map reference of all gun positions could now be ascertained to an accuracy of one metre, and this was part of the GPO Ack.'s duties. Since targets could also be identified by map references, predicted fire became possible.

With the map reference of both gun position and target known, it was not a difficult matter to compute the line and range using simple trigonometry and log. tables. Alternatively, the target could be plotted on the 'artillery board', which already had a metal arm and arc reflecting the gun position on the ground.

There was, however, a small complication arising from the huge diurnal temperature range in the desert, which could reach as high as 100 degrees Fahrenheit. During the hottest part of the day, the heat would cause the air to expand, so reducing its density and offering less resistance to the passage of the shell. If the computed, or plotted, range to the target was, say, 18,000 yards, (i.e. the actual distance on the ground) the gun would overshoot, possibly by 800 yards. A correction therefore had to be applied, and the range set on the gun would be, say, 17,200 yards, the extra 800 yards of 'carry' being provided by atmospheric conditions. The GPO Ack. could work out the correction for any range, since every four hours a 'meteor telegram' would be received from the survey regiment giving the necessary data. At night the opposite condition applied (there could be a thin film of ice on water at dawn), and it might be necessary to put, say, 18,200 yards on the gun to hit the target.

The main key to the successful use of co-ordinated fire power in the desert was the 4th Survey Regiment, Royal Artillery. This was a Territorial regiment like our own, and hailed from Gateshead. A warm appreciation of its work is given by Lieutenant-General Horrocks.[1]

A survey regiment, the 'intelligentsia' of the artillery, had a remarkable range of responsibilities. Besides its main function as the ultimate survey authority, the regiment would play a navigational role in mobile operations where maps were lacking. Using triangulation, it would establish co-ordinates of survey beacons by which all artillery regiments could accurately fix themselves on a common system of co-ordinates, as at Alamein. Another of its duties was preparing the meteorological data for artillery units. Finally, the survey regiment would operate the flash-spotting and sound-ranging equipment.

For co-ordinated massed fire, a simple organisation was all that was required. This involved (1) the means of identifying accurately a target (map reference) which justified such massive treatment; (2) passing this information to all relevant artillery units by means of an efficient and reliable signals network. These concentrations of fire were called 'stonks'. The receipt of this word would immediately establish signals priority. Within minutes, all batteries would report ready to engage the target. Fire orders had to be passed to each troop so it could compute its line and range. Thus, co-ordinates permitted the marriage of individual locations and collective purpose. The effect was devastating. The field regiments of many divisions (each with 72 guns) could be engaged. To this formidable total could be added one or more medium regiments, each of sixteen guns. (On rare occasions, the 3.7in anti-aircraft guns could also be used in a field role.) This extraordinarily powerful and flexible instrument could have a dominating influence. The enemy had nothing like it for effectiveness. All this exemplifies the growing professionalism under Montgomery.

A further example of integrated fire power was the remarkable counter-battery organisation, manned by the 4th Survey Regiment. Hitherto, counter-battery fire by both sides had mainly consisted of engaging enemy batteries by direct observation, i.e. when an OP was able to pick out a gun flash and locate it accurately. Normally this would be engaged by the troop of four guns, but, if warranted, heavier fire could be brought down by the battery. With the establishment of the counter-battery organisation, we had a much more powerful and effective instrument in that the organisation actively sought out the hostile battery location, and could then call for a much heavier concentration of fire.

Everyone who served at Alamein will recall the tubular steel flash-spotting towers, some forty feet high, set in a straight line at kilometre intervals and striding across the desert from north to south. The position of these towers was fixed with great accuracy. The spotters from the survey regiment would be in position on platforms on top of the towers, protected by sandbags. As soon as enemy gun-flashes were spotted, instruments would fix accurate bearings. Each tower was in signals contact with the Counter-Battery Office. and by noting the time of flash one could be sure that the bearings related to the same battery. The intersection of these bearings on plotting gave the enemy location with great accuracy. A code number would then be allotted, together with the map reference, and lists would be compiled and circulated to artillery regiments by the Counter-Battery Office. Medium regiments tended to specialise in counter-battery work because of their longer range and heavier shell. A similar procedure was followed by the sound-rangers: using a line of equally spaced microphones with the time intervals indicating distance from source in an analogous manner. In practice, sound-ranging was less accurate and used infrequently, but we did have one very successful sound-ranged shoot on a hostile battery.

These methods of seeking out the enemy guns had an obvious limitation. If the hostile battery remained silent, i.e. 'masked', for example after a move, there would be no flash or sound to be detected. Here the air photograph was invaluable. Batteries which had not yet fired could still be located by the skilful interpretation of air photographs. If the enemy position was already known, the photographs provided useful confirmation or additional information, e.g. number of guns.

The data collected needed frequent revision, because batteries moved and the lists had to be revised. (Counter-battery work played a key role in the opening phase of the October battle.) If enemy guns made a nuisance of themselves, the Counter-Battery Officer (CBO) would quickly identify the culprit, and within minutes it would be deluged with fire. This rapid and massive retaliation must have been an intimidating experience for the enemy gunners. We were frequently shelled ourselves. In this deadly game of 'hide-and-seek', my impression was that we won 'hands down', although the enemy's relative ineffectiveness may have also been the result of shell stringency. Ammunition was seldom a problem with us, particularly at Alamein, where we were much nearer to our bases. Nevertheless, with both sides seeking out the other, the gun position was obviously a dangerous place, with bombing and machine-gun attacks an additional hazard.

Besides concentrations of massed fire and counter-battery work, a further example of predicted fire was the creeping barrage. This will be discussed later.

It will be apparent that the surveyor specialists played a crucial role in performing, as professionals, in the essential function of fire control and the establishment of a realistic relationship between guns and targets. This was true equally of observed and predicted fire, although different skills were involved. There were only two specialists in a troop, one at the OP, the other at the gun position. There were usually four or five at the battery command post, so there was a tiny reserve in case of casualties.

The troop specialist, an NCO, had a technical responsibility far exceeding his rank. Indeed, he assumed control of all technical matters if the officer was a casualty, or was absent for any other reason, i.e. he took over the command post and directed all fire. This would seem to conflict with the army's hierarchical command structure, but there was seldom any problem: the artillery took a severely pragmatic attitude to the position. It would be an interesting research project to ascertain how other armies dealt with the question of technical professionalism at the working level. (Specialists were often commissioned.)

Predicted fire in the Normandy and Reichswald battles followed the principles here enunciated (although there was no need for meteor correction). As Horrocks points out, the 4th Survey Regiment, RA, provided the same essential function as at Alamein.

SOME RELATED MATTERS

During the period after Alam Halfa until towards the end of 1942, we had a role in the training of junior subalterns fresh from OCTU. An artillery troop, as we have seen, was a small, taut, relatively self-contained unit controlled by the GPO, the GPO Ack. and the troop sergeant-major, who, among other duties, had the task of leading the troop to its new gun position which would be reconnoitred by the GPO and his assistant. A trainee GPO was therefore something of an embarrassment, he was definitely *de trop*. Nevertheless, we did our best to help him and make him familiar with command post procedure, and encouraged him to visit the guns, particularly when firing, but not to make a nuisance of himself to the detachments. One necessary task he was given was to check the zero-line of the guns with a prismatic compass on occupying a new position. A farcical situation always developed with the 'discovery' that all guns were off line! In every case, the trainee officer had forgotten to allow for magnetic variation. When this was pointed out, he would kick himself for having forgotten such an elementary point. (The difference between grid – true – North and magnetic North should have been inculcated at OCTU.)

The fuses used were almost invariably of the impact variety, and were activated by the rotation of the shell in flight. Very rarely, fire orders would be cancelled after the gun had been loaded with the live shell. The crew had to remember this, and the drill was to leave the rammer against the breech as a reminder. If the order to move was given with the gun loaded, the No. 1 (a full sergeant) would report this, as it could be hazardous, particularly if the move was over rough ground. The GPO would then order 'Empty Gun', and it would be fired at the last target engaged, or, if for some reason this was not wise, a fresh target would be given. To move with a loaded gun was a last resort.

Care was always taken not to hit a fuse-tip, although this was normally safe. A gun crew of one of our troops accidentally knocked a fuse in loading and, unfortunately, it was defective. The shell exploded in the gun pit, and many men were killed or horribly mutilated. We heard that an army photographic unit recorded the dreadful event, and used it for a poster to be displayed in ordnance factories as a sombre warning of the terrible result of carelessness in manufacture. I cannot vouch for this because the regiment was seldom re-united, except, perhaps, at the end of a campaign, and we never discussed 'shop'. Nevertheless, I have no doubt the tragedy occurred. It was strange how our horizons were bounded by our own four guns, even 'B' Troop, who were often in view, seemed a world away.

The regiment was, however, almost invariably fully operationally co-ordinated as a result of good communications. We were in touch with our OPs and battery HQs by radio. The latter was also in touch with RHQ, which, in turn, was linked to Corps and AGRA (Army Group Royal Artillery). Whenever things stabilised, telephone lines were invariably laid, and the radio link kept in reserve, e.g. if lines were cut by shell-fire. The telephone was much more reliable and secure, as well as needing less powerful batteries. (We had facilities for charging wireless batteries.)

The recoil of a gun is extremely violent, the force generated being equal and opposite to that propelling the shell. This shock is taken by the hydraulic buffer-recuperator system. Even so, the gun would run back, possibly damaging the crew, unless the carriage was firmly anchored by the spades, which would bite into the ground when the first round was fired. The crew would normally dig to make sure the spades were properly bedded-in, particularly on hard or rocky soil.

A novelty was the air shoot. Early in August 1942, an RAF corporal with a wireless set and operator was attached to us for a few days. Two Spitfires then appeared, one to protect the tail of his colleague who would be seeking an enemy battery or other target to engage. The planes would fly in circles, and we could generally tell from their position on the circuit when the fire orders would come. The first shoot was moderately successful, but had to be abandoned when visibility deteriorated. We tried again next day, but the event was a fiasco because the pilot kept his radio on 'send' and so could not receive our signals. He therefore failed to be observing at the critical moment. The cost and difficulty of this method seemed to outweigh the advantages, but the method improved considerably later. We never experienced the low-flying Auster spotter planes with Royal Artillery officers as pilots. These planes were very vulnerable, even to small arms fire, and soon ceased to be used for artillery purposes.

* * * * * * * * * * *

Montgomery understood the full power of artillery, and he ensured that the many weeks of preparation for the battle in October should exploit all its potentialities. The counter-battery organisation was brought to a peak of perfection for the great trial ahead. This was never again equalled, because in the desert there were specially favourable circumstances for locating enemy guns. In the event, all aspects of predicted fire were thoroughly employed, and, in the familiar setting of North Africa, observed fire as well. Heavy concentrations by many batteries had devastating effects on the enemy.

The awesome power of artillery and its tremendous flexibility – switching rapidly from one target to another – made it the dominant force on the battlefield. The intense activity of the four and a half months at El Alamein, mainly under Montgomery's command, was the equivalent of a graduate finishing school, and gave our artillery there a unique advantage compared to regiments still necessarily unengaged at home.

NOTES

1. B. Horrocks, *Corps Commander,* p. 155.

PRELUDE TO OCTOBER

After Alam Halfa our time was taken up by preparations for the great October offensive. But first, each man received a well-earned four-day leave in Cairo. Soldiers tend to live for the present: tomorrow is another day. The city seemed to us a wonderful place, with facilities to suit every taste, and we became quite fond of it. No-one thought we should never see the place again; at least not at His Majesty's expense. Money was plentiful, even for gunners, because pay had been accumulating after months in the desert, where, of course, there was nothing to spend it on. I was particularly well funded because my civilian pay was being made up, and I had opened an account at Barclay's D.C.& O (Barclay's Bank, Dominion, Colonial and Orient). I therefore booked in at a good hotel, rather than an army camp, and lived it up for a few days. Unfortunately, none of my specialist friends had a similar place on the leave roster. I bought a Rolex watch for seven Egyptian pounds (!) and a box of 'Punch' Havana cigars. Perhaps I had a premonition that this was a farewell visit.

A major problem with mounting a surprise offensive in the desert was the question of concealment. The RAF was establishing air superiority, but this could not guarantee immunity from overflights by the enemy. Since it was impossible to conceal our movements, the overriding aim was to deceive, and a comprehensive deception plan was devised by Charles Richardson of the Royal Engineers, who had a first-class degree in engineering and was obviously a man of imagination. Huge dummy lorry parks were constructed, giving the impression of large concentrations of troops in misleading positions. The highlight was the construction of a false pipeline, complete with dummy pumping stations, running roughly south-west and progressing slowly, but inexorably, each day. (The 'line' was of empty petrol tins.) Needless to say, this was left unfinished when the battle began. For this and other reasons the enemy was completely deceived both about the timing and the location of the attack, so surprise was achieved.

The artillery, too, had a part to play in misleading the enemy by making our position in the relatively empty south seem stronger than it was, and by indicating that we might be contemplating an enveloping movement, along the lines of Gazala and Rommel's attempt at Alam Halfa. Montgomery never had any such intention, realising that our armour was ill-fitted for such a role and was unlikely to be successful.

The timing of these diversionary attacks in the south reveals a great deal about Montgomery's thinking. The first of our southern jaunts took place on 25 August, i.e. less than two weeks after Montgomery assumed command of the Eighth Army, and *before* Alam Halfa. This shows clearly his serene confidence in the outcome of that battle, and that he was already beginning the deception programme for October. Few commentators have stressed the importance of this early development, which shows a commander in total control of himself and the situation. (On this first trip we fired 160 rounds as a troop.) From August to October we were very active, with single troops moving south to temporary sniping positions in the Munassib, Muhafid and Ragil areas. We much enjoyed the sense of freedom which these expeditions involved. It was rather fun temporarily to leave our congested area for the empty desert through the gap in the minefield at 'Hungerford', and to be entirely alone. We would generally take up a position near the line of telegraph poles which ran through Deir el Ragil in the direction of Himeimat. The latter peak commanded an excellent view, and as the enemy also had other vantage points, it was always possible that we would be shelled, which slightly soured the experience. The conical peak of Himeimat therefore seemed ominous. These excursions by many regiments had a serious purpose: they confused the enemy about our strength in the south and also gave the opportunity to engage targets out of range from 'home'. This was the very area through which Rommel had advanced during the Alam Halfa battle.

In September, after that engagement, we were again in the area, to attract attention away from the north where our main blow was to be delivered. On this occasion we were three days on our jaunt, each night leaguering for safety within the minefield. On the last day, we were ranged on to an enemy battery by one of our field regiments which was out of their range. The inevitable retribution followed: we were ranged on by a single 170mm gun (about 7in). This made a big bang and a lot of black smoke, but was not too accurate nor sustained. On these detached operations we were more concerned about the guns than ourselves, because they were not dug-in, while we had slit trenches. Sometimes sandbags were placed to protect the pneumatic tyres from bomb or shell splinters. Early in October the exercise was repeated, and we were in support of the 7th Armoured Division in a local attack on a strongpoint with anti-tank guns. We returned 'home' on 3 October, having hopefully helped to create the impression that we were strong in the south and that the enemy could expect trouble there.

A second grand theme of the lengthy interlude was training. Montgomery was not satisfied with the state of training of much of his army, but time did not permit of any comprehensive effort. What was of great concern was the problem of the deep minefield belts, which had to be crossed before reaching the main enemy defences. Intensive training therefore took place for armour and infantry, under simulated conditions approaching reality. This included the problem of traffic control to avoid congestion on the approach to the minefields. Tanks and vehicles would be very vulnerable in single file through the narrow minefield gaps. The leading elements would be from the Royal Engineers, with an officer following a compass bearing for a stated distance, while a following party would use electric devices, or prodding by bayonet, to locate and mark the mines. Another party would then lift the mines, being wary of booby-traps, and place them to one side. The edges of the gap (some 16 yards wide) would be marked by the Military Police with white tape or picket lights. 'Gapping' would be a difficult and hazardous operation at night under fire, made even more difficult by smoke and dust. Tanks and vehicles could provide easy targets while so restricted.

There was no specific training needed for the artillery in the type of battle envisaged. When not engaged in our deception tasks in the south, we were fairly busy with concentrations, counter-battery fire and observed shooting. What could be done, however, was to give us a training exercise of which we would have no advanced knowledge, and so we would be judged on the manner of our reaction.

The GPO was sent off to a rendezvous by map reference, to collect orders and then to join the troop. I was instructed to lead the troop to one of the empty spaces in the south. This was rather disconcerting because I did not have a good sense of location. The map reference given was in the 'empty quarter', which was pretty featureless. Then I recalled that south of the army's well-populated area, in solitary isolation, was a petrol drum with the map reference thoughtfully painted on the side by the survey people. By great good fortune, I had noted its co-ordinates and from the map I could easily ascertain the bearing and distance to our destination. I knew how to get to the petrol drum from our previous southern deception tasks: one knew the regimental and other signs on the way, and hopefully not many had moved. Once arrived at our intermediate staging post, the rest was easy.

We duly arrived at the map reference to find the battery and troop commanders awaiting us (to my great relief), so we settled down pending the arrival of the GPO. As the minutes passed, it became apparent we were not going to see him, so the BC called me over to tell me that enemy tanks were approaching us. Meanwhile, the No. 1s were attentively watching, and when I bawled out for them they came tumbling out of the gun tractors pretty fast. Having had a few seconds to collect my thoughts, I told them the exercise was 'enemy tanks approaching', and ordered action with Charge III and 'gun control', which involves firing over open sights when the order 'Fire' is given. (Charge III provided the flattest trajectory and highest muzzle velocity.) When the guns had unlimbered, I sent the tractors farther back while I waited until I judged the supposed enemy was near enough, and gave the order to fire. Everyone bustled around. The No.1s lined up on the imaginary tanks and did some suitably hectic simulation. After a time, the BC seemed satisfied and sent us 'home'. (The unfortunate GPO was so sheepish about it that it would have been tactless to refer to the incident. He was posted a few months later: poor map-reading was a common 'crime'.)

This exercise made me think very hard about a direct tank attack on a gun position. It was rare for artillery to engage tanks over open sights, although engaging them indirectly was common enough. Nevertheless, there had been instances where field batteries had been so involved, and had been overrun. Vulnerability was at a maximum where a troop was isolated in the open with little protection for the crews from close gunfire. Under those circumstances, casualties mounted, making it increasingly difficult to service the guns. Obviously, the position would be greatly eased if guns were dug-in. The risk of casualties would be less, but care would have to be taken to ensure that the guns could clear the parapet. We all had absolute confidence that the 4.5in would have been a superb anti-tank gun, even without solid shot, for its high muzzle velocity and heavier shell would have made it lethal. Against that, of course, it would have less facility for rapid traverse. (The 88mm, being originally designed as an anti-aircraft gun, had 360 degree traverse.) These reflections were never, so far as I am aware, put to the test with medium guns, with the unique exception of our 'C' troop, which had fired over open sights at Matruh on 28 June.

After Tobruk, where so much artillery was lost, the Eighth Army relied on 25-pounder field regiments, with the sole exception of the 7th and 64th Medium Regiments. So quite literally we became indispensable, and were never out of action until the end of the Sicilian campaign.

The pending battle, like most battles, would largely be fought at night, but the guns would also be active during the day. With the prospect of so much hectic activity there was concern about strain and loss of sleep. The gunners were flexibly-minded, and informally divided the detachments so that half were on duty in quiet periods, although all would be involved at high intensity times when much ammunition would be expended.

There was particular concern about the GPO Ack., since he was the sole specialist at the gun position. If he became a casualty, the battery command post could find a replacement, but since he had to be fresh and mentally alert at all times to deal reliably with target computations and so on, the real problem was seen as the question of relief. We were instructed to select an intelligent gunner and train him in the simplest tasks, because as an ex-elementary schoolboy he could hardly be expected to master trigonometry and log. tables. The arrangement did not work very well, since one tended to act on the safe side and be reluctant to delegate. I presumed this was a regimental, not an Army, order and, in my opinion, it was an exaggerated fear. A young, fit man could take a great deal of strain when keyed-up and still be alert mentally. Also, one could catnap at times.

A special problem was relieving the OP. This was a job involving great strain on occasions: one had to be constantly alert and attentive to target possibilities even in quiet periods, and, of course, the risk was great. (Nearly all our officers who were killed were on OP duty, and naturally they tended to be the best, those who could be least spared.) After our recent exertions, it became imperative to relieve our OP teams. Although I had not been exactly idle myself, I relieved our OP Ack. two or three times in September and October, and he replaced me at the gun position. It was at least a change of scene. The OP was at Point 63 on Ruweisat Ridge, the key feature of the Alamein position. The OP itself was a tiny slit trench cut out of the rock by a compressed air tool. There was a shelf with two Mills bombs which we eyed rather gingerly, never having used one of the things, and we had our rifles. Nearby were some burned-out tanks, the relics of earlier fighting. The enemy was generally very quiet during this interregnum, and I was surprised how few signs there were of our own infantry. One could only catnap, and we slept fully clothed. Sometimes we were warned that a patrol was out, and when we 'stood-to' at first light one could hear the scraping of boots and the clink of accoutrements as the familiar 'tin-hats' appeared reassuringly on the sky-line. Sometimes the infantry forgot to tell us, which I did not much enjoy!

We would spend the day constantly surveying the desert stretching away to the Rahman track in the distance, with the sun glinting on the windscreens of the enemy transport, which, unfortunately, was out of range. One could see the blood-soaked features of Deir el Shein and Miteiriya Ridge, but owing to lack of elevation (the OP was the highest point we had), the landscape seemed very flat and the mirage effect often made observation difficult. One morning I spotted what I took at first to be an enemy working party of some thirty men, or rather half-men, for they were standing in a slit trench. If ranged on in the usual way they would immediately go to ground, so I looked over the records of other targets engaged in the area, judged the appropriate line and range, and called for five rounds gunfire from our supersonic guns. With good fortune we were right on target, and I saw no more of the enemy that day, or succeeding ones. It was only later that I reflected that, through much experience, we had become professionals: we thought in terms of ballistics, trigonometry, killing at a distance. Only gradually did I realise that some of these men might be dead or maimed. During a war one cannot think too much in such terms.

THE BATTLE OF ALAMEIN[1]

s already emphasised, no Eighth Army man regarded the disconnected engagements of July 1942 as a battle. Rommel had been handicapped by his desperate supply position, and we had temporarily blocked him, pending his more serious attempt at Alam Halfa. (This did not mean that there had not been some heavy fighting and casualties.)

Our approach to the October battle was fraught. Our diversionary expeditions to the south had ended early in October. Breech troubles and minor breakdowns of buffer-recuperator systems were becoming more frequent, and the troop artificers were kept busy. Because of the acute shortage of medium guns and the need for range and weight of metal, all our fire was on Charges II and III, imposing the greatest recoil shock. Analysis of our ammunition expenditure showed the balance was on Charge III, so the frequency of breakdowns was readily explained. We had first fired our new guns on 20 June, and experience was to show that the 'life' of a medium gun was some 2,000 rounds, after which it would require radical attention in the excellent machine shops of the RAOC in Alexandria. All our guns were at about this limit for the second time.

A naval gun of 4.5in calibre had a life of only 500 rounds, because with its mechanical hoist and other aids its rate of fire was very intense, generating great heat and friction. They wore out quickly. For an army medium gun of this calibre, lacking mechanical aids, 'intense' fire was only 2rpm and could only be maintained briefly. After the previous round, the chamber had to be swabbed out, the next round loaded and rammed home, the correct charge inserted, the breech closed, the percussion tube inserted, the lanyard placed, the line checked by the layer and the gun fired – all in 30 seconds. Even a first class detachment could not sustain such a rate for long. 'Normal' rate of fire was a single round per minute and could be easily maintained.

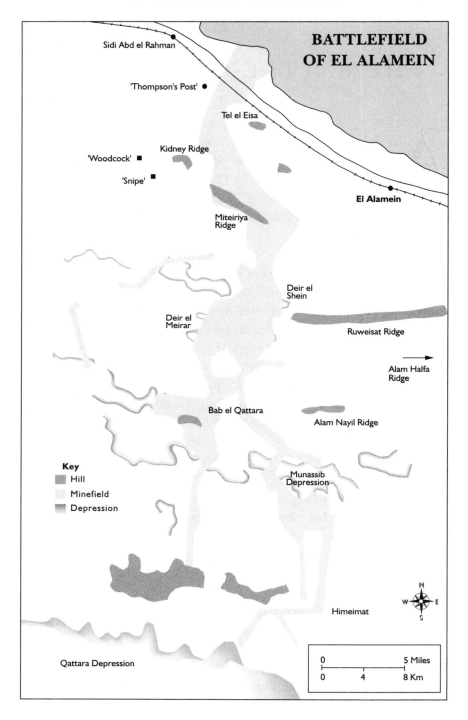

On 8 October 'A' Sub. gun was condemned by the ordnance people and was replaced a few days later by a new, or reconditioned, gun. (A troop of four guns comprised two sections of two guns each, so a sub-section was one gun – often referred to as a 'Sub.', ie. detachment.) And on 10 October it was noticed that 'B' Sub.'s piece was distorted near the muzzle end, i.e. the damage to the inner rifled lining was so serious that it had affected the piece itself. The gun was too dangerous to fire, and it was taken out of action. Calibration of the other two guns showed that they were shooting badly. We were clearly in no state to engage in a major battle, and all our guns were progressively replaced before it began. (I have no record or recollection that we had time to calibrate these guns.) The artillery was well managed and directed, and all the regiment's guns were replaced in time: the need had been foreseen. It would clearly be folly to engage in a major battle with clapped-out guns, particularly since, if successful, we might advance far to the west and end up a long way from our repair base. (Some time after the battle, an RAOC mobile workshop, with a powerful generator and some ancillary repair vehicles, formed part of the regiment. Its importance was shown by the fact that it was commanded by a Warrant Officer, Class I, i.e. equivalent to a regimental sergeant-major.)

As part of our preparation, an aggressive counter-battery programme was launched between 18 and 20 October. On the first day our three guns fired 169, 198 and 93 rounds. ('B' Sub. was still out of action awaiting its new gun.) Inevitably this intense fire provoked retal-iation. A 105mm battery – the lightest calibre I recall being used against us in North Africa – shelled us on 19 October, but not very effectively. In the afternoon 'C' troop was shelled by two 170mm guns, which turned their attention to us a little later, followed by a repeat. This was heavy and accurate, but we suffered no damage and only one minor casualty. This was due to luck and the fact we were well dug-in.

There were many occasions when we were shelled, sometimes heavily and accurately. This may suggest that our own counter-battery fire was also fairly ineffective, but this is not the case. In fact, we had been remarkably fortunate, and sustained few casualties and little or no damage. The 212th Battery, in the same area, had sustained much more serious damage and casualties. Moreover, the enemy fire was invariably by a single troop or battery: there was no equivalent of our co-ordinated mass fire through CBO. There were no flash-spotting towers. A heavy bombard by us must have caused a great deal of damage and lowered the morale of the enemy gunners.

On 20 October we completed our contribution to the harassment of the enemy artillery when we used up the last of the ammunition, and later that night the troop moved to its battle position. The gun sergeants and a few men remained, however, to fabricate dummy guns, using lengths of telegraph poles for the purpose, and placing camouflage nets over to give the impression that the troop had not moved. They then left for the new position to continue the digging overnight and to familiarise themselves with where the ammunition was buried. Work continued each night, the gun pit walls being revetted as usual with sandbags. The command post was also dug-in. Camouflage nets were always in position before dawn and movement by day was kept to a minimum.

The battle position was near the sand-dunes, between the coastal road and the sea. It was surveyed-in meticulously, with, unusually, the map reference of each gun being noted. The zero-line specified was 260 degrees, and the zone to be covered was 330 degrees to 190 degrees, i.e. 70 degrees either side of the zero-line and 40 degrees either side of the traversing gear limits. In other words, wide deflections were envisaged, necessitating manhandling of the six-ton gun. There was nothing unusual in this, and it was accepted as part of the gunner's life. The gun pits naturally incorporated this fan-shape. There was a *canard* that, with widely separate fronts during the battle, the guns were in difficulty. This is ridiculous, and, indeed, insulting. We were especially solicitous for the infantry and never let them down. At the most there was cursing if major changes of deflection were frequent, which was natural enough, but that was all.

23 October was a day of great expectancy. We knew that our preparations had been exceedingly thorough: nothing had been left to chance. There was a personal message from the army commander to be read to all troops, stating that we were ready for 'one of the decisive battles of history. It will be the turning point of the war'. This proved prophetic, at any rate as far as the western Allies were concerned. We were well equipped and supplied, and so long as everyone did his duty, the message continued, the

outcome was not in doubt. It ended with the typical Montgomery flourish that 'the Lord mighty in battle' would give us victory. I always had difficulty in suppressing a smile at the style, with its mixture of cricketing and biblical metaphors. But the simple direct message we were to learn must always be taken seriously. During the day our CO addressed us, passing on the gist of the strategic and tactical briefing which had been given to senior officers. Montgomery always believed that men fought better if they were 'in the picture', and he was unquestionably right. Strangely, this obvious insight had not been vouchsafed to his immediate predecessor, nor, it may be added, to some other generals later. (At the beginning of the Normandy campaign the ordinary member of XXX Corps did not even know the name of his new corps commander.)

Zero hour was 22.00 hours, and the artillery was to open up at 21.40 hours. Thus the enemy would have only 20 minutes' warning of the impending attack. This gave us the supreme benefit of surprise, because the deception plan had been remarkably successful in concealing the time and place of attack. (Rommel was on sick leave in Germany at the time.) There were 824 field guns involved, i.e. all the divisional field regiments and a number of independent ones, and 48 medium guns (apparently a third regiment had just arrived from the U.K). There were no heavy guns. We naturally awaited our detailed orders with some impatience, and it was not until about 19.00 hours that our instructions arrived. The description that follows must have been typical of every troop command post.

Our orders comprised 45 serials, a list of map references, with timings, 43 of which were enemy batteries, the remaining two being priority infantry targets. (The divisional field regiments presumably had a much higher proportion of infantry targets.) The GPO Ack. would sit in a quiet corner and compute the line and range for each of the targets. With such a large number, plotting would be impracticable, because the artillery board, which would already have some targets plotted, would get too crowded and confused. The meteor correction would be applied to each calculation. The information would have to be transcribed to a gun programme sheet for each gun, and the No. 1s would then be invited to the command post to be presented with their orders. Were the sheets clear? Were there any questions? There were none. Watches were synchronised, and torches checked, including a spare. Then with expressions of 'Good Luck!' the sergeants – Kirby, Patterson, Wilson and Vowles – left for their guns. They had time to make themselves comfortable so as to be able to read their programmes and control their detachments. George Vowles exercised a calm authority. He was the best No. 1 in the troop, and, I believe, the battery. He subsequently became head printer of *The Times*.

The plan had been well conceived with execution delegated. From receipt of orders to end of programme, the whole Eighth Army artillery was controlled by its specialist-surveyors and senior NCOs.

We came out of the command post as the sun was setting. It seemed unusually quiet. I thought I heard a dog bark. We were joined by our battery commander, Major Eason, who had formerly commanded the troop and wished to witness our contribution to the spectacle about to explode before us. (He would be manning an OP at first light.) He was a highly competent OP operator, completely fearless, with extraordinary powers of leadership. The men would follow him anywhere without question. He was the brother-in-law of Lieutenant-Colonel R. L. Syer (our first fatality in Greece), but his promotion owed nothing to that, being due to sheer merit.

We were counting the minutes, when the guns along the whole line opened up with deafening crashes and brilliant flashes. The horizon was alive and aglow. Everyone was keyed-up. A solitary aircraft came over and hopefully dropped a bomb into our gun flashes. It exploded harmlessly, deep in the sand-dunes. Shortly after, there was an extraordinarily brilliant flash and we ran over to the gun concerned, wondering what could have happened. The explanation was very simple – only the charge had been loaded, not the shell! This naturally occasioned much laughter and ribbing. We had known nothing like this before, nor were we to experience it again.

The programme finished at 03.00 hours on 24 October. The guns had been in action continuously for 5 hours and 20 minutes. There was, of course, little time to relax, because at first light both sides could judge the results of the night's work. Calls for fire came in rapidly: we fired three 'stonks' and engaged a number of targets indicated by our forward

Above: A 5.5in gun in action in the desert. The gun is not dug-in and there is no camouflage. The large number of shells shows a major action is proceeding or pending, perhaps the creeping barrage during 'Supercharge', fired at 01.05 hours on the night of 1/2 November 1942.

Below: 6pdr anti-tank gunners in action during a practice shoot.

Above: General Leese, commanding XXX Corps, General Montgomery, commanding Eighth Army, and General Lumsden, commanding X Corps.

Below: 25pdr field gun in action as Eighth Army advances. This splendidly designed gun was the backbone of the British artillery. Rommel's praise fits it admirably.

Right: A gun of the author's battery (311/64th Medium Regiment) at Mersa Matruh, 26 June 1942, immediately before the encirclement and breakout.

Below: Abandoned enemy gun position. The author saw several such examples after the Battle of El Hamma in Tunisia.

Right: Ceremonial inspection of 64th Medium Regiment, RA, by Winston Churchill, near Tripoli, 4 February 1943.

Below: A knocked-out German 50mm anti-tank gun.

Opposite page, bottom: A German quadruple gun encountered in Sicily in August 1943.

Above: A British heavy gun (155mm) in support of 50th Division attacking Tilly-sur-Seulles, an operation in which the author's regiment also participated in June 1944.

Below: A 25pdr gun firing smoke to cover an infantry advance at Tilly-sur-Seulles. Note the muzzle brake indicating the gun also had an anti-tank role.

Opposite page, top: A 4.5in medium gun being prepared for action in the Caen sector, July 1944.

Opposite page, bottom: The ubiquitous Bofors anti-aircraft gun, so successful – particularly in North Africa – in dealing with the Ju 87 dive bomber.

Above: The woods, small fields, hedges and sunken lanes of the bocage countryside, her exemplified south of Caumont, show it was excellent defensive country for fanatical Panze troops and was a formidable obstacle to our advance.

Below: A medium gun leaving the Falaise area en route for the Seine, on completion of the battl for Normandy, 9 August 1944.

OP. During the opening phase of the battle, the four guns of our troop fired 310, 238, 376 and 263, an average of 297 rounds per gun. (The discrepancies arose from minor faults requiring the attention of the artificer.) Assuming a similar performance from our comrades, our regiment alone fired nearly 5,000 rounds that night. This was a remarkable effort on the part of our gunners, and was representative of the artillery as a whole. Unlike naval gunners, we had no automatic hoists and other aids. Everything depended on human muscle power.

The initial attack clearly illustrates the enormous difficulty of, and hazards actually encountered in, a night battle in minefields. Heavy fire, smoke and dust caused confusion. Navigation officers and many others were casualties, picket lights had gone out, vehicles had strayed from the marked 16-yard gaps, causing others to follow: many were damaged by mines. So, there was often considerable uncertainty as to location, leading to strong differences of opinion. Moreover, the landscape was flat and almost featureless. Many of the ridges and depressions, so clearly marked on maps, might be practically indistinguishable on the ground. Some units had, as planned, successfully gapped a second minefield, but were unaware that a new, intermediate belt had been constructed, so that they over-estimated their advance. We were in some cases short of our objectives, and the uncertainty of position, which occasionally persisted for days, made it difficult for Intelligence to be accurately informed, and risky to arrange artillery programmes. When artillery support was requested, because of inaccurate observer locations, the fire sometimes came down where it was not expected.

It was difficult for a single troop of guns to form an impression of the wider picture. We received reports from our OPs, but their information was inevitably local and partial. Sitreps from RHQ, having originated with Corps, were more reliable. We were clear that the New Zealanders had done a remarkable job in establishing themselves on the forward slopes of Miteiriya Ridge, while the South Africans had also done well in taking their section of the ridge. The 51st Highland Division was inexperienced, and was held up by a number of strongpoints. They had sharp differences of opinion with the 1st Armoured Division about exactly where they were; and were later vindicated. The chief disappointment was that the armour had failed to establish itself beyond

Miteiriya Ridge, and so was not shielding the infantry to enable 'crumbling' of the enemy infantry to proceed. The armour had never relished their role as infantry support, and the narrow approaches through the minefields, necessitating their advance in single file, made them very vulnerable to anti-tank gunfire. They lacked determination and professionalism (e.g. they saw no need for liaison with artillery). In effect, they were not obeying orders. Montgomery was woken up during the small hours of 25 October, and at a conference with corps commanders reiterated his order for the armour to resume the attack.

Montgomery was, however, a realist, and felt the need to think again: he had been too optimistic about the potential of the armour. He realised that the brunt of the attack would have to be borne by the infantry. The armour's lack of determination for which there was some justification, was shown by the grim index of casualties. In the first two days of combat, X Corps (the armour), had suffered some 450 casualties, less than half the losses of XIII Corps, and only a tenth of those of XXX Corps. These facts were duly noted by Montgomery.

He remained confident of the outcome and, as the sign of a great commander, completely changed the direction of the attack. The Australians were to make a strong thrust to the north, while Miteiriya Ridge was to be held defensively and strongly. The new attack would alarm Rommel (who returned on 25 October) and would provide opportunities for which a strong reserve would be built up. The NZ Division would lead, but since it was only two brigades strong and had suffered 800 casualties, it would be rested and supported by the 151st Brigade (50th Division) and the 152nd Brigade (51st Division). Apart from one brigade, the 10th Armoured Division would also be withdrawn, while the 7th Armoured Division in the south was warned it would be required to support.

No time was lost in implementing the new policy. The 9th Australian Division, with all three brigades, their own artillery and the support of two field regiments and two medium regiments (of which the 64th was one), attacked during the night of 25/26 October, taking the enemy completely by surprise, and captured Point 29. In such low, flat terrain this was a valuable vantage point. Pressure was maintained to advance further to the north, and on 28/29 October, a powerful attack was made with the support of 200 field guns and all three medium regiments. Our programme comprised 31 infantry targets and nine hostile batteries. It provoked fierce counterattacks; the salient was very narrow and vulnerable, but the Australians maintained their threat, curling east across the railway and coast road, and almost cutting off the enemy in 'Thompson's Post'. Rommel was concerned for the safety of Sidi Abd el Rahman, the hinge of his position and key to his supply line. He brought up both his Panzer divisions, the 90th Light Division and the 164th Division, as well as Italian forces. This exactly suited Montgomery, who thus held the initiative, while the enemy concentration provided the opportunity for devastating attacks by the RAF, which had radio ground crews to ensure accuracy, and, of course, by heavy artillery fire. Meanwhile, the 1st Armoured Division was attacking Kidney Ridge. There was desperate fighting, particularly around the strongpoints 'Woodcock' and 'Snipe', and much heroism was displayed. These names acquired for us an ominous ring. Nevertheless, these struggles served further to distract Rommel from the great threat pending.

This was to be known as operation 'Supercharge'. Montgomery intended that the NZ-led attack should be delivered to the north through the Australian position, but his staff convinced him that this would be unwise: the latest intelligence reports showed that the Germans were concentrated precisely to meet this threat. So, reluctantly, Montgomery changed the direction of the attack towards the west and south-west, to be delivered from the north of Kidney Ridge. This was at the junction of the two Allied armies, usually a weak point, with the Italians predominant. The attack was to be led by the New Zealanders with their faithful 9th Armoured Brigade, and with the 151st Brigade on the right and the 152nd Brigade on the left.

We were aware of the impending attack, and had already surveyed a new position 7,000 yards to the west. This was done with great care, the map reference of each gun being established. We did not move, however, until 1 November. The centrepiece of 'Supercharge' was to be a classic infantry creeping barrage, a development of the First World War. (It was a further example of predicted fire, outlined in Chapter 9.) There were to be 45 'lifts' of 100 yards, at three minute intervals. The duration was 147 minutes, with pause lines. The total frontage to be covered, with other regiments, was 4,000 yards. Our guns were deployed in the usual diamond formation, but the resultant fall of shot would have been most inappropriate for a barrage, so corrections were made to ensure our rounds fell in a straight line. Infantry were trained to keep close to a barrage, even at the risk from any 'shorts', since the enemy would be briefly in a state of shock and unable to use his weapons. They could be easily dealt with while so vulnerable, but if the advance was held up for any reason, the barrage would be moving inexorably forward and would become of decreasing value to our infantry. In that case, the attack would almost certainly fail.

The zero hour was 01.05 hours on the night of 1/2 November and our zero-line was 270 degrees. Our 'orders' consisted of a 'trace' of a rectangle with the co-ordinates of the four corners indicated. This was then fixed accurately to the artillery board. The rectangle was divided into four columns, 'A' troop taking the right hand 'lane'. Line and range could easily be ascertained for each lift, meteor correction applied and gun programmes prepared.

The barrage went very smoothly from our point of view, and we hoped fervently that our attack had prospered. We embarked immediately on a counter-battery shoot which kept us busy until 06.25 hours. It was confirmed that the infantry attack had been successful, but the armour was having a tough struggle to establish contact with the hard-pressed 9th Armoured Brigade in the van, which was integral to the New Zealand Division, and was suffering substantial casualties. Some of the heaviest fighting was in the north of the salient where the 2nd Armoured Brigade was having a tough fight on the Rahman track near Aqqaqir.

We were thrilled to hear, however, that the Royals with their armoured cars had broken through to the south-west, and were creating havoc and consternation in the enemy's rear as far west as Daba. This was the beginning of the end, indicating that this was the weak spot in the enemy defences. It was attacked by the armour and the 152nd Brigade, and by 3 November the armour, too, was in open country. The enemy rear was also dislocated by the South African Armoured Car Regiment and the Honourable Artillery Company, with SP 105mm guns, known as 'Priests'. The battle was, in effect, over. We engaged in an area shoot, but firing soon ceased as targets became out of range. Our BC reported on 4 November that enemy dumps were being blown up, and wireless intercepts showed that the Germans were commandeering all transport for themselves, leaving the Italians to march into captivity. This was ruthless but justified on military grounds. Prisoners were coming in in large numbers, unfortunately mainly Italian. Meanwhile, the Germans were in full retreat to Fuka and were being mercilessly pounded by the RAF as they fled along the coast road. Our role seemed effectively over: there was nothing within range. After days of intense effort and little sleep, we realised that a great victory had been won. Montgomery's message of 23 October had been fulfilled. We were profoundly relieved and grateful, but not exultant. The full implications had yet to sink in.

During the day we heard that X Corps, under Lieutenant-General Lumsden, was to pursue the enemy with the New Zealand Division and ourselves. We were naturally gratified that we and not the 7th Medium Regiment had been selected for the pursuit, but we attached no particular signficance to this; attributing it to the toss of a coin.

We moved through the minefield gap. Progress was appallingly slow because the gap was so narrow and the surface had been churned up not only by gunfire and bombs, but also by the wheels and tracks of innumerable vehicles. By 08.00 hours on 5 November we contacted the 8th Armoured Brigade and the NZ Division ten miles south of Fuka. Plenty of Italian prisoners were again in evidence. At dusk we leaguered a few miles further west for the night, not having been in action. (It was near the point where we had been ambushed at the end of June.)

Early on 6 November there was some excitement about light fire from the enemy, to which our 6-pounders and machine-guns replied. We continued towards Bagush.

At dusk rain began to fall and this continued pitilessly throughout the night and the next day. We had not seen anything like this in the desert before. The downpour was heavy and incessant. Pools of water were lying and the ground became a quagmire. All vehicle movement was impossible, but our spirits remained high in these miserable circumstances. The sun appeared on the morning of 8 November, and we dried our clothes and blankets. Towards evening we tried to move a short distance, but the going was damnable, and several vehicles were bogged-down. We were unable to move until the next morning, when the going finally improved. We had lost two precious days, and our experience must have been typical of the vanguard.

There has been widespread criticism of Montgomery because of the slowness of the pursuit. In particular, it was said he had over-insured by assembling a far too large and unwieldy force to deal with a disorganised and broken opponent. In addition, the advance had been needlessly complicated administratively by including the New Zealanders from XXX Corps, when the armour came from X Corps. This was bound to cause problems and impose delay. There is substance in both these contentions.

Both Montgomery and his critics may have given insufficient weight to the psychological factor: the battle had been keenly contested and every yard of ground had been gained at great cost. It was, perhaps, expecting too much of the Eighth Army's powers of flexibility to suddenly assume the role of pursuer, where speed, rather than hard slog, was what was required. Furthermore, the critics treat the torrential rain as if it was a mere passing shower of no consequence, whereas it was surely a mitigating factor.

Montgomery was determined that there should be no repetition of the 'Benghazi Stakes'. He paid great attention to the questions of balance and logistics, not only to regain Cyrenaica, but also for his army's formidable and novel bound round the Gulf of Sirte. The Eighth Army captured Tripoli on 23 January 1943, three months to the day from the opening of the battle of Alamein. In this controversy, Montgomery had certainly the last laugh!

* * * * * * * * * * *

The final comment on the role of our artillery in the battle comes most appropriately from the two opposing commanders. Rommel has left on record his opinion of the part played by our gunners in his defeat: 'The British artillery demonstrated once again its well-known excellence. Especially noteworthy was its great mobility and speed of reaction to the requirements of the assault troops.'[2] This was the verdict of a great soldier in the agony of defeat. He could not conceal his admiration. No tribute could be greater than this.

Montgomery, (in a report to General Brooke) said: 'The artillery fire has been superb and such a concentrated use of artillery fire has not been seen before in N. Africa. We could not have done what we have done without the artillery and that arm has been wonderful.'[3]

The 'well-known excellence' of the British artillery came from 48 medium guns and 824 25-pounder field guns, which fired over a million shells in the twelve-day battle.

NOTES

1. A good account of the battle is that of Michael Carver, and this can be supplemented by reference to Nigel Hamilton.
2. Churchill, Vol. IV, p. 539.
3. Hamilton, Vol. I, p. 835.

THE PURSUIT

By 11 November 1942 we were at the Egyptian frontier, and acquired a fine German trailer kitchen in good order. We also obtained some *knäckerbrot* and German potato supplies in Bardia. On the 13th of the month our 'C' sub caught us up with a new gun and some reinforcements. We were busy in clearing up and maintenance. We had a visit from Brigadier Weir, the CRA of the NZ Division, on 23 November, which presaged the beginning of a very close and happy relationship with that fine division. (We beat the 6th NZ Field Regiment 8–0 at football.) Speed of advance was entirely determined by logistics and the need for our services.

Progress was leisurely, as the army awaited the opening of Benghazi port and the establishment of dumps. Montgomery was determined not to repeat past mistakes which showed lack of balance and lack of logistic preparation. For some days we were halted at the Bay of Bomba, before entering once more the green hills of the Jebel. The nights there, I remember, had a magical quality: all was unusually peaceful, as the war had moved far to the west. As one lay at night on the barren ground gazing into the infinity of the vast blue-black vault above, with the stars apparently larger and more brilliant than they had ever seemed before, it was impossible not to feel a sense of wonder and awe and of the insignificance of man. The silence was so intense it was palpable. I was reminded of a remarkable passage by T. E. Lawrence in *The Seven Pillars of Wisdom*, where he speculates on man and the emptiness of a world devoid of everything but desert and sky; and how this inevitably conjures up the divine. Hence the desert begot Islam. Yet, he might have added, Islam, like Christianity, is a derivative of Judaism, which also shows the profound influence of the wilderness on the sense of the numinous, whether in patriarchal times, or during the Israelites' later sojourn in the desert of Sinai. The infinity of the void has in like manner spawned other cosmogonies, while cosmology and philosophical speculation have been similarly inspired. Each night I felt some such emotion and awoke purged and refreshed to face the war. This feeling is so vital and important from a human standpoint, yet is so trivial and insignificant when seen in a wider setting.

By 27 November we were near Benghazi, which we by-passed, and two days later we were in the Agedabia area, almost two years from our first visit. On 4 December we were in the Suera area. Next, we 'found' the enemy and recorded some targets. The succeeding days were quiet with a little 'sniping'. The enemy rearguard then withdrew, but on 12 December they delivered a small attack on the Highland Division, which was beaten off and prisoners taken. The Germans soon abandoned the strong Mersa Brega/Agheila position because they feared an outflanking march by the NZ Division.

For some two months we had subsisted on tea, bully beef and biscuits. After bully beef for breakfast, lunch and dinner, one found its charms diminishing rather rapidly. I made a vow (which I have not kept) never to eat the stuff again. In contrast to the somewhat dismal Christmas on the bleak plateau outside Bardia the previous year, the army really had pulled out all the stops to give us a memorable meal this year, and everyone was cheerful and appreciative on Christmas Day after three bottles of beer a man. Unfortunately, it rained heavily towards evening and some of the tents were flooded out.

On 27 December we arrived at 'Marble Arch', so called because a Roman-style arch had been erected by Mussolini's latter-day legionaries. It was decided we ought to smarten the enemy up a bit, and for a few days we engaged in what we called 'pistol gun' shoots. These consisted of detaching a single gun and constantly changing position and harassing our opponents. On 8 January we carried out a couple of airshoots with Hurricanes, which were quite successful.

Next day the 212th Battery and RHQ prepared to advance along the coast road, but the 211th Battery was lucky and we were attached to the NZ Division. We passed Nofilia and caught up with 'our' division some sixty miles further west. The obsession of the former command with battle groups now found its full and logical flowering by enlarging the concept and retaining the division as nucleus with unitary command exercised by General Freyberg. The division had been 'beefed up' by tank and other units, besides our guns, and the old problem of infantry distrust of armour was overcome. This reinforced division was powerful, integrated and very mobile: it formed the basis of those decisive 'left hook' flanking manoeuvres.

We moved in desert formation, strongly reinforcing the naval metaphor. The group must have been at least a mile across, with armoured cars in the van closely followed by tanks, in one of which was General Freyberg. Very often our battery commander was also allotted a tank as forward OP. Then came lorried infantry, closely followed by the artillery. To the flanks was a screen of anti-tank and Bofors guns. The supply echelons brought up the rear. The whole division moving like some naval convoy, with pennants flying from the aerials of the armoured cars, was an impressive and stirring sight. Everyone enjoyed these operations and morale was high; the only snag was the occasional visit by the Luftwaffe.

If we bumped into the enemy we would halt while the armoured cars dealt with the situation. If the opposition was more serious we might be brought into action. This was achieved remarkably quickly. The BC would signal the zero-line, which as we were advancing west-wards was normally about 270 degrees. By the time the guns had unlimbered we were ready to give them the line and report ready to fire. (The gun tractors carried 60 rounds for immediate use.) As soon as the BC had a couple of rounds on the ground he would engage. With the guns slightly behind him, registration was unnecessary. In the advance through Tripolitania we had no maps, of course, unless someone had an old school atlas, but this was of no consequence with observed fire. (See Chapter 9.)

We were glad to see the country turning green, with a few trees, but it was becoming more hilly and rugged – good defensive country. On 16 January we ran into enemy shelling and there was some strafing by Me 109s as well as a few bombs from Stukas (Ju 87s). This was the expected stand to protect the Homs-Tarhuna line. The enemy was well sited in a wadi and difficult to observe. It was decided that the NZ Division was to carry out a left hook, with which we were delighted to be involved. We had to proceed in single file along a wadi to Sedada and then swing west towards Beni Ulid. There was a heavy attack by Stukas and Me 109s.

Some New Zealanders were killed, but although there were some near misses, we sustained no casualties or damage. The going was difficult and progress slow. On 17 January there were plenty of RAF Kittyhawks in evidence, and we heard that the Highland Division and the 22nd Armoured Brigade were west of Misurata. We halted for maintenance and a clean-up. The track ahead of us was heavily mined, which did not facilitate matters. All the signs were that the enemy intended to hold the Homs-Tarhuna line: there was a reserve of tanks at Azizia, some twenty miles to the south-west of Tripoli. At night on 19 January we reached the road at Beni Ulid, a clean little town with an old fort commanding the road. There was good going along the road north-west to Tarhuna, but as well as becoming more rugged, the country was intersected by deep wadis. Our objective was Azizia, while the 7th Armoured Division, following a path roughly parallel to our own but a little nearer the coast, had a shorter route along the direct road from Tarhuna to Tripoli.

By 21 January the country was assuming a civilised appearance, with small Italian settlements, each with an artesian well. The colonists were still in occupation and seemed a bit nervous, but were not unfriendly. Apart from officials, I doubted whether their fascism was more than skin-deep. The going through the hill country was good, and we swept west to Gasr Gharian, where the Luftwaffe put in a brief appearance. We had only fired a few rounds on this march. We emerged the next day onto the plain, with the going soft and hummocky, and went into action against a rearguard at Azizia. With such an obvious threat to all their troops still to the east, the enemy was withdrawing in some haste along the coastal road. We moved forward, but the going was very soft, and the enemy slipped away – but not before some tanks shot up our infantry patrols in Azizia. On 23 January we moved into pleasant green country around Tripoli. The 7th Armoured Division entered Tripoli from the south, closely followed by the Highland Division coming along the coast road. The town formally surrendered in the afternoon, as did some tanks. No attempt had been made to hold the defences; there was an anti-tank ditch across the road with the bridge intact.

We had advanced 1,400 miles, as the Army Commander reminded us in one of his special messages. With great tact, he said we must not forget all those who had worked so hard for success on our line of communication who would not have the opportunity of 'triumphal entry into captured cities.' The taking of Tripoli marked a definite phase in the desert war. The capture of this base was as big a disaster to the Italians as the loss of the Delta would have been to us. It symbolised the end of the Italian Empire in Africa, and was therefore of enormous significance. It meant much to the Eighth Army, which had twice before reached the very gates of Tripolitania, only to be counterattacked and driven back in confusion while it was weak and off balance awaiting the build-up of supplies.

On 2 February we rejoined the regiment. Daily leave passes were issued but rather sparingly I feel, because I only remember one visit to Tripoli, which had been the object of our hopes for so long. My only memory is of a pleasant palm-fringed esplanade, with Bofors guns spaced at regular intervals against the inevitable air attacks on the harbour.

One night, when camped outside Tripoli, an army kinematograph unit drew up, a screen was unrolled on the side of a lorry and we were regaled by *Holiday Inn*, including Bing Crosby and 'White Christmas'. That cursed, vacuous tune haunted us for months thereafter. I remember more vividly a news film with pictures of wartime Trafalgar Square and the familiar buses. As a London regiment, we found this deeply nostalgic after our long and eventful exile.

There was to be no triumphal entry into Tripoli for us; that was an honour deservedly reserved for the infantry. But we had not been forgotten; our long and active contribution had been noted. Some special acknowledgement was talked about and rumour was rife. Somehow boot and brass polish materialised and we smartened ourselves up. There were ample supplies of paraffin, and the guns were thoroughly cleaned and made spic and span, together with our gun tractors, which were the mobile homes of the gun crews, not merely the haulers of heavy loads. The 7th Medium Regiment, Royal Artillery was also sharing in the honour, and all thirty-two guns were lined up accurately by director and given the same elevation, with the tractors meticulously aligned in rear. It was a most impressive sight. On 3 February, we were arranged in our appropriate groups, with officers and NCOs in front, and were duly inspected by Lieutenant-General Lumsden. It was clear this was only a rehearsal for something much more momentous next day. There was a story that the prime minister was on a visit to Tripoli, and so there was considerable excitement when, next day, we paraded in front of the guns which were our *raison d'être*. Sure enough, it *was* a ceremonial inspection by Mr Churchill, in his air force uniform, accompanied by our regimental commander, Lieutenant-Colonel J. Hunt, with Generals Montgomery and Alexander and some staff officers in attendance. The prime minister stopped for a moment, and I found General Alexander looking me straight in the eye with a broad smile. When standing rigidly to attention one is expected to stare straight ahead, like some visionless stone idol. I am afraid I smiled back! Presumably our active contribution from January 1941 had been remembered: in particular, we had become indispensable after the fall of Tobruk as the only two surviving medium artillery regiments, correspondingly hard-worked and always totally reliable.

Both our regiments were conscious that a great honour had been paid us, and we did not forget. As far as I know, we were the only two artillery units to be so singled out during the whole of the war. The fact that Muhammad had come to the mountain seemed more significant than partaking in the victory parade in Tripoli. The artillery does not normally receive much acknowledgement, whatever it does, it is said to be just doing its job. It was warming to have such a mark of appreciation.

TUNIS-BOUND

After the ceremonial inspection there was naturally a sense of anti-climax, a period of boredom while the port of Tripoli was slowly brought into use and supplies built up as a preliminary to an assault on the Mareth Line. This was a fortified position prepared some years before by the French in case of an invasion of Tunisia by Italy. To make matters worse, the weather was cold and wet, and many men had coughs and colds.

The delay in fully opening up Tripoli enabled the Germans to forget the Eighth Army temporarily and concentrate on the Anglo-American force which had landed on 8 November 1942 (Operation 'Torch') in French North Africa. Some twenty miles west of Gabes on the coast are the impassable Chott Marshes, and the area between was known as the 'Gabes Gap'. Just to the south is the Mareth Line, and a little beyond Gabes is the wadi Akarit, which had also been fortified. This narrow gap with its two fortified lines, analogous to Alamein, was thus going to be a tough nut for the Eighth Army to crack. Each would require well-prepared assaults. With this strong position in his hands, Rommel could afford to concentrate on US II Corps and the First Army. He therefore determined to inflict a heavy blow with the DAK and the 10th Panzer Division. (In view of the 'Torch' landings, Hitler had at last sent reinforcements to North Africa.) A familiar story was enacted – veteran troops against inexperienced ones. Fierce attacks were made on Sbeitla and Kasserine, and US II Corps was broken. Four thousand prisoners were taken. This disaster occurred despite the many tactical 'Y' wireless intercepts showing Rommel's intentions. Only with difficulty was the front stabilised. Part of the explanation was with the high command, which was also inexperienced, although General Alexander was appointed General Eisenhower's deputy and was responsible for all operations in Tunisia.

These events precipitated moves by the Eighth Army. Our regiment crossed the Tunisian frontier on 20 February. We stopped the night at

Ben Gardane. On 22 February we moved towards Medenine some fifteen miles in front of the Mareth Line. Because of heavy traffic the surface of the track broke up, and we were unable to get the guns forward until next day, when our reconnaissance party had prospected further west. For a few days we kept up desultory fire with divisional salvoes to confuse any possible enemy flash-spotters who commanded the higher ground. (With salvoes, unlike gunfire, all guns fire simultaneously on a signal) We had been preparing our attack to take the pressure off the Americans and the First Army. By the end of the month we were in a pleasant position in the wadi Tessar, with the winter rains providing opportunity for bathing. This was intended as a sniping position on the Mareth Line but we withdrew on 2 March to a position further east.

Having delivered one successful blow, the Germans thought they could do the same to the Eighth Army before it completed its preparations for the assault on Mareth. In addition to the faithful 15th and 21st Panzer divisions there was the 10th Panzer Division for the assault, followed up with infantry. Fortunately the German plans were known and circulated to us on 2 March, with an indication given of our countermeasures. Mines were laid to the west of Medenine, and the orientation of our line was changed to meet the threat. The Highland Division in the north held the line of the wadi Tessar against a feint attack expected from our old adversaries, the 90th Light Division. The 201st Guards Brigade was to the north-west of Medenine, with the 5th NZ Brigade forward and the 6th NZ Brigade holding the village itself. The 7th Armoured Division held part of the front, with the 131st Lorried Infantry Brigade on the left of the 201st Guards Brigade. We awaited the attack with perfect confidence. It was to be another defensive battle very like Alam Halfa, even including an exhortation from Monty himself. Essentially it was to be an artillery battle. The Eighth Army had a great capacity for learning and there were a number of improvements compared with Alam Halfa. *All* anti-tank guns, including those with infantry units, had been carefully co-ordinated and sited in interlocking positions with pre-arranged zones of fire. At last we had taken a page from the German book, and our 3.7in anti-aircraft guns were deployed in an anti-tank role. Besides the field artillery, we had been joined by a

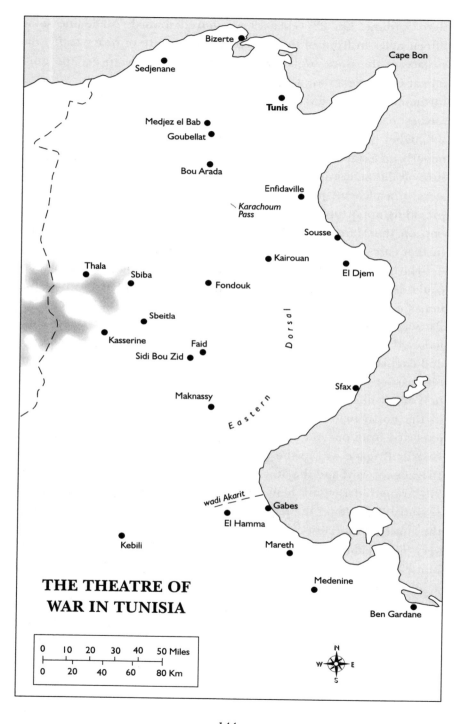

**THE THEATRE OF
WAR IN TUNISIA**

third medium regiment, the 69th Medium Regiment, Royal Artillery. Altogether, Montgomery disposed of over four hundred guns of all types capable of a fully co-ordinated role. We were not to open fire prematurely, but to let the enemy get to close range first.[1]

On 3 March at 03.00 hours the field artillery opened up on some moving lights, and at daybreak we engaged a suspected battery. The attack was still deferred and was now expected further south, so after dusk we moved in that direction, establishing a battle position and dumping 200 rounds per gun. Our zero-line was due west. It was fairly quiet on 5 March, but we were intensely sorry to see a Spitfire shot down by a Me 109. The pilot did not bale out.

The attack duly opened early on the misty morning of 6 March, and seemed at first to be of a mainly probing character. We had a large number of defensive tasks prearranged, and at 07.15 hours received our first SOS call. The Black Watch lost one of their positions, but successfully counterattacked an hour later. The tanks ran into heavy fire and were severely discouraged, while the infantry suffered heavily when they debussed and began to advance. Tanks and infantry were brought to a halt before our main positions. The 15th and 21st Panzers attacked the Guards and the 10th Panzer attacked the New Zealanders at Medenine. The attacks intensified. Many concentrations ('stonks') were fired, and we put down a 10 rounds per gun regimental bombard on a reported Panzer HQ. All attacks were repulsed. We had averaged 116 rounds per gun; the field regiments had also had a busy day, but the next day was quiet. The enemy was licking his wounds. He had suffered severely and had failed really to get to grips with our F.D.L.s (Forward Defence Localities). He had had enough and decided to withdraw. Forty-six tanks had been knocked out, mostly by artillery fire. Our losses were light both in men and tanks. Once again, it was a perfectly controlled defensive action, but some of the credit, as we now know, must surely go to the 'Ultra' decryptographers. The 5th AGRA units (the 7th, 64th, 69th Medium Regiments, RA and the 4th Survey Regiment, RA) were gratified to receive a message from the GOC 7th Armoured division thanking us for 'the quite exceptional support you gave us yesterday. It was a most decisive factor in sending the Boche flying in all directions. I am most grateful to you for the excellent arrangements you made and the tremendous job of work done'. Such acknowledgement was extremely rare.

On 11 March our positions were taken over by the 51st Medium Regiment, RA, another new arrival. As a precautionary measure we occupied a position near Medenine vacated by a New Zealand field battery. A further move was clearly envisaged and we spent the day quietly on maintenance.

The Eighth Army faced a difficult task because the Mareth line was an immensely strong position, possibly even more formidable than the Axis defences at Alamein. The fortifications had long been prepared by the French, and included reinforced concrete strongpoints. The Matmata Hills enhanced the obstacles and gave excellent observation. The position had been further strengthened by a line of forward defences, including extensive minefields. Finally the wadi Zigzaou formed a natural anti-tank barrier, aided by ample water and marshy patches. In the rear were the usual two Panzer divisions waiting to see at which point we would attack. General Messe, who had assumed command after Rommel's final departure from Africa on 9 March, had the reinforced 90th Light and 164th Divisions and four Italian infantry divisions.

It was considered that the position could not be turned, but Montgomery, foreseeing a possible need, had sent the Long Range Desert Group to reconnoitre a route for a flank march. They had found a difficult, but just practicable, track through 'Wilder's Gap', named after one of their officers who discovered it.

XXX Corps attacked 'Horseshoe Hill', about ten miles north-west of Medenine, with the 50th and 51st Divisions and the Guards Brigade. Deep minefields proved a problem, and the attack was a failure. This should have proved a warning to Montgomery. On 20 March, a direct attack was put in across the wadi at Zarat, in the coastal sector. This also was repulsed with heavy losses, especially in the 50th Division, and our precarious bridgehead was lost. That this was the direct responsibility of Montgomery is the view of his official biographer, Nigel Hamilton: 'Fame, adulation and a growing feeling of infallibility after Medenine all contributed to a dangerous over-confidence in his own tactical genius.'[2] Fortunately, Montgomery recognised his failure, and was able to deal with the situation by switching attention to the outflanking force he had already been moving into position at 'Wilder's Gap'.

We had taken no part in the dramatic and serious setbacks on the coastal sector because we were part of the sizeable force (27,000 men with 200 tanks) under Freyberg which was to undertake a 200-mile outflanking march, aiming to discomfort the enemy by threatening his rear. This was to become the decisive thrust. We were delighted to be back under New Zealand command. We were in a secret concentration area when Montgomery learned from 'Ultra' that the Germans had discovered our whereabouts. He therefore ordered the march to take place, even in daylight. Our route lay south through Foum Tatahouine and then swung sharply north through 'Wilder's Gap', and on 19 March we were given the scheme of attack and moved roughly north-west after dark. In spite of the previous reconnaissance, the going was bad, with many sticky patches. Progress was slow as we were frequently getting stuck and had to dig to place sand-channels under the wheels. In bad patches the process had to be repeated. In the worst places, one could take an hour and only move 100 yards. At daylight the going was still very difficult, with many intersecting wadis. We were attacked by a lone fighter-bomber, which some said was American. At nightfall we set up a gun position about 25 miles from El Hamma, our destination to the rear of the Mareth defences.

It was a busy day for us on 21 March. We engaged targets at extreme range, but moved forward later in the morning, and by early afternoon occupied our third battle position. A tense struggle was still raging at Mareth, but the enemy was now getting worried and looking over his shoulder. We supported an attack at 22.00 hours which was successful, with 300 Italian prisoners taken, and we remained ready with a number of defensive fire targets, but these were not required. Two paths had been cleared through the minefield. It was quite a busy day and we averaged 88 rounds per gun. The intensity slackened somewhat next day, but the attack was going well, with prisoners at midday about a thousand. We were intrigued by an Intelligence report that the natives were pro-German and that many had enlisted. This seemed a strange story, and I do not know whether it was ever confirmed. Pressure was maintained successfully over the next day or two, but in view of the setback at Mareth it had been decided that X Corps under General Horrocks, with the 1st Armoured Division, should follow a parallel route so that a massive and decisive blow could be delivered, General Horrocks assuming overall command. The 69th Medium Regiment was with this force. The Germans had little option but to switch much of the DAK and 164th Division to our front, but they, of course, had the benefit of interior lines.

Freyberg felt he needed a much bigger artillery support for this assault, but this would have imposed delay while additional guns and ammunition were brought forward over a most difficult route. The solution was the rapid and imaginative use of air power.

The main attack at El Hamma was delivered on 26 March, with zero hour at 16.00 hours. The RAF was to be used as low-level flying artillery, and under the inspired leadership of Air Vice Marshal Broadhurst, this technique was devastatingly successful. Waves of Kittyhawks, Hurricanes and Spitfires came in low from the west, so that the defenders had the sun in their eyes. The operation was under the control of RAF officers with the forward troops. It was a remarkable exhibition of the precise application of air power and was most exciting to watch. Meanwhile, the field artillery fired a creeping barrage which helped pilots to locate targets accurately, while our task was to fire twenty concentrations on enemy batteries. The 8th Armoured Brigade moved forward very quickly to exploit while the enemy was still dazed, and the NZ motorised infantry was also well up. Our expenditure rate for this active and exciting day was 96 rounds per gun.

On the following day, 1st Armoured Division was in the area of El Hamma, clearing up enemy pockets in the hills. The 'B' Echelon of 21st Panzer Division was captured. Seventy-five tanks had been rushed to this front, of which thirty-one had been destroyed. We were still finding targets, and averaged 60 rounds per gun.

The reduced resistance at Mareth had enabled the 7th Armoured and 4th Indian Divisions to capture Hallouf and Toujane in the centre of the Mareth Line, and they were now moving roughly parallel to us, although still well to the east. My battery moved at dusk. On 28 March we were able to see something of the damage inflicted: abandoned equipment – including a 105mm battery – lay everywhere, some of it destroyed, some in full working order. Sixteen 88mms had been accounted for by our guns and tanks. There had obviously been a hasty withdrawal. There were many dead, the burial parties not yet having been organised. So the miscalculation at Mareth had been rectified by this brilliant outflanking thrust.

As a rude reminder that the Luftwaffe still had some punch, we were bombed, although casualties were few. On 29 March there was rapid progress towards Gabes, which was occupied by the Highland Division at midday. Our speed of advance had curtailed the usual delaying tactics. We by-passed the town, moving north towards wadi Akarit, the last obstacle blocking the gap between the Chott Marshes and the sea. Progress was slow because of road congestion, and it was not until the small hours on 30 March that we pulled in to a gun position west of Oudref. We were shelled by a single gun of heavy calibre. It was not clear whether the enemy contemplated a delaying, or a more sustained, defensive action, but the wadi was reputed by the Germans to be the strongest *natural* position in North Africa. One of our intelligence reports suggested, however, that it was not so formidable.

The next day, there was a congratulatory message from Monty to NZ Corps and X Corps 'on the splendid results achieved by the left hook. These results have led to the complete disintegration of the enemy resistance and the whole of the Mareth Line is now in our hands.'

In early April we learned that the NZ Division was being rested and would not be involved in the attack on Akarit. By coincidence it seemed we would also be *hors de combat*, due to a shortage of 4.5in ammunition. This, however, was soon overcome. On 4 April we were able to carry out a calibration shoot to ensure that wear factors were not causing any inaccuracy in performance, and the next day we moved to our battle positions. The nature of the ground dictated that this would be an infantry/artillery battle. From our patrolling activity we noticed that the Young Fascists held the coastal section, and I hoped they would be suitably chastised. Next in line was the 90th Light Division, with three Italian Divisions on their right, while the 164th Division was furthest inland.

To achieve surprise, our attack was delivered at night, which was moonless. It was launched by the 50th, 51st and 4th Indian Divisions, together with the 201st Guards Brigade. Our only tanks were elements of the 7th Armoured Division. It was obvious that thrusts by US II Corps and our IX Corps (the First Army) to the east would have been helpful to our enterprise, but these did not materialise.

Our attack seemed to meet its objective and achieved considerable tactical surprise. We fired an extremely heavy programme aimed at hostile batteries, and many concentrations were brought down on infantry targets and strongpoints. Considering that they held the high ground and commanded much better visibility, it was surprising there was so little counter-fire: presumably our bombardment had inflicted severe damage and disorganisation. Nevertheless, a single 170mm round, aimed apparently at random, fell on our 'A' Sub. and there were many casualties, some serious. The gun, however, was undamaged and remained in action throughout that hectic day, strangely firing more than its sisters. We were encouraged to see a number of Ju 87s shot down by our Bofors guns, and there was a successful night attack by the Indians. The Highland Division and the Indians had specially distinguished themselves in savage fighting, and gaps were breached in the enemy line. Much of the enemy FDLs were in our hands. It was a spectacular victory. Our contribution was the exceptionally heavy expenditure rate of 223 rounds per gun, the highest achieved with the exception of the great October battle, and other artillery units also had high rates of usage. This was essentially an infantry battle. Gunners always had the greatest admiration and respect for the infantry: they are the true heroes of war. Consequently, we always felt specially solicitous towards them, were always trying to envisage their problems and were ready to help at any hour of the day or night. We must have greatly facilitated their task at Akarit.

At last we had penetrated onto the plain, into open country. As we moved forward, we were impressed by the strength of the Akarit position and were amazed how quickly our infantry had dealt with it. We went through a gap in the minefield and advanced northwards. The next few days witnessed some minor engagements, but our progress was quite steady. There were reports that the much-famed Tiger tank had put in an appearance, and this was later confirmed. On 8 April contact was made with US II Corps, and the next day we bumped into an enemy rearguard north-west of Sfax. We were credited with having accounted for two tanks. Our advance continued into pleasant agricultural country, with olive groves and flowers in the villages. Sfax was entered on the morning of 10 April. The 6th Armoured Brigade from the First Army was reported to be in Kairouan, the Moslem holy city, and a link-up was imminently expected. On 11 April we were intrigued to see on the horizon a huge black blob, which as we approached materialised into the magnificent Roman amphitheatre at El Djem. To my regret, we passed tantalisingly close but were not allowed even a five-minute halt. One did not need a classical education to feel a keen sense of deprivation.

On 12 April we entered Sousse, a large flourishing town with a busy *souk*. The natives were friendly, and it was easy to buy eggs. In fact, it smacked of liberation, the French being particularly welcoming, with flowers, pretty girls, and much waving of the Tricolour. We were halted on the coast road north of the town, where there was a long delay. There were some houses on the left of the road, one of which was more imposing than the rest, surrounded by a high wall and a locked gate which gave on to a courtyard. One of our 'experts' on such matters pronounced that this was the local brothel. He was right! There were two young girls in the courtyard, and with a little encouragement they were persuaded to lift their kaftans. At this moment the column moved ahead, which was, perhaps, just as well!

Finally, we arrived on the plain immediately before the jagged hills beyond Enfidaville. There were plenty of peas and beans in the fields, a welcome addition to our diet. Because the enemy had excellent observation, we were concerned about lack of cover, so we continued to reconnoitre, and did not bring in the guns until we had found somewhat better cover. Mosquitoes and biting insects were a problem and I hoped that I would not again succumb to malaria.

Here there was yet another example of the crass stupidity of 'green' troops. Some units of the newly arrived 56th Division came into place near us. Although we were obviously overlooked, to our astonishment they erected a huge marquee as their officers' mess. Retribution was swift. They were accurately shelled, suffering casualties. We felt this served them right, but their close proximity meant that some of the shells fell near us, fortunately innocuously. We now know that the army commander also formed a low opinion of this division and it was soon cannibalised.

On 19 April all was quiet, and we dumped 200 rounds per gun. Our attack was directed towards the high ground to the north of Enfidaville, which Monty likened to the north-west frontier of India, it was so rugged. The 4th Indian and New Zealand Divisions had a difficult task, and we were heavily engaged in support, interspersed with counter-battery and AGRA shoots. We averaged 152 rounds per gun that day. By 08.15 hours the next morning, the Guards Brigade occupied Enfidaville. The Indians and the New Zealanders were not advancing as fast as expected; the hills were very broken, with jagged peaks and precipitous sides, and on 21 April the enemy put in some very heavy counterattacks. But, by nightfall the New Zealanders had taken their objective, Takrouna, a high dominating peak, a magnificent achievement. The opposition had been tough, some 300 prisoners being taken from the 47th Grenadiers, a crack unit, while the Italians were from the Folgore (Lightning), a parachute formation and one of their better divisions.

Intelligence sources were able to explain why the enemy resisted us and the First Army so bitterly. Reports showed that there were 95,000 Germans still in Tunisia, but only 30,000 Italians, whereas the Eighth Army was used to fighting an enemy with a greater proportion of Italians to Germans (roughly half and half). If the Germans chose, they could make the end of the campaign extremely bloody and costly. Indeed, jetties were being built along the Cap Bon peninsula, so that supplies could still be landed if they lost Tunis.

Our efforts at Enfidaville were intended to divert attention from the First Army attack, code-named 'Vulcan', which opened on 22 April in the Medjez–Goubellat sector, and petered out on 28 April. It was a costly failure, although it gained some useful ground and resulted in heavy German losses. The Eighth Army continued to exert pressure to help the First Army. My troop was down to only two guns, the other two having been condemned by the Ordnance people as exceeding the limits of wear, i.e. they were unsafe to fire. We had a visit from the corps commander on 23 April, who told our BC that the fact we had been in action for so long had been noted and would be borne in mind when the question of relief or leave arose. This was good to hear, but nothing came of it. We took it stoically.

It is necessary at this point to introduce more serious matters into the narrative. We had had a new GPO some weeks before who seemed a decent sort, and who impressed by gravely introducing us to a large brown hen called Clara, in memory of a Walt Disney creation. He told us that Clara laid an egg every day, and that the command post staff could enjoy this feast in turn. Clara never failed with the morning offering, and was perfectly at home with us. She pecked away quite happily in the sand for what sustenance she could find, and seemed to enjoy crushed army biscuits. When we had to move, our truck would at first go quite slowly. Clara would cluck with alarm at the sight of her 'home' retreating, and with a run and a squawk she would land on the tailboard and make herself comfortable in her box. She accompanied us to Sicily, and seemed to enjoy the change of scene. Towards the end of that campaign, however, I saw some ruffians from the 7th Medium Regiment eyeing her up rather enviously, and Clara disappeared shortly afterwards, presumably into their cooking pot. We were very sad at her presumed demise, not merely for the loss of the eggs, but because we had grown quite fond of her. I felt Clara deserved an Africa Star!

* * * * * * * * * * *

On 25 April we put down some defensive fire for the Guards Brigade and the New Zealanders. We then moved east of Enfidaville, but, owing to soft saltmarsh, it was a difficult position. We had to detour over some bridges, but these proved too weak to take the guns, so they had to use a still more circuitous route. The cover was not good and the mosquitoes were a frightful nuisance. The next few days were frustrating, with frequent changes of position and plans; we became rather irritable. This unsatisfactory position arose from the failure in the west and conflicting ideas about what should be done about it. A firm decision was at length taken at Montgomery's suggestion, and it was with relief that we learned that the 4th Indian and 7th Armoured Divisions, with the 201st Guards Brigade, were to move secretly to the First Army front to join IX Corps, to be commanded by Lieutenant-General Horrocks. The Corps was to put in an attack which was intended to finish the war in Tunisia, and the 64th Medium Regiment was to be part of this force. We began to wonder whether the choice was deliberate. Normandy was to show convincingly that it was!

At 03.30 hours on 1 May we bade farewell to the mountains on the Enfidaville front, and moved on to the Kairouan road, where we bivouacked. We passed through the town at midday and halted for the night at Sbeitla. The next day, we threaded our way through Le Kef, a picturesque and lively place, stopping for the night well beyond the town, where we were joined by our 'B' sub, who had had a replacement piece fitted to the existing gun carriage. Already we had covered 220 miles, our long southern detour being necessary for security reasons.

Our reconnaissance party left early the next morning, 3 May, for the Medjez el Bab valley. We found a good position with satisfactory flash cover. The zero-line was to be 70 degrees, i.e. roughly east-north-east. The guns were safely in a 'hide' and were not to come in until next day, so we had ample time to dig in our command post. We met some First Army men who seemed to have plenty of everything, in sharp contrast to our rather impoverished state. We were intrigued to find just behind us some 7.2in howitzers, for no one in the Middle East had seen a British heavy gun before. All was quiet next day and all our guns came in with their various mechanical or hydraulic aliments cured, to everyone's great satisfaction. There had been talk of dumping 400 rounds per gun, but this was not achieved, and there were frequent changes in the dumping programme.

On the night of 5 May we were instructed not to fire except on call, although the 212th Battery did. The attack proper began on 6 May, the main thrust towards Tunis comprising the 4th Indian, the 4th British and the 6th and 7th Armoured Divisions. The Indians, with the 22nd Armoured Brigade in support, secured two objectives. Everything was going to plan and there seemed a complete absence of enemy artillery. A third objective was taken and we fired a concentration on a road junction. Two First Army Divisions (the 4th and the 6th Armoured) were involved, but the decisive thrust was essentially an Eighth Army affair, both in design and execution. An inspiring message was received from the prime minister, encouraging the First Army fighting alongside the Americans and the French forces which would lead to final victory. There was no mention of the Eighth Army, which we charitably, but perhaps dubiously, explained by the need to keep our presence secret. (Although we were temporarily part of the First Army we still regarded ourselves as Eighth Army).

The attack was a complete success; in fact it was ridiculously easy, and one could hardly justify the use of the term 'battle' for such a simple 'pushover'. We had only fired 30 rounds per gun, an extremely modest allotment. We were naturally elated at our victory, presaging the end of the North African campaign. On 7 May we moved forward to a position on the plain of Tunis near Massicault, but fired very few rounds, and this only at extreme range as the enemy withdrew. We went forward again, near St. Cyprien, where there were many abandoned civilian cars which the Germans had requisitioned. There we heard that our troops had entered Tunis. The first to enter were the 11th Hussars, 7th Armoured Division, immediately followed by four of our OP vehicles.

Our satisfaction at our success rapidly gave way to profound sorrow when we heard the terrible news that Major Eason, our former Battery Commander, had been killed at an advanced OP by what must have been one of the last shells fired by the enemy. It was particularly poignant that, after having seen so much dangerous and distinguished service, he should be killed at the very end and in such an anti-climax of an action. For the regiment he was irreplaceable. He had recently been promoted second-in-command, and we tried to comfort ourselves by the thought that he would have soon been lost to us anyway because he would have certainly merited further promotion. A day or two later some of us paid our last respects when we came upon his temporary grave, marked by a rough wooden cross with clumsy pencil lettering. He was the brother-in-law of our late colonel, so that the family had twice been afflicted by tragedy. We had great sympathy for Mrs Syer, who was more than just a name for us.

The position remained somewhat unclear. Would there be isolated pockets of resistance? Between us and the Americans and the French on the Bizerta side there were many Germans. In addition, they were supposed to be in some strength in the Cap Bon area. In the event, all was fairly peaceful. Whole formations were surrendering intact, including the 15th Panzer Division. They must have felt it fitting that they surrendered to the 7th Armoured Division, their old and respected opponents. The 6th Armoured Division moved across the base of the Cap Bon peninsula in case any Germans were thinking of a desperate last stand, and we were in support while the Navy blockaded the coast. The threat never materialised: the enemy obviously felt that under the circumstances, surrender was no dishonour. It was not so much a collapse of morale, but a spontaneous recognition of the futility of further resistance. It was an astonishing end. There were 150,000 prisoners, with over a thousand guns, of which 180 were 88mms, and 250 tanks (including Tigers), plus innumerable vehicles.[3]

It is not out of place to record our respect for the high professional skill of the 15th and the 21st Panzer, and the 90th Light Divisions. They proved formidable opponents who always just managed to avoid containment and slip away. Now, at last, they were accounted for. One must note that the Eighth Army was understandably 'uppish' about the slow progress of the Anglo-American forces after 'Torch', but candour forces us to admit that their opponents were predominantly German. Had we met an opponent with a similar composition of forces, our victories in the desert might never have been won. The North African landings forced Hitler to send reinforcements. Had he had the wit to spare similar forces to strengthen Rommel, the outcome might have been very different.

It was time to go back 'home'. As we left the plain of Tunis, by a more direct route than we had used to get there, we saw many happy civilian refugees making their way home, with many signs of friendliness and gifts of wine. We arrived back in the Eighth Army area around Sfax and located ourselves some 25 kilometres north of that town. Almost everyone was hoping to have leave in Cairo, but this was totally unrealistic. It was unreasonable to expect the army to mount a substantial logistic effort over a vast distance merely to give men a well-deserved leave. The centre of gravity had inevitably moved west. The regiment therefore did the best it could, and towards the end of May it set up a rest camp, with daily leave passes into Sfax. We also had a pleasant position near the sea. During our whole period in the army so far we had never had a sergeants' mess: we now repaired the deficiency, acquiring a marquee and a piano! Hitherto the only 'perk' had been a bottle of whisky a month, supplies permitting. Now that a much shorter link with the UK had been established, there was beer and we began to receive First Army-type rations, making an acquaintance with 'compo' (composite) rations, which included such delicacies as tins of Irish stew, meat and vegetable stew, tinned fruit, rice pudding, cigarettes, even toilet paper. Compo came in boxes for 14 man-days. We felt we were wallowing in luxury.

The Eighth Army was now very professional as a result of accumulated, and often painful, experience. Naturally, there was some tension between us and the First Army, who thought we were insufferably conceited, like our army commander! I remember encountering a medium artillery regiment from the First Army going in the opposite direction to us along a main road. They were led by their battery commander, who we immediately recognised as having been with the regiment for a time back in England. He clearly recognised us too. He wrinkled his nose in ill-concealed disapproval of the half-naked brigands comprising my battery, many sitting on the roofs, hatless, some with coloured handkerchiefs round their necks. By contrast his own men looked a very sober lot, all correctly dressed, with webbing and brass polished. Ships that pass in the night, apparently little in common, mutually uncomprehending. For myself, I quite enjoyed the comparison and the evident signs of displeasure. I knew to which unit I preferred to belong!

Towards the end of June we moved to Sousse, an embarkation port, and received new guns. I recall we had a one-day leave pass to Tunis. This proved to be very French with boulevards, cafés and many *flaneurs*. I found a bookshop and bought Voltaire's *Vie de Louis XIV*. We were soon reminded that there were more serious matters in hand.

NOTES

1. D. Belchem, *All in the Day's March*, pp. 143–8.
2. Hamilton, Vol. II, p. 186.
3. Churchill, Vol. IV, p. 697.

SICILY

O n 6 July 1943 we calibrated – a clear sign of impending action. On 10 July the invasion of Sicily began, with the Eighth Army landing on the south-east corner of the island, while the Americans landed further west. So once more we set foot in Europe, but this time, unlike in Greece, to stay.

We moved to an embarkation area and all vehicles were water-proofed. This involves sealing the engine with a special tape and attaching a pipe to the exhaust to bring it well clear of the waterline. There was apparently no immediate need for our services, a satisfactory lodgement having been obtained, and it was not until 22 July that we embarked on an LST (Landing Ship, Tanks), and sailed next day. The crossing was smooth and uneventful, and on 24 July we disembarked on

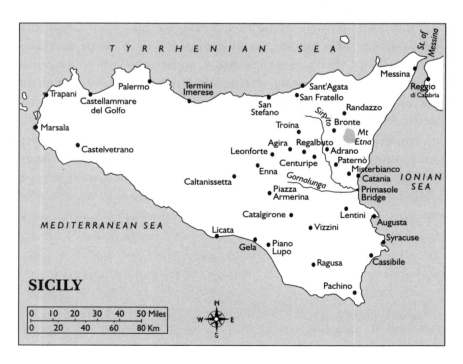

the beach near Pachino, where we de-waterproofed. We moved quickly from the beachhead, passing through Syracuse and taking up a position to the north, where we spent the night. Next day we advanced to Lentini and then swung west, where we caught up with the war at Catalgirone and engaged a regimental target at Regalbuto.

The 15th Army Group was commanded by General Alexander, with two prima donnas responsible to him, Montgomery with the Eighth Army comprising XIII Corps (Dempsey) and XXX Corps (Leese); and Patton commanding the US Seventh Army, with II Corps (Bradley), now battle-hardened after its experience in Tunisia. It was not a harmonious arrangement.

The dominating physical feature as far as the British were concerned was the Mount Etna massif which approached the east coast north of Catania, meaning that advance along the narrow coastal plain was not a practicable proposition as an immediate objective. The Eighth Army was therefore forced to sidestep to the west, and fight its way over the black lava slopes of Etna, with its hills, straggling villages and narrow roads. It was excellent defensive country; moreover, the opposition was now wholly German.

We spent 26 July quietly, but we fired a night programme in support of the 1st Canadian Division at Agira. (It was here we learned that Mussolini had been overthrown and a new government formed under Badoglio.) Agira was occupied, and on the next two days we secured Castelnuova. On the last day of July we were in support of the Seaforths and fired a counter-battery programme at midnight. On 1 August Regalbuto was taken. Attention was now centred on Centuripe to the east; our infantry was in the outskirts on 2 August and there was bitter street fighting all next day before the town fell at last light. We now had axial vent trouble on some of the guns, while cracks developed on the trails because of the rocky nature of the ground. With so much sloping ground, platforms had to be dug before the guns could be brought into action. The devoted work of our artificers and a nearby Ordnance workshop, which had welding equipment, enabled us to surmount our problems.

A bridgehead had been secured over the river near Centuripe towards Adrano. We carried out harassing fire tasks on road junctions and were particularly busy on 5 August, with regimental targets controlled by

AGRA, and 'A' Troop doing the ranging. 'Stonks' were put down, including one on a *nebelwerfer* position, which was our first encounter with these particularly nasty weapons. They fired a cluster of low velocity, high trajectory rockets (reducing the value of digging-in) and emitted a frightful moan. Hence they were known as 'Sobbing Sisters' or 'Moaning Minnies'. They were greatly feared, and caused many casualties. The next day, General Montgomery spoke to our BC confirming that Paternò and Catania had been taken, and we moved into the rugged country near Centuripe, where we fired a midnight programme, in support of the 78th Division, directed towards Adrano. The field artillery barrage crept up to the town, which fell next day. Over the course of the next few days we advanced, seeing the devastation in Regalbuto, where bodies were still being dragged from the ruins. However, we were saddened to hear that 'B' Troop had been bombarded by a *nebelwerfer*, killing five men. Later on, our OP armoured car was hit by a *nebelwerfer* and was completely destroyed, although no-one was hurt. We had an account to settle with these compound mortars, and were therefore pleased when an RAF jeep arrived to link us with two Spitfires to carry out airshoots on these deadly nuisances. We believed the engagement was successful. It proved the prelude to a busy day, with serial bombards and harassing fire tasks. Our infantry was now north of Bronte and only eight miles from Randazzo, on the north coast.[1] Things were now beginning to take a more favourable turn, and by 13 August it was reported that Randazzo was in our hands and that the Americans were advancing east along the coastal road from Palermo. They were also making seaborne landings on the northern coast, threatening to catch the Germans in flank and rear. Meanwhile, with their many preoccupations, the enemy was unable to stem the north-ward advance of the 50th and 51st Divisions along the narrow coastal plain from Catania. The race for Messina was now on. As a consequence, there was doubt whether the Germans were still in range of the 211th Battery, and our sister battery was definitely out of range. We saw both Bronte and Adrano, but the devastation was less than at Regalbuto.

The war in Sicily rapidly drew to a close, but with the Italian main-land so invitingly near it was essential to keep up the momentum and cross the Straits of Messina before the enemy could recover. By 28 August we were in position near the coast, and at 11.00 hours the 211th

Battery, aiming at three 170mms, fired the first shells to land on Italy proper. It seemed an excellent way of announcing our presence. For several days we were engaged in counter-battery work across the straits, with a heavy programme on 3 September of 176 rounds per gun, starting at 03.45 hours for a zero hour of 04.30 hours. The attack on the straits went in with the 5th Division at Catona and the 1st Canadian Division at Reggio di Calabria. It was supported by no less than five medium regiments and twelve field regiments, together with anti-tank guns. The Navy supplemented this with a monitor (15in guns), the cruiser *Orion* (8in guns), five destroyers (4.7in guns) and rocket craft. In my opinion this was a prodigious over-kill, but then I was not one of the assault infantry. The attack, perhaps not surprisingly, was successful and the lodgement established. Next day the straits were alive with bustling craft of all types busily ferrying supplies across.

There was a seventeenth- or eighteenth-century fort on a bluff near us, overlooking the straits. It had some huge mortars, some 15in across, with piles of cannon balls from another age, and commanded a magnificent view over the straits it was designed to protect. It was most picturesque, and would have been the perfect setting for a performance of *Tosca*, with a superb battlement from which Floria could make her spectacular and tragic exit. In the grounds was a huge fig tree, and I could sit in the branches with quantities of luscious fruit easy to hand, and before me one of the most beautiful vistas in the world, the setting of the mythical Scylla and Charybdis. This was a real sybarite's life. (Sybaris, an ancient Greek city famed for its luxury, was not far away, towards Taranto.)

But life was not all sweet. Stagnant pools bred malarial mosquitoes, and at one stage the equivalent of a whole division was incapacitated by the disease. Vigorous countermeasures were taken, including the issue of individual small tents fitted with mosquito nets.

There was day leave into Messina, which proved an attractive place with a glorious setting. We could hardly walk in the town without being accosted by small pimps, touting the attractions of their 'sisters', very nice, very cheap! I was determined to set foot in Italy, and found my way to the harbour where an obliging Royal Engineers sergeant gave me a place in a DUKW, a small amphibious vehicle. Apart from the army, Reggio di Calabria was fairly deserted. I enjoyed the counter-view across the straits towards the island. I noticed that bananas were growing in some of the gardens, but they seemed of an inferior variety.

We soon left by the coast road for the Catania area, stopping briefly to enjoy the view of snow-capped Etna from Taormina. Catania is a large city with many grandiose public buildings in ornate style and some fine piazzas. It also has some frightful slums. It is a musical city, the birth-place of Bellini. I bought a gramophone and some records which we added to some we had 'liberated' from the Germans, and soon the camp was echoing to the voices of Beniamino Gigli, Tito Schipa and Toti dal Monte. At least it was a change from Lynn, Shelton, Crosby and Sinatra.

Cigarettes and bully beef were universal media of exchange. It was well understood that the price of a woman was one tin, the result of poverty and the scanty food supply. The economy had broken down, the men were absent and children had to be fed. Thus the supply of sexual services was assured, while soldiers, who had perhaps not had relations with a woman for years, provided a ready demand. Thus we had the conditions for a flourishing market: Adam Smith and David Ricardo would have approved, or would they? I once saw a girl with a large basket go into a brick hut near us. There was soon a small queue, each man clutching a tin of the vital commodity. After she had left they told me that some smart lads had purloined some of the tins she had earned and then paid her with them when their turn came. I told them what I thought of them in no uncertain terms. They had behaved despicably. Even in such matters the proprieties should be observed! This petty meanness reminded me of another example. Much earlier on, in the desert, men had dried used tea-leaves in the sun and bartered them with the Arabs for eggs. The trick was soon rumbled. But dishonesty is a universal failing. We bought some bottles of Woodhouse marsala, correctly labelled and sealed. The contents proved to be a disgusting raw *vino*. Closer examination showed that the bottom of each bottle had been cut off, and the contents and bottom replaced. I never discovered how this was done.

One day there was a great 'buzz' going around that Monty was going to address the troops. We smartened up and were driven into Catania. We marched into one of the largest piazzas, where the whole of XXX Corps was crammed. Soon after, Monty arrived. (This was only the second time the regiment had seen him.) He was brief and to the point. We had done a good job and earned some reward: he was sending us home! This was momentous news, totally unexpected, and we felt rather dazed. Astonishment and delight were followed immediately by the realisation that we had been selected to spearhead the looming invasion of north-west Europe: there was a price to pay which was to have serious consequences.

Monty must have addressed us almost immediately after receiving specific permission from the UK. As we now know, in mid-September he wrote to the CIGS: 'I would like to suggest to you that, for the good of this war as a whole, you ought to ship 30 Corps home to England. It at present consists of

30 Corps H.Q.
30 Corps troops
50 Div.
51 Div.

The whole lot are in Sicily and I see no possibility of employing them in this campaign (Italy). In the Corps troops you have an AGRA which is probably unequalled anywhere for knowledge and experience; it is

7 Medium Regt.
64 Medium Regt.
4 Survey Regt.'[2]

Thus the real reason for sending us home was 'for the good of the war as a whole'. Monty spelled out precisely what he meant: 'These units have fought together for a year and are a great team. It seems to me that if you get home to the U.K. the Corps HQ and the Corps Artillery and the two Divisions of the Corps, *and you keep the whole party together as a Corps*, then you will have a Corps that has taken part in every type of fighting, which is a superb team, and which could be a model for the whole army in England to study. To break up such a weapon would be a thousand pities – such an experienced Corps would be worth untold gold when it comes to a cross-Channel venture.'[3] In the event, the 7th Armoured and 1st Airborne Divisions were also sent home.

All this seemed obvious and straightforward to Monty, but it was not so viewed by most of those intimately concerned. There was much resentment at this preferential selection for the hazards of spearheading the invasion. Monty had shown a good understanding of soldiers' psychology, but on this occasion he had misjudged the situation. Sometimes the resentment led to ill-discipline and men were arrested and charged.

'Many of the British troops were inevitably tired. By bringing home divisions such as the famous 'Desert Rats', the Highland Division, and the Geordies of the 50th Division, Monty had hoped to leaven the otherwise green formations of Dempsey's Second Army. But was this wise? ... was he asking too much of men who had risked their lives and lived with death for too many months and years to relish the "great adventure"?'[4]

* * * * * * * * * * * *

And so it came to pass. By early October we embarked for Algiers to await the next convoy to the UK, having abandoned our guns and vehicles. We tarried a short time in Algiers and then left for home, arriving after an uneventful voyage at Liverpool by early December. Our corps commander, Lieutenant-General Leese, had preceded us and came on board to welcome us over the ship's loudspeaker system and to wish us a happy Christmas leave at home, a charming gesture from the commander-designate of the Eighth Army in Italy.

We had already realised that life in the UK had been hard, with much bombing (including of Liverpool), but even so the people seemed curiously listless as we marched through the streets. We were not expecting a triumphal return with bands playing, yet they just looked at us with indifference, noted our sun-tanned faces and 'Africa Stars', and concluded, rightly, that we were destined for the Second Front, and went on with their business.

NOTES

1. Bronte was the town near which Nelson had the estate bequeathed to him by the grateful Bourbon King of the Two Sicilies, Ferdinand IV.
2. Hamilton, Vol. II, p. 428.
3. Hamilton, Vol. II. The 64th Medium Regiment, RA and the 4th Survey Regiment, RA were Territorial Army units. They had advanced a long way along the learning curve since their two hours a week at the local drill hall.
4. Hamilton, Vol. II, p. 616.

HOME

Our dispersal was speedy. There were happy reunions with wives, families, girlfriends. There were some marriages. Others pondered the ruins of affairs which had not withstood the strain of a three-year absence, with the prospect of no return. We knew there had been much privation and that the bombing had been severe. For a mainly London regiment, this would have been brought home painfully by family experiences and the visible evidence. Yet, although grim, home morale was sound; the war might not yet be won, but the outcome seemed certain. Hope was now rationally sustained. Oddly, it was our own morale which came into question. The general effect of our homecoming as veteran troops was to soften us, to 're-civilianise' us. Some even wore civilian clothing on leave, if it had survived the attention of the moths!

At the end of our leave we were based in Felixstowe, being billeted in requisitioned empty houses, furnished only with 'blackout' and bare electric light bulbs, and with no heating. We were without guns or equipment of any kind and had few vehicles. Presumably it would have been a poor use of scarce shipping to send them home when they would have a valuable replacement function in Italy, while there were ample supplies in the UK. Life was terribly dull: we had nothing to do and we were greatly bored. Men spent each day playing cards, reading or sleeping. In the evening there was the pub, the cinema and wenching. Every weekend men went home, with or without a leave pass. Many townspeople were hospitable and invited us into their homes, which was much appreciated. A local radio dealer had a good collection of gramophone records (78 rpm) and had, for those days, what would be regarded as hi-fi equipment. He was very ready to collaborate, and I gave a concert every few weeks. These were highly successful, attracting audiences of nearly one hundred people, not limited to my own regiment and including 'the locals'.

Yet our life of boredom was hardly the most appropriate preparation for the invasion. Nothing could disguise the fact that we were steadily becoming demoralised. A high standard of professionalism had been built up as a result of our many and varied experiences. Even when out of action for a spell, as in Syria, the fact that we were an integrated unit, a group with a corporate personality having clearly defined tasks to occupy our days and living in a strange, rather exotic land, maintained our morale. We were, too, proud to be part of the Eighth Army – a status we had now lost.

At many points in this book I have given examples of the indifferent performance of 'green' troops, both British and American. Given battle experience, and progress the hard way up the learning curve, these same troops could become transformed and give a good account of themselves. Our own experience abundantly confirms this observation. Perhaps a minor part of the reason for sending XXX Corps home was genuine altruism, but the compelling reason, as we realised, was to have experienced troops for the exacting and difficult task which was represented by the invasion. The high command obviously thought, as Monty had underlined, that it would enormously complicate matters, and possibly place the whole vast enterprise in jeopardy, if the invasion forces consisted wholly of untried troops, no matter how well trained. Experienced troops were necessary to spearhead the invasion; so reasoned the military mind.

All this seems obvious enough. Yet there is a counter-argument, that has received less attention, relating to the psychology of those concerned. The men brought home from the Middle East had faced death many times. Some had been wounded, all had comrades who had been killed. The initial joy at the news of going home was soon replaced by the sour reflection that preferential selection was being exercised for the next bout of slaughter in favour of those who had already experienced it. Very understandably, this crystallised into such thoughts as: 'Why should I again be put at risk, when there are all those blighters at home who have never seen a shot fired in anger?' I could detect this feeling in my own regiment to some extent, but it was much more marked among the infantry and armour, who had so often met the enemy face-to-face. Lieutenant-General Sir Brian Horrocks makes the same point: the veterans 'begin to feel it is time they had a rest and someone else did some fighting.'[1] As a consequence, some divisions and units resented what they felt was unfair and discriminate treatment and, as events were to show, performance in some instances was adversely affected. These views were slightly irrational because the alternative – the Italian campaign – was itself a difficult and costly operation.

As will be seen, in our own case we overcame any possible disability arising from resentment by a sheer effort of will and the recognition that our high priority was inevitable, and, for our own good, we had better get used to it.

Our experience was typical of former Eighth Army units. To this was added boredom, the futility of existence pending the receipt of equipment, and lack of enthusiasm for exercises, all of which we shared. This was aggravated by the feeling that 'we know it all'. Little attempt was made in many cases to adapt to the very different environment to be met in western Europe. The desert was poor preparation for the bocage, the hedged small fields, woods and sunken lanes of Normandy.

At this time the regiment again nominated me for OCTU. This was gratifying; moreover, if I was accepted and completed the course I would be preserved from all the hazards of the invasion. This placed me in a quandary: I regarded the pending operation to liberate Europe as a noble one; I had been with the regiment since its inception almost five years before, and had seen much action with it. It was quite painful to feel I would not be part of it. I therefore attended the selection board two-day assessment in a state of great indecision. Something about the atmosphere, however, helped me to make up my mind, and I deliberately gave absurd answers to written questions. I was duly rejected, with something like relief. Almost at once the regiment showed it retained its confidence in me by sending me as its representative on a course at the School of Artillery at Larkhill.

Our Intelligence sources had become very concerned at the German developments in mortar warfare, particularly the dreaded *nebelwerfer*, which we had encountered in Sicily. Intelligence forecast, correctly, that these would pose a serious threat to our forces. Work was therefore proceeding energetically on effective countermeasures. These depended on means of locating accurately these pestilential nuisances, so that they could be dealt with primarily by the artillery. The course I attended covered the new countermeasures, and I was one of some thirty officers and NCOs to be inducted into the mysteries of the 'Four-Pen Recorder'. This system was essentially a development of sound-ranging. Four microphones were placed equidistantly in a straight line across the FDLs to pick up the mortar reports, and the resultant four electrical impulses actuated four pens marking lines on a rotating drum. (Something like a barograph.) The mortar report caused a squiggle to appear on the paper, one for each of the lines, but since the microphones were at different distances from the originating source, it was possible to translate the various squiggles into distances on the ground, and so pinpoint the mortar. (The paper was calibrated in standard distance divisions.) Presumably this equipment would not be operated at regimental level, but by the sound-rangers of the survey regiment, so the object of the course was to ensure that one specialist in each regiment at least had a nodding acquaintance with the system, and would pass the information to colleagues. To my surprise, I was not asked to inform anyone of what I had learned, but we never encountered the equipment in Normandy. (I doubt whether it was practicable in the close bocage country.)

Boredom, merely waiting (and that for something unpleasant or unknown), was not good for morale. Everyone suffered; officers and men. A feeling must have developed that something had to be done to bring us to peak fighting pitch, but this was very difficult in a theatre where the field army, unlike the RAF and the Navy, was not yet engaged. By early spring we had our full complement of guns and vehicles, and we carried out some exercises in the countryside. It was terribly difficult to work up any enthusiasm. We had been in action countless times, and there was no type of artillery activity with which we were not familiar. It was difficult to enthuse over mere exercises, pretending to fire at imaginary targets. This was the sort of thing we had done in 1940, and it seemed a retrograde step. The 'masters' were being sent back to school.

Fortunately, there were two factors bringing us back to concert pitch. One was the realisation that the invasion was imminent, we were clearly destined to play an early role, so we had better reconcile ourselves to the

inevitable and steel our resolve. The second factor was the need to calibrate our new guns. This meant a trip to the firing camp in Redesdale.
We had, of course, done *that* before, too, but at least for two weeks we
were living under approximately active service conditions, cut off from
the softer civilian world, and again firing guns. It was like putting on an
old, favourite suit of clothes. We were also put on our mettle. There was
a certain natural resentment in the rest of the army at these cocky
Eighth Army veterans, with their insufferable air of superiority. We
appreciated that the IGs themselves had probably never been in action,
and so would be extra zealous in putting us through our paces and
seizing on any shortcomings. We were therefore quite spontaneously
determined to put on a good show, and I believe we passed out this
second time with flying colours. The firing camp thus did us nothing but
good, and helped greatly with our rehabilitation. This process was also,
of course, assisted by the passage of time. As spring began to move
towards summer, it was no longer possible to keep at the back of one's
mind the impending invasion. With increasing imminence came a
sharpening of our sense of direct participation in great and necessary
events: indeed, of impatience. I cannot speak directly for other veterans
units, but I believe that by D-Day we were indeed back to concert pitch
and ready for whatever lay ahead.

NOTES

1. Horrocks, p. 24.

169

INTO EUROPE[1]

Our new CRA came to address us, an elderly man with flowing white hair, standing on the bonnet of his Jeep in the approved Monty style. We knew of course that Monty was to command the Anglo-American invasion force initially. We did not know we had a new corps commander, Lieutenant-General G. C. Bucknall, who had commanded the 5th Division in Sicily and was Montgomery's nominee. It did not occur to anyone to ask who our corps commander might be: I suppose we thought it was still General Leese, who had welcomed us home from the Middle East.

Leave ceased during May, and shortly afterwards the guns and most of our vehicles disappeared for waterproofing and embarkation. Before the month was out we followed. The camp was close to the London docks and was surrounded by barbed-wire; security was tight and there was to be no leave except on the most extreme compassionate grounds. We lived in Nissen huts. The period of waiting was very trying, and we were bored. There were no recreational facilities whatsoever. The only break in the boredom was provided by a School of Cookery sergeant who demonstrated the US individual pack of concentrated, dehydrated rations, which fitted neatly into a mess-tin and was to see us through the first 48 hours, pending the arrival of normal supplies. There was a tiny metafuel stove for heating water for tea or porridge.

It was with great relief that we embarked on a Liberty ship on the night of 3 June 1944 (guns and vehicles had been stowed in reverse order of use) and sailed downstream to anchor off Southend, where a substantial convoy was assembling. As is well known, the weather forecast was bad, and General Eisenhower had postponed the operation for 24 hours, so we spent 5 June in enforced idleness. We sailed during the small hours of 6 June and rounded the North Foreland in line astern. It was a beautiful clear day. As we entered the Straits and were approaching Dover a heavy battery at Cap Gris Nez opened fire with a salvo of four guns, bracketing perfectly the ship immediately ahead of us. She hove-to with black smoke pouring from her centre section. As good artillerymen we expected the next salvo to straddle us, but there was no further firing. A small RN escort vessel belatedly put down smoke between us and the French coast, and our voyage proceeded uneventfully. We heard later that the damaged ship had been towed into Dover harbour. I often wondered what effect the withdrawal of that ship had on the invasion plans. It clearly meant a great deal for the unit aboard, who found themselves unexpectedly not taking any active part. They had, however, sustained casualties.

Progress continued peacefully. The ship's loudspeaker system relayed the BBC news and broadcast a statement from the Supreme Commander, General Eisenhower. Apparently the landing was going well. We opened our sealed orders, which evidenced the meticulous and detailed planning of the operation. These included local large-scale maps and air photographs of the particular field our gun position was to occupy. Every unit must have had equally specific and detailed instructions. I memorised our photograph very carefully, even down to the individual trees. We were to land at Arromanches, which was at the right of 'Gold', the most westerly of the three British beaches. At night the vast fleet moved towards the assembly area, before standing-in southwards towards the coast of France.

We had a good breakfast next morning (D+1), the last full breakfast for some time. The sight from deck at dawn was awe-inspiring, with hundreds of merchant ships of all shapes and sizes, and various types of landing craft conveying troops and vehicles to the shore. A few cruisers and destroyers were engaging targets in support of the army. There was a total lack of enemy aircraft. We anchored about half a mile from the shore. 'A' Troop was to disembark first, and I suppose that the armoured cars belonging to our battery and troop commanders would have preceded us, but my recollection is that our troop command post truck was in fact the first off. We were called forward, and we went over the side down a rope ladder with wooden slats. There was a small landing craft waiting, rising and falling some eight feet in a heavy swell. As the landing craft came up we stepped gently off the ladder; no-one was so silly as to step off at the wrong moment and risk a broken limb.

Hardly had we arrived when we looked up to see our truck swung out on the derrick and beginning its descent. The operators were extremely skilful; it was said they were London dockers. The slings were released at precisely the right moment, and the vehicle dropped gently to the deck. The craft was quite small, and we represented a full load. We immediately cast off, and the young sub-lieutenant R.N.V.R. in charge headed for the beach. We boarded our truck and started the engine, and as soon as the landing craft grounded, the ramp came down and we drove through shallow water to the beach. The landing had been as simple and trouble-free as the one in Sicily; a tribute to skill and careful planning. We were also lucky: XXX Corps had not met very determined opposition.

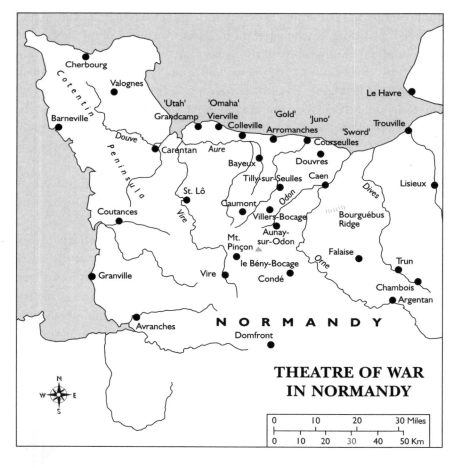

THEATRE OF WAR IN NORMANDY

172

I think I was the only one who had been to France before; indeed, I had been in Normandy at Easter, 1939 when Mussolini had invaded Albania. I had a love for France, but it was clear that even the less romantic of the party felt the solemnity and nobility of the moment as we stepped ashore. We had come to liberate a Europe 'groaning under the Nazi tyrant's heel'. Reality, however, is more prosaic, and what happened next was sheer bathos. The naval beachmaster had halted us just above high-water mark. We noticed a large gilt tin lying half-buried in the sand, with the familiar WD mark on the lid. We eyed it warily: some said leave it alone, it may be booby-trapped, to which the answer was: 'what have our engineers been doing this last 24 hours?' I suggested that although the Germans were undoubtedly thorough and painstaking, they could hardly have littered all the possible invasion beaches with WD tins. It must have been dropped by a preceding truck. I picked it up. We discovered later that the first thing we had liberated in the invasion was a tin of soya-link sausages! Alas for romantic notions. We put these aside as we were called forward, de-waterproofed and passed through a marked gap. We saw little of the town of Arromanches, but it seemed not badly damaged, and was deserted by the civilian population. We soon found our track, as indicated on the air photograph, and arrived in the field which was our destination. We settled down to await the guns. From the sea came the occasional boom of naval guns, while two or three miles to our south, towards Bayeux, there were some warlike noises and a few bursts of machine-gun fire. It was idyllic and peaceful; hardly what we had anticipated. If things went wrong we had our rifles, for what they were worth. We felt a little lonely, because the other troop gun position truck was some distance away. The Luftwaffe risked a few night raids on the beaches, but we already had plenty of Bofors guns in position, and there was quite an impressive display of red tracer. Our guns arrived next morning. Apparently the unloading had taken longer than expected; a heavy swell was running, and it had been quite a tricky manoeuvre to offload gun, tractor and crew on to the 'Rhino' ferry, which was a long, powered, floating platform. (It seems the 'Rhino' continued to give trouble.) Apparently XXX Corps' advance was continuing, and it would be pointless to occupy our designated position at Arromanches, so at dusk we moved inland a mile or two, and, watched by our brigadier, occupied a position and recorded night lines.

From the artilleryman's point of view Normandy was not an interesting battle. It consisted of a long, hard slog in support of our infantry and armour, meeting fanatical resistance from a resourceful and determined enemy who fought hard for each yard of ground, for which he exacted a heavy price. The bocage country with its many woods, small fields, hedges and sunken lanes was ideal defensive country, and particularly unsuitable for armour, which had difficulty in deploying. We found a number of well-constructed and concealed foxholes, all carefully and meticulously designed and finished, from which a handful of men could enfilade our infantry with automatic fire. They were difficult to detect, and when located the occupants might have melted away. Sniping was a real problem. The area was congested, there were virtually no opportunities for outflanking movements which had so enlivened our activities in North Africa. Until the Arnhem operation, there was no scope for drama, for the regiment to show any dash or initiative. There were now many medium regiments: we had lost our scarcity value. It was as if the prima donna had been relegated to the chorus. Counter-battery fire was restricted by the close, wooded and undulating character of the bocage, which made flash-spotting and sound-ranging difficult. As a consequence the counter-battery organisation was much inferior to what had been experienced in North Africa after Alam Halfa. Apart from observed shooting, the main thrust consisted of huge concentrations and programmes in which, until we became out of ships' range, the Navy was also involved. These concentrations must have been devastating, and the Germans were particularly fearful of the naval guns with their great accuracy and calibres up to 16in.

Many farms were abandoned, and the stench of dead cattle killed by bombs or shell-fire was overwhelming, coming from many bloated corpses with legs stiffly in the air. Gradually this unpleasantness was dealt with, and the unfortunate animals were bulldozed into the ground.

One of our men had found a cask of Calvados, quite typical of farmhouses in this orchard country. He filled his water-bottle with the fiery liquid, which attacked the enamel lining of the bottle. He drank the stuff and was dead in a day or two from lead poisoning. This bizarre death was our first fatal casualty. I wondered how it was reported to his family.

Some houses and villages were still occupied, and a brisk trade developed in butter, eggs and cheese, especially Camembert, which was always in perfect condition. Many men found this plenty rather odd, believing occupied Europe was starving. The fact that we were in a prime dairy area, with huge surpluses it could not dispose of because of the surrounding enemy ring, seemed not to have occurred to them.

* * * * * * * * * * *

XXX Corps, like the Americans on 'Utah' beach, had had a fairly easy landing on 'Gold' beach, and the 50th Division had soon advanced inland. It was, however, a little behind schedule, and did not take Bayeux until D+1, 7 June. This was the first place of any size to be liberated. It was virtually undamaged, and was soon to have a visit from General de Gaulle. The Division had had its share of Eighth Army nostalgia and resentment at the prospect of spearheading the invasion, but, like ourselves, it had come to terms with reality and was to give a good account of itself. Montgomery was pleased with the men's performance, and they maintained their reputation.[2] (The performance of the 51st Highland Division was unsatisfactory. 'It is not battle worthy. It does not fight with determination and has failed in every operation it has been given to do,' Montgomery said.[3] As we shall see, the 7th Armoured Division also performed poorly.)

The 50th Division, advancing southwards, crossed the Caen–Bayeux road and advanced towards Tilly-sur-Seulles, where it encountered stiff opposition from the Panzer Lehr, one of Germany's finest armoured divisions, and for long a thorn in the Second Army's side. The infantry had the support of the 8th Armoured Brigade, and we were frequently in action on their behalf. The place was bitterly contested and it was not until 19 June that the Seulles valley was finally cleared.

Meanwhile, dramatic events were pending of which we had no inkling.

The US 1st Division had had a very bloody reception on 'Omaha' beach, because the enemy's 352nd Infantry Division was at that moment engaged in an anti-invasion exercise. By a most gallant effort involving many casualties, the Germans were overcome, and the 1st Division was rewarded with a virtually unopposed march to Caumont in the south. This was a little to the west of the Allied boundary, and indicated that the German defences were not yet organised. As a result of bad weather, our unloading programme was in arrears, and the air interdiction activity was restricted. Rommel had thus been able to bring up panzer divisions to 'rope off' our lodgement: the front seemed to be congealing. The unexpected gap provided a glittering opportunity to exploit to the south and open up the prospect of advance into the Falaise plain. (It was in fact the last opportunity.) The 22nd Armoured Brigade (of the 7th Armoured Division) was therefore ordered to side-step westwards of the Germans at Tilly, and to move to the Caen–Caumont road, then turn east and take Villers-Bocage, an important communication centre. The brigade advanced without incident, and early on the morning of 13 June drove unopposed into Villers-Bocage. This was a complete surprise, and the town was *en fête* at its liberation. Troops parked their vehicles in the main street and joined the happy crowd. Meanwhile a squadron of tanks and a company of infantry were similarly parked on the road to Hill 213, a little to the north-east. Unfortunately, they were observed by some Tiger tanks, one of which, under Captain Wittmann, approached the town unobserved, using a bocage hedge as a shield. His Tiger emerged into the high street, where he caused havoc and much damage to the 22nd Brigade's tanks and vehicles before withdrawing. Captain Wittmann later returned twice with other Tiger tanks. On the last occasion some defence had been organised and some of the Tigers were put out of action, but their crews, including Wittmann, escaped on foot. The advance party near Hill 213 had many casualties and were taken prisoner. The Brigade thought it prudent to withdraw towards Tracy-Bocage, where the US artillery rendered notable assistance. But without reinforcements the position was untenable, and the brigade withdrew. So a wonderful opportunity was lost.

This fiasco was the most graphic example of the questionable policy of sending home experienced troops for the invasion. Any unit less likely to be useful for operations in the close bocage than the 'Desert

Rats' would be hard to find. They thought they knew everything, they were swollen-headed, ill-disciplined, and made no effort to adjust mentally to a very different environment. From now on they were the least regarded of our three armoured divisions. (The Highland Division shared most of these defects.)

There has been a great deal of debate about Allied strategy in Normandy. In fact it was made for us by circumstances. The effect of the appalling weather, quite unpredictable for the planners, was to slow down our build-up of troops and resources, while giving Rommel time to bring in reinforcements, notably panzer divisions. They naturally concentrated these against the British in the eastern sector, since a breakout there would cut off the rest of the German Seventh Army facing the Americans, and threaten an enveloping movement to the east. The British therefore found themselves hemmed-in by many panzer divisions. With some desperation, several attempts were made to break out or to distract the enemy so that this tank concentration should be pinned down in the east, thus improving the American likelihood of a breakout and an envelopment movement further west.

In furtherance of this policy, after the dismal fiasco at Villers-Bocage, Montgomery decided to attack the Odon valley, where fresh panzer divisions were arriving (Operation 'Epsom'). There was a delay in launching this attack, which was to be by VIII Corps under Sir Richard O'Connor of Benghazi fame, who had escaped from an Italian POW camp. The delay was principally occasioned by the great storm of 18–20 June, the US 'Mulberry' harbour being completely destroyed and ours seriously damaged. The intention was to cross the Odon and threaten the German positions south-west of Caen. VIII Corps would attack from the 3rd Canadian Division sector, I Corps protecting its left flank and XXX Corps its right flank. The main thrust was to be led by the 11th Armoured Division, with the 15th Scottish, 43rd Wessex and 53rd Infantry Divisions.

As a preliminary, XXX Corps was to attack Rauray and hopefully advance to Noyer. This attack was to be by the 49th Division. We were to support it, and there would also be very heavy concentrations for the main attack from the artillery of the three corps.

The attack by the 49th Division made good progress but failed to take Rauray, which was held by the formidable Panzer Lehr. We had been heavily engaged all night on 27 June, and feeling the need for a break, I wandered into a field a few hundred yards away. There I saw the corpses of some eighty of our men, covered by blankets and arranged neatly in two rows. They were from the 49th Division. Their first action: no doubt inexperience accounted for some of the deaths. I could see many of the limbs were distorted under their merciful covering, and guessed many were victims of *nebelwerfers*. Soldiers become accustomed to death, but the sight of our own dead is always intensely moving. I thought of the families, all unsuspecting, of the dreaded telegram. My sombre thoughts were interrupted by a padre with a face the colour of beefsteak, who asked me with a bright smile if I was looking for anybody. 'No,' I said curtly, and walked sadly back to our gun position. It was about this time that Captain Edwards, our 'B' Troop commander, was killed by a shell while acting as an OP officer with our armour. We were very sad: he was an original member of the regiment.

The main attack was now developing. The Germans had correctly anticipated it, and the Odon was held by the 21st, 12th SS and Lehr panzer divisions. The attack opened with exceptionally heavy artillery support, and the 11th Armoured Division crossed the Odon, the 15th Division capturing a bridge intact. The armour crossed the Orne and on 29 June, after very savage fighting, captured Hill 112. To distract and seriously damage our dispositions, the 9th and 10th SS Panzer Divisions attacked north-eastwards towards Cheux. This was critical but the German counterattack was decisively defeated. Either General Dempsey (commander of the Second Army) was unaware of this success and thought the counterattack was still to come, or he thought our salient too narrow to withstand attack, for he ordered the withdrawal on the Odon front, and so the battle ended on 30 June. (We lost 400 tanks, although many were recoverable.)

It was about this time that we realised that XXX Corps had been reduced to only one medium regiment, ourselves, instead of the usual two.

This surprised us enormously, because the Corps was one of the assault formations. We were very puzzled, not to say, bewildered. There seemed no shortage of medium regiments. No explanation was ever vouchsafed and the matter remained completely inexplicable, a mystery. However, if the Corps was to have only one medium regiment, it was very gratifying that the choice had fallen on us. The earlier instances of preferment had seemed due to chance. It was now clear that the preferment had been deliberate, not random.

The Germans were giving less importance to artillery and were increasing the emphasis on rocket-type projectile, multi-barrelled mortars, the *nebelwerfer*. They had a very high rate of fire, had a small flash, were mobile, and were very difficult to locate, especially in the bocage. They came in three sizes with ranges from 5,000 to 8,600 yards. There were five of these regiments in Normandy, each with 60–70 of these fearsome weapons. Our concern was shown by the 4-Pen Recorder development, but I doubt whether this was ever deployed. For one thing it would be difficult to place and survey the microphones in such dense and close country. The only remedy was to saturate a suspected *nebelwerfer* position with gunfire.

Shortly after this vicious encounter to take Rauray, we occupied a new position and were astonished to find a Mk. VI Tiger tank only 100 yards from our pivot gun. It naturally attracted a great deal of attention. As far as we could see it was quite undamaged, and we assumed it must have run out of fuel and been abandoned by its crew in some haste. We remembered the alarm caused in Tunisia by its presence, and we could now understand why. It obviously completely outclassed the Sherman, which had been at the forefront of Allied tank development as recently as Alamein. German technology had clearly effected a revolution. All our tanks, including the new Cromwell and the Churchill were now obsolete.

The close examination of the Tunisian Tigers, so foolishly made available by Hitler, was a very sobering experience for the Allies. The invasion was only about a year away, and there was no time to develop a comparable tank. Under the circumstances, it was creditable that two partial countermeasures were devised. The 17-pounder anti-tank gun, as lethal to tanks as the 88mm, was formerly only issued to Royal Artillery regiments. This gun was installed in the turret of a Sherman, and one of these modified 'Firefly' tanks was issued to each of our tank troops. 'Fireflies' proved an effective counter to German tanks, particularly if they were mistaken for Shermans, but, of course, they still had the disadvantage of the vulnerable Sherman chassis, and they were few in number. The other countermeasure was the rocket-firing Typhoon of the RAF. They hunted in pairs, locating heavy tanks usually with the aid of ground observation. It was a thrilling sight to see them dive almost vertically before releasing their rockets very nearly at ground level.

So although enjoying numerical superiority, we were technically vastly inferior, and this factor largely explains most of our setbacks. When hit, the Sherman was likely to burst into flames, and many tank crews were incinerated. With sardonic humour the Germans christened the Sherman the 'Tommy-cooker'!

The magnitude of our disadvantages needs to be outlined. The Tiger was a monster weighing 54 tons: its frontal armour was 100mm thick and it was almost impossible to knock out except from the flank, since its side armour was thinner. Its 88mm gun (20lb shell) could penetrate 102mm armour at 1,000 yards. The Mk. V Panther, which many consider to be an even better tank than the Tiger, weighed 45 tons and had a 75mm gun (14-pounder) which could penetrate 118mm of armour at 1,000 yards. Its frontal armour was also 100mm thick. The Mk. IV Special's gun could penetrate 84mm of armour at 1,000 yards, and its own armour was 80mm thick. Half the German tanks were Mk. IVs, nearly 40 percent were Mk. Vs, and Tigers made up the balance of the force. In contrast, the frontal armour of the Sherman was only 76mm thick. 'It could be knocked out by any German tank at 1,000 yards.'[4] At best, the Sherman's 75mm gun could penetrate 74mm at 100 yards! This dreadful litany makes clear what a magnificent and courageous achievement was that of the 11th Armoured Division in their action in the Odon valley.

It cannot be overemphasised that the failure of the British to break out from the eastern sector (quite apart from the weather-induced delays) was the result of the vastly superior technical quality of German tanks, nearly all of which were concentrated on the British front. Critics who miss this crucial point should not be taken seriously.

Montgomery was condemned to launch a series of attacks (with huge bomber resources and the artillery of several corps) because it was essential to keep the panzers firmly anchored to the eastern front. This would give the Americans the opportunity to break out from a front relatively free of panzers. The attacks were foredoomed to fail, but could still be claimed as strategic successes. (Hypothetically, had the weather in the Channel been 'normal' and our build-up on schedule, we could well have broken out on the British front before the main force of panzers could arrive).

In pursuance of this policy of maintaining maximum pressure, Operation 'Charnwood' was planned to capture Caen. It was to be carried out by I Corps with the 3rd British, 3rd Canadian and 59th Divisions, and was to be preceded by 'carpet-bombing' on a large scale. There were two armoured brigades in support, and a heavy artillery programme. The objective was to secure a bridgehead south of the Orne, in which case VIII Corps would renew its operations on the Odon. As a preliminary, on 3 July Carpiquet village was taken, but not the airfield, which was held by the 12th SS Panzer Division. The intense bombing and shelling of Caen caused cratering and blockage from ruined buildings, so it was a mixed blessing. The attack was successful, although at heavy cost, but gave us only the northern part of the city, but Colombelles, with its steelworks and blast furnaces, which gave excellent observation, remained in enemy hands.

The next phase was Operation 'Goodwood', timed for 18 July to precede the US breakout attempt (Operation 'Cobra'). Our attack was to be launched southwards from the Orne bridgehead to complete the envelopment of the city, seize the Orne crossings and break in to the Falaise plain, dominated by the Bourguébus ridge. The attack was preceded by even heavier bombing and artillery support, and was to be delivered by the three armoured divisions led by the 11th Armoured Division, supported by infantry and independent armoured brigades. It was impossible to conceal the preparations, and the Germans were fully alerted. The jumping-off area was so narrow and congested that the armoured divisions had to leave in sequence, not simultaneously. XXX Corps was not engaged but we were, because of our range.

Terrible damage had been inflicted by the bombing on the German defenders; Tiger tanks had been blown over like chaff and casualties had been heavy. The 11th Armoured Division had left on time, 07.30 hours, but found the cratering and damage to roads a problem. When they reached Cagny, they came under heavy fire from a troop of 88s which had emerged unscathed from the bombing. The enemy was soon joined by heavy tanks and 88s from Bourguébus. The attack was halted and many tanks were knocked out, with little effective means of dealing with the problem. They badly needed the support of their infantry brigade, but this had been ordered by Montgomery to protect the flanks of the advance by taking the villages of Cuberville and Demouville. 'Pip' Roberts, commander of the 11th Armoured Division, had bitterly opposed this order, but had been overruled. When the Guards Armoured Division arrived, at about 11.00 hours, the battle was effectively over. (The 7th Armoured Division did not appear until early evening.) Since further 88s, as well as Mk. V and VI tanks, had reinforced Bourguébus, there was nothing to do but accept failure.

The operation was seriously misconceived. The constrictions of the jumping-off area were so serious that congestion was inevitable and the full force (750 tanks) could not be delivered in a single blow. Furthermore, it was impossible to conceal preparations on such a scale, so surprise could not be achieved. The enemy accurately predicted the form of the attack, and had devised appropriate defensive measures. Since the operation proceeded from his vantage point at Colombelles, he also had good visibility.

What is very strange is that our planners seemed not to have heard of the laws of probability. They assumed that all opposition would be totally obliterated by the bombing. We had been shelled and bombed many times, yet it was exceedingly rare for a gun to be hit. Moreover, the artillery had probability tables so that the number of rounds needed to hit a target with certainty, if the gun was properly laid, could be calculated. By the laws of chance, some 88s or heavy tanks would survive, to which we had no answers.

The Americans launched their break-out attempt on 25 July, after delay caused by bad weather. It was a repeat of 'Goodwood', being preceded by heavy bombing, some of which fell on the US 30th Division as well as on the Panzer Lehr Division, for which it was intended. The attack on St. Lô was successful, and after stiff fighting to the south-west, US forces advanced steadily until they reached Avranches, at the foot of the Cotentin peninsula. General Patton, with armour and motorised infantry of the US Third Army, had not yet been engaged, and he proved a brilliant exploiter of the situation.

This was obviously a good time for the Allies to strike, while the enemy was distracted. The Canadian Army was formed on 31 July and given the task of advancing along the main road to Falaise. In effect it was a continuation of 'Goodwood', and after hard fighting, and initial bombing, Tilly-la-Campagne was captured. The operation was carried out by II Corps, under Lieutenant-General Simonds, who was thrusting and imaginative, e.g. he removed the guns from SP gun vehicles, so converting them into armoured personnel carriers for the infantry. The operation was codenamed 'Totalize', and was spearheaded by the Canadian and Polish Armoured Divisions. Sadly, owing to navigational errors, our troops were twice bombed by our own air force. The familiar pattern repeated itself, and although slow progress was made, the attack ground to a halt on 11 August because of fanatical resistance and the huge technical superiority of the enemy tanks and 88s.

Co-ordinated action was also undertaken by the Second Army, with VIII Corps attacking le Bény-Bocage and heading towards Vire so as to threaten the flank of the Seventh Army, which was increasingly concerned with the American advances to the south-west (Operation 'Bluecoat'). XXX Corps was also involved, and was to strike south to protect the flank of the Canadians who were advancing so painfully towards Falaise. Its main objective was Mt. Pinçon, some ten miles south of Villers-Bocage. The initial objective was Aunay-sur-Odon, but progress by the 'Desert Rats', the 7th Armoured Division, was so painfully slow that Dempsey's patience, already strained by the Villers-Bocage fiasco, snapped. With Montgomery's agreement, Dempsey sacked the division's commander, the 22nd Brigade commander and Lieutenant-General Bucknall, commanding XXX Corps. The new corps commander was Lieutenant-General Horrocks, who had been seriously wounded in North Africa and had only just recovered. He took up his appointment on 4 August, and performance soon began to improve.

For some weeks our intelligence had been emphasising the importance of the 1,200ft-high Mt. Pinçon as a possible focal point of German resistance, and the name had begun to seem sinister. We reached the area on 6 August, expecting some savage fighting, but early in the morning, in heavy mist, some tanks of the 13th/18th Hussars came across an unguarded track and decided to take a chance. They drove up the track to the summit of Mt. Pinçon without opposition. Tanks can take, but cannot hold, a position, and they were feeling very vulnerable until infantry of the 43rd Division soon reached them. And so, easily and unexpectedly, the hill was ours. Horrocks then was accompanied by his CCRA, who directed some very heavy concentrations from the hill on the enemy, with which we were involved.

These concentrations were so heavy and sustained that Horrocks (of all people) says that the help of clerks and cooks was needed. This is nonsense – the gunners invariably met every demand, however prolonged and intense. (There were two clerks per battery – and no cooks!)

Meanwhile, Patton at Avranches had soon decided that he needed to detach only one corps to advance to Brest, and turned the rest of his army eastwards towards the lower Seine, directing his XV Corps on Argentan in a bold move to envelop the German Seventh Army. Hitler now intervened, seeing the opportunity of cutting the American forces in two by attacking westwards towards Mortain. This effort was repulsed by stout defence and the use of close air support. The position of the Seventh Army was now very precarious and they engaged in a desperate withdrawal to the east. Unfortunately, General Bradley, US overall commander, ordered Patton to halt at Argentan because he feared that XV Corps would be exposed to a larger and desperate German retreating force. Bradley had also overestimated the Canadian–Polish speed of advance towards Falaise. Patton was furious, for the gap between the Allied forces had yet to be closed.

Some very desperate and bloody fighting took place, with the Americans eventually advancing from Argentan, and the Canadians and Poles inching their way south to Trun against desperate men with superior weapons. There was the danger of the Allies fighting each other, and artillery observers were directing fire towards themselves. The Polish armour managed to advance south-east of Trun to Chambois. The gap was still not finally closed, and they fought a magnificent defensive battle to hold Hill 262, a little to the north-east, which was in the path of the retreating enemy.

Field Marshal Model had succeeded von Kluge (who had committed suicide) as commander of Army Group B, and he introduced a novel feature, learned on the Russian front, of bringing back formations which had already escaped to aid those troops still trying to escape the closing jaws. Thus the indomitable Poles were attacked front and rear at Hill 262, but in spite of heavy losses they held to their task. Eventually the gap was closed, and much of the Seventh Army was taken prisoner. How many Germans escaped is still a matter of controversy. The Allied armies were thus able to continue their advance to the Seine, and the battle for Normandy had been won.

* * * * * * * * * * *

With the Americans sweeping towards the Seine, the way was open for general advance. My regiment crossed the Orne at Thury-Harcourt, some ten miles east of Mt. Pinçon, as XXX Corps formed the southern-most British formation. We passed through Argentan and saw much evidence of the havoc wrought on the escaping columns by our fighter aircraft. Many of the German vehicles were horse-drawn, which surprised us very much. Our experience had been with panzer and motorised infantry: we had not realised most infantry divisions were not yet mechanised. The lines of burned-out and blackened vehicles were a grim sight. We were directed towards Évreux, and were to cross the Seine west of Paris at Vernon, where the 43rd Division had established a bridgehead. Everyone was delighted to be free of Normandy and the accursed bocage country. It was wonderful once more to have freedom to move. Intoxication was in the air, stimulated by joyous scenes and welcoming crowds in towns and villages, no doubt grateful for having avoided the destruction inflicted on their unfortunate compatriots in cities like Caen and villages such as poor Aunay-sur-Odon, reduced to a heap of rubble.

We stopped for the night of 28 August in a small village on our approach to the Seine. Towards evening a few of us wandered over to a large farmhouse in search of eggs. Eggs proved to be not the only attraction: there was an extremely pretty blond in her early twenties who was flirtatious, and some of the men were weighing up the amorous possibilities. A group of some six tough-looking individuals then arrived, clad in berets and black leather jackets, and carrying Sten guns. Clearly the Maquis, and almost certainly Communists, who were usually the core of the Resistance. Obviously, their business was not with us, but with mademoiselle. They had come to arrest her. She became agitated and tearful, and the gallant British were about to intervene to save the damsel in distress. However, I had an inkling of the truth, and told my people pretty sharply not to interfere. We surely did not want an incident with the Maquis; moreover, they were armed and we were not.

That evening there was great excitement in the village square. We joined the throng, our curiosity aroused. There were many patriotic speeches, interspersed with cries of 'Vive de Gaulle', 'Vive Roosevelt', 'Vive Churchill', with rhythmic clapping of the Morse 'V' sign between each invocation. In the centre of this animated throng sat three women on chairs, two in their forties, stolid and phlegmatic, and our pretty mademoiselle, quite distraught. It was clearly a public trial, revolutionary justice was to be done. I looked for the *tricoteuses* and listened for the tumbrels! To the villagers, the women's guilt was already abundantly established: the three had shown sexual favours to the hated Germans. Sentence was a formality; we were gathered for the execution. The two older women were dealt with first. They were perfectly submissive, with expressionless faces, as a burly man with a large pair of shears cut off their locks. Another man then ran clippers over their heads until their skulls were as bare as billiard balls. They then turned to the girl, who was screaming and hysterical. She struggled but the same treatment was meted out. Once sentence had been carried out the victims were permitted to depart amidst the jeers of the villagers. We returned to our vehicles in sombre mood, now aware of some of the subterranean tensions in occupied France. As we progressed through the country we sometimes noticed women with kerchiefs tied tightly around their heads. We now knew what it signified.

We duly crossed the Seine at Vernon and moved towards Amiens. Everywhere there was the heady wine of liberation, and joyous, expectant, welcoming crowds. Occasionally odd pockets of resistance had to be cleared up. Normally they were false alarms, but if confirmed could most appropriately be left for the local Resistance to deal with. Similar scenes took place in Belgium. The war seemed really over, but there was one grim reminder. By the side of the road was a knocked-out Tiger tank. It had caught fire, and one of the crew had been trapped by the flames as he sought to escape. His body lay sprawled halfway out of the turret, completely carbonised it seemed, with his bare, smooth, blackened head.

The Guards Armoured Division had been directed on Brussels, amidst wild scenes of jubilation. The destination of our column, which was led by the 11th Armoured Division, was Antwerp. Remarkably, the port and its installations were undamaged: all equipment was in perfect working order. This, we were soon to find, was rather academic, because access to the port, some miles inland, was blocked by the German presence on both sides of the Scheldt estuary. The city itself had suffered some damage from V-1 rockets. There were grim pictures in the local newspaper office of piles of the resultant dead. We halted near some modern houses on the outskirts of the city, and I talked to a young, extremely friendly, married couple. They asked me about the war as we had seen it, and seemed quite upset when I mentioned in passing that for most of the last three or four years we had lived rough, sleeping on the ground in the open. It took some time for them to realise that this was as it had to be. They then pressed me to stay the night with them and 'sleep in a real bed' and have a meal. I gratefully accepted, and later that evening I arrived *chez eux* with a tin of corned beef and some cigarettes. Madame managed a highly creditable meal and they produced some wine. I thanked them profusely next morning and went back to the war.

Liberation had affected our high command and the planning staffs. An air of crass over-optimism prevailed: the war would be over by Christmas! This led to serious errors of judgement. One less serious error was the failure to clear the enemy out of the suburb of Merxem. More important, the obsession with crossing the Rhine meant that other matters tended to be neglected. Thus, much of the Fifteenth Army had been able to slip away from its mainly non-combatant role in the Pas de Calais and make its way along the coast, crossing the mouth of the Seine with little interference, and occupying the Scheldt estuary in some strength. A long and difficult operation was necessary to clear the river so that the port could be belatedly opened in early November. These troops were, in due course, to oppose us when we began our drive through Holland towards the Rhine. All these misjudgements resulted from the delusion that after Normandy the Germans were 'finished'. Already the failure at Arnhem was foreshadowed.

NOTES

1. A good account of the battle for Normandy is given in Carlo D'Este's *Decision in Normandy*
2. Hamilton, Vol. II, p. 690.
3. Hamilton, Vol. II, p. 715.
4. P. Delaforce, *The Black Bull*, p. 12. (A black bull was the divisional sign of the 11th Armoured Division).

DESTINATION GERMANY

T he difficulties and sacrifices in Normandy had been succeeded by the exhilaration of liberation, with its sweeping advances. A grim phase was about to begin with a different topographical factor dominant: innumerable water obstacles and inundations. We were about to embark on 'the war of watery wastes'. The Germans would be fighting on interior lines, near their borders. For some time to come we would still be dependent on distant Normandy beachheads for supplies. Inevitably, there had to be a pause until Antwerp port was available. Moreover, the obvious threat to the Fatherland strengthened still more enemy determination, while the July attempt on Hitler's life increased the fanaticism of SS units. Wehrmacht officers had to be zealous in the execution of their duties if they were not to arouse suspicion of treachery. The German army had always been good at improvisation, and it hastily assembled formations from the wreckage of the Seventh Army and from the Fifteenth Army, which had been less strenuously engaged. Paratroop regiments were brought in, in an infantry role, together with units formed from men on leave or recuperating from the Russian front. When XXX Corps moved east, it was faced by paratroops under General Student, a formidable opponent, who had commanded the 1940 operation against Rotterdam and had directed the airborne invasion of Crete.

On 7 September the Guards Armoured Division crossed the Albert Canal at Beeringen. Resistance was stiffening, and we were held up in the town: our guns helped repel an attack by Panther tanks. There was to be no carefree advance into Holland. Resistance was strong in Bourg Leopold and at Hechtel, and the 11th Armoured Division was brought over to strengthen our thrust and protect our right flank. The Irish Guards seized the De Groot bridge over the Meuse–Escaut Canal by a brilliant *coup de main*, cleverly shielding their presence behind a large power station which received its coal supplies via the canal. We had to shell Hechtel heavily before we could get through to relieve the gallant captors.

XXX Corps edged up to this bridge and secured a shallow foothold on the far side of the canal. During a short lull, opportunity was taken to organise bath parties using the workers' showers in the power station. This was very welcome. Bourg Leopold had been a Belgian Army cantonment, and Horrocks called a conference there to acquaint senior officers with the plan for 'Market Garden', which XXX Corps was to spearhead on the ground. It was here that we belatedly learned that 'Jorrocks' had taken command of the corps. We were delighted he was back.

We were staggered at the audacity of the plan: perhaps foolhardiness would have been a more appropriate term. The risks seemed immense. The whole of the First Airborne Army was to be used to capture and hold the intervening river bridges. XXX Corps was to charge single-mindedly up the main road to Arnhem, to link up with them. Then it was to turn east, outflank the Ruhr, and finish off the war

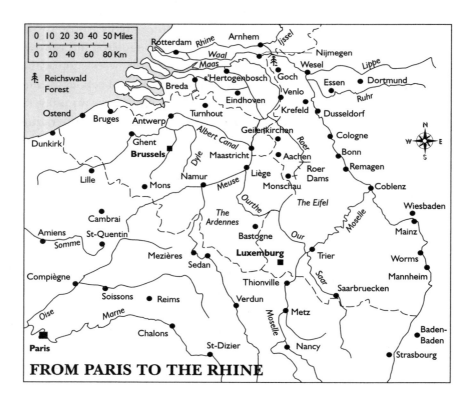

FROM PARIS TO THE RHINE

190

in 1944! The corps would comprise the Guards Armoured Division, the 43rd Division, the 8th Armoured Brigade and a Dutch Brigade. We were hopeful, but somewhat sceptical. The advance to the canal had been strongly contested, hardly consistent with the view that the Germans were exhausted. Just to emphasise that the war could still be grim, one of our despatch riders, a likeable lad, an ex-Barnardo's boy, had been killed by a stray shell from harassing fire on the Hechtel cross-roads, miles to our rear and, one would have thought, a relatively safe spot. It was a stark reminder of the random effect of harassing fire, which we had ourselves inflicted many times.

I have had little to say about our role in Normandy because our part, although substantial, was generally unremarkable. We were part of a massive artillery effort. We sometimes engaged targets by observation, but were frequently involved in large, co-ordinated, anonymous concentrations. Naturally we did not stand out. Like every other artillery unit we did our duty, and there was nothing very remarkable in that. We were, however, destined to play a significant role in 'Market Garden', which has earned us at least a footnote in the history books.

In preparation for the attack, the regiment moved into the shallow bridgehead beyond the Meuse–Escaut canal on the night of 15/16 September. We had surveyed-in and camouflaged extra carefully, and since we were in small arms range, we kept a low profile. We were not to fire until zero hour: it was vital our presence should not be suspected. The object of being so far forward was, of course, to give maximum support for the maximum time to our armoured thrust. General Horrocks had perfect observation from the power station roof, and very wisely did not confirm zero hour until he had actually seen the Allied airborne armada. This was fixed at 14.35 hours on Sunday, 17 September, and some 350 guns opened up at 14.00 hours with a rolling barrage. Opposition was fierce, and progress was slow. To our surprise, a lone glider carrying men of the US 101st Airborne Division landed in our bridgehead quite close to our guns. Presumably the tow-rope had parted prematurely or there had been a navigational error. The men calmly disgorged from their glider, mounted their jeeps and drove north to join their colleagues.

Our advance was disappointingly slow, not at all the rapid thrust we had hoped for. The Guards stopped for the night at Valkenswaard, only six or seven miles ahead and still comfortably within our range. We were well short of Eindhoven. There was not a lot of point in pushing too far ahead because the bridge at Son over the Wilhelmina Canal had been blown, and this needed the attention of our engineers. The next day, the armour linked up with the US paras at Eindhoven. The delay was frustrating, we knew we were behind schedule.

The opposition was tough. General Student was at Vught, as we now know, only a few miles to the west of the landing zone of the 101st Airborne Division. He had a grandstand view of the operation, and, as a parachute operation specialist, was well qualified to take quick countermeasures with his rather grandiosely titled Parachute Army. In defiance of all security considerations, as well as common-sense, a copy of the operation order for 'Market Garden' had been brought into the area by a glider crew, and very quickly was captured and in Student's hands. The information was no doubt very rapidly communicated to Field Marshal Model, commander of Army Group B. By a similar stroke of ill-fortune, he was actually at Osterbeek, almost in the landing zone of the 1st Airborne Division. He was in an ideal position to react positively and authoritatively. Already, if we had but known, the enterprise was doomed. The 9th and 10th Panzer Divisions were recuperating after their punishing losses in Normandy, and refitting just north of Arnhem, while a little beyond, at Apeldoorn, was a Tiger training battalion. Paratroops, with their relatively light weapons, were at a huge disadvantage.

Our pencil-thin advance made slow progress. Counterattacks against our single road became more determined and frequent. The US paratroops and our armour and infantry had to deal with these dangerous intrusions. An artillery unit on the road is very vulnerable, and we would have had to rely on small arms fire if there had been any difficulty or delay in getting off the road and deploying. Fortunately this did not happen, but some of our supply wagons were not so lucky. The attacks on the 82nd Airborne Division, which had captured the crucial bridge over the Meuse at Grave, were particularly severe, the Germans bringing many men over the frontier near Grosbeek, on the approaches to Nijmegen. The 82nd had to keep their landing zone clear for the second wave, and this delayed attempts to capture the Nijmegen bridges. Not until 19 September did this division and our armour enter the town, where there was stiff fighting for the approaches to the bridges. The road bridge was captured next day as the result of a combined operation, with a detachment of US 82nd Airborne Division making an assault crossing under heavy fire a mile downstream and then seizing the northern end of the bridge. This gallant action enabled the armour to rush it. (The attack had been delayed while assault boats had been extricated from the column on the road and brought forward through the congestion.) Since the Germans were expecting to need the bridge for counterattacking, they had not blown it up. All attempts to advance north beyond Elst failed: the road was raised above the level of the polder, meaning that the tanks could not get off the road to deploy and were a sitting target. The route to relieve the 1st Airborne Division was blocked, and their position looked increasingly desperate.

Meanwhile we had been moving forward slowly, in part perhaps because there was no immediate need for our assistance. We crossed the Meuse at Grave marvelling that this huge span was still intact, a tribute to the splendid action by the 82nd Airborne Division. The countryside was still littered with their parachutes. We halted once more a mile or so beyond the bridge, when fate intervened.

The 1st Airborne Division had landed west of Arnhem, but there was no reliable news about them. The Second Army was not fully aware of their desperate plight, although the silence must have been worrying. There had been an almost total breakdown in communications. The signallers had tried strenuously but without success to get through on their allotted frequency, then they appeared on our net (frequency). It is axiomatic that wireless, unlike an army telephone, is highly insecure, so everyone is trained to imagine that the enemy is listening to one's every word. So, an artillery unit may use radio for fire orders, but is very circumspect about passing tactical or other information. The signallers could recognise each other's voices, so an interloper, even if speaking immaculate English, would at once be suspect. When, therefore, our RHQ signallers received messages in clear from an unauthorised station, they reported to an officer what was happening. Our adjutant took over, and at once realised that the caller was genuine : he thought he recognised the voice as that of Lieutenant-Colonel Loder-Symonds, the CRA of the 1st Airborne Division, and a personal friend. To make sure, the adjutant asked the caller for the first name of his wife. 'Merlin,' was the answer. The adjutant then asked if she had any favourite sport. 'Falconry,' was the reply. In this highly unorthodox way *bona fides* were established, and the Second Army was informed that we were in contact with the 'missing' division. We were ordered in no circumstances to lose contact, and Second Army signals came onto our net. After giving a situation report, Loder-Symonds naturally turned to us for fire support.

This was coincidence enough, but fate played yet another trick. Of all the units in XXX Corps the 'Red Devils' could have contacted, we were the only ones who could help them. Indeed, initially, only the 211th Battery could reach them. They called for supporting fire on various targets, which, we were disconcerted to see, were all about 20,000 yards, our maximum elevation. Our guns had not been calibrated since we left England; there had been no opportunity during the hectic Normandy days, and there had been much barrel wear as a result of continuing heavy action. We had no reason to suspect that any gun was shooting 'wild', but it was possible that all were inaccurate, particularly at extreme range. Fortunately our concern was groundless: they reported we were 'bang on', and throughout the succeeding action they commented on the great accuracy of the fire. The battery certainly presented an unusual sight with all guns near 45 degrees' elevation, giving the appearance of an anti-aircraft battery.

It was immediately obvious that we would have to move forward to make the range more comfortable and to bring the 5.5in battery into range. Reconnaissance vehicles had already left to reconnoitre new positions. There was, of course, no question of leaving the airborne troops without support while we moved, so we leap-frogged, a troop at a time, the rear troop not moving until it heard that its partner was already in action. Our progress was no longer slow. We had the highest priority, and moved at speed the few miles to Nijmegen. Our new position was to the west of the town on some allotments just beyond a row of typical, small, brick houses. The locals were delighted to see us and were very excited at their liberation. We made it clear in a friendly way that we had no time for civilities, and were almost immediately in action. After the first ranging round, there was a queer, slithering noise: many of the roof tiles had been displaced and were gently sliding down the boarded roofs, sticking in gutters or plopping to the ground. Strangely all the windows were intact. The Dutch were very good about the damage to their homes, telling us not to worry, and to get on with the war! (We would, of course, have continued firing even if the houses had collapsed.) We were soon joined by the 212th Battery with their 5.5ins, and continued to engage targets throughout that day, Thursday 21 September. The 1st Airborne Division had been isolated in its shrinking perimeter since 17 September, and ours was the first succour they received from the Second Army. Sadly, it was all they were to get during the remaining days.

Because of our close contact, we were beginning to form some impression of the terrible plight of the airborne division in the perimeter. However, we did not know that (in what was probably the most brave, and desperate, defensive action of the whole war) Lieutenant-Colonel Frost's gallant band at the northern end of the Arnhem road bridge had already been silenced by overwhelming odds. While the prospects were grim, we were determined that our support should not be found wanting. From 21 to 25 September (the night of the evacuation) we were entirely at the disposal of the airborne division, at any hour of the day or night, although most activity was by day. There was no real sleep, however; all one could do was to loosen bootlaces and catnap, with one ear tuned to the signaller's earphones. At the first crackle of activity we became alert, warning the guns and waiting for fire orders.

The effect of our fire on the first day is described most graphically and authoritatively by Major-General R. E. Urquhart, the commander of the Airborne Division. Once he knew contact had been made with the 64th, he warned his brigade commanders to prepare lists of targets. 'Thus started one of the most exciting and rewarding artillery shoots I have ever experienced. From a range of about eleven miles, these gunners proceeded to answer our calls with a series of shoots on targets nominated by Loder-Symonds some of which were no more than a hundred yards out from our perimeter line. It involved certain risks, but the situation merited their being taken, and in the afternoon the shelling had had a quite noticeable effect on the Germans. Hearing the whine and the tremendous blast of these medium shells – there is surely no more terrifying noise in war – we felt glad the 64th were on our side.

And now, supported by a battery of heavies, these gunners broke up several attacks supported by self-propelled guns on the eastern flank.'[1] This is praise, indeed, and there is more of the same, but this is not my purpose in quoting Urquhart.

Many commentators have remarked on the reference to 'heavies', noting, quite correctly, that there were no heavies in XXX Corps. Some have assumed that Urquhart must have been mistaken; while others have invented a mysterious 155mm battery. The reader will appreciate at once the source of the confusion. The 64th, being an ex-Eighth Army regiment, had mixed batteries, whereas most medium regiments were standardised with 5.5in guns. We had initially opened fire with the 211th Battery (4.5in guns) and were joined a little later by the 212th, our sister battery (5.5in guns). They had been following us and, because their maximum range was 2,000 yards less than ours, took a little longer to find a position. So Urquhart is vindicated. He was an experienced officer and could appreciate the difference between a bursting 56lb shell and an 86lb one. So this minor mystery has been caused by confusion on the part of the commentators.

Urquhart's comments are also interesting because they draw attention to a unique, or very rare, instance where the observer of artillery fire is virtually in the target area. No wonder the description is so intimate and vivid.

Much more important, however, is the lack of perspective in Urquhart's remarks, shown by his eulogy of the 64th's gunners, which has been followed by many military historians. It is a failure to understand the role of artillery, which it is one of the purposes of this book to correct. An example will make clear my meaning. At Alamein on one occasion, a flight of RAF planes caused a troop of 88s to open fire in their anti-aircraft capacity. They thus betrayed their location, and were spotted by our OP, which ranged on them accurately at 19,000 yards, inflicting serious damage, as air photographs confirmed. We would have thought it exceedingly odd if praise had been heaped on our gunners for their remarkable accuracy in carrying out fire orders. The credit for this successful engagement surely lay with the OP.

At Arnhem the regiment was completely 'blind'. It was not practicable to deploy OPs for the simple reason that the whole of the ground between the Waal and Lower Rhine ('the Island') was in enemy hands. (Even if we had had OPs there, we could not have risked fire: both parties were so dangerously intermingled that we would have needed observers in the direct combat zone if we to avoid killing our own men.) Much had gone wrong in the planning of the operation, but someone had had the foresight to see that the airborne troops might need to contact XXX Corps artillery. Hence Loder-Symonds, their CRA, had a small team of experienced OP officers. They became our 'eyes': we were for a few days the 1st Airborne Medium Regiment. (Urquhart acknowledges that the targets were nominated by his CRA.) So began a remarkable collaboration with men and guns they had never seen, which was made effective by adherence to common and well-used procedures. We merely carried out the fire orders they issued. Of course, every man knew of their desperate predicament and, perhaps there was, therefore, a little more zest than usual, but essentially we were carrying out their orders in support of our infantry, our essential and abiding duty. So I suggest we need to adjust our perspective and give more credit to the airborne OP officers, and a little less to the artillery. It is a strange irony that it falls to a former member of the 64th to set matters in proportion.

We heard that the road south of Nijmegen had been cut. No-one seemed unduly concerned: we only had in mind our responsibilities to our people isolated west of Arnhem. Some of our ammunition lorries had narrow escapes, but ammunition was never a problem: so vital was our support that ammunition was flown in by DC-3s – presumably a landing strip had been extemporised somewhere. The position was becoming increasingly desperate. Intelligence reports showed that the armour and the 43rd Division could not advance northwards and, instead, the infantry turned off the main road just north of Nijmegen, striking north-west through Oosterhout, towards the Polish parachute brigade which had recently landed at Driel, roughly opposite to the Heveadorp ferry. The intention was to bring out what was left of the airborne division under cover of darkness on 25/26 September, while we put down a heavy protective curtain of fire. Only some 2,000 were rescued.

On the conclusion of the battle General Urquhart paid courtesy calls on those with whom he had been in closest contact. He included the

RHQ of the 64th Medium Regiment 'whose gunners had sustained such brilliantly accurate long-distance shooting in our interests, and but for whom we would almost surely have been wiped out.'[2]

We were naturally depressed at the outcome, although we had come to see it was inevitable. We had done our utmost, but much more than one artillery regiment was needed to overcome faulty conception and planning, poor intelligence, and sheer bad luck. The hopes for decisive victory in 1944 were seen to be in vain. We were, however, most gratified to receive a visit a few days later from Lieutenant-Colonel Loder-Symonds. He had evidently recovered from his ordeal and wanted to thank us for all we had done. He told us we could not imagine what it meant to them to have this tangible support. It had done wonders for morale. He thanked us for the promptness with which we had met all calls for help, and, above all, was impressed by the extraordinary accuracy of our fire, citing the many close targets they had engaged. He concluded by saying that the 1st Airborne Division wished to show their appreciation in a graphic way: they wanted us to wear their 'Pegasus' badge as a memento of our association. We were deeply conscious of this honour, which brought home to us just how much our support had meant to them. A few days later a supply of 'Pegasus' badges arrived, one for each man. Since we were already liberally supplied with shoulder flashes – 21st Army Group, XXX Corps' leaping boar and our regimental sign (a black elephant on a red background) – there was no room for an additional badge (which was rather large) on the upper arm, especially for NCOs who had also to accommodate their stripes. It was therefore decided that the 'Pegasus' should adorn our lower left sleeve. We proudly displayed our new badge, but the inevitable happened. Someone noticed! It was totally irregular for a division to bestow honours – least of all to the artillery which had no battle honours or colours other than its guns. Was it not its job to be everywhere, was not its motto 'Ubique'? These arguments were unanswerable; away went our 'Pegasus' badges. Our resentment at losing the badges did not last, but we always remembered being given them; we may have lost the tangible evidence, but the gesture, much appreciated, could never be expunged.

To leave our worm's eye view for a wider perspective, the reasons for our failure may be outlined. The euphoria of liberated, cheering crowds and the exhilaration of our rapid advance led our top brass to believe that the Germans were 'finished'. Their power of recovery was totally underestimated. Montgomery was probably smarting under the charge of over-caution. He would do something spectacular, to emulate Patton's great dash and to demonstrate the correctness of his view that the advance should be on a narrow, rather than a wide, front. Moreover, the First Airborne Army had been actively pressing to participate in the battle, and their clamour was satisfied by 'Market Garden'. Many times operations had been planned and then cancelled because of the speed of our advance. All those frustrated plans meant that the one finally adopted might be hurriedly planned. The Dutch Resistance warned of the presence of panzers in the area of the landings, but these warnings were played down. The nature of the ground between Nijmegen and Arnhem had not been properly assessed, and worst of all, the planners had arranged for the landing eight miles west of the road bridge – a fatal defect. The difficulty of keeping the single road clear was under-estimated. The lesson is that lightly equipped airborne troops should not be landed so far from their objective and main support that they could be dealt with in isolation. (The Germans never again risked paratroop operations after their costly experience in Crete.)

* * * * * * * * * * *

We were next involved with VIII and XII Corps in the widening of our narrow salient westwards towards Antwerp, and the clearance of the area between Tilberg and s'Hertogenbosch during October. After Arnhem any operation seemed an anti-climax.

XXX Corps' front was quiet, and since it had borne the brunt of the battle, leave to the UK was instituted. I came home via Brussels, where I was able to buy some silk things in the NAAFI shop and some black hothouse grapes in Boulevard Adolphe Max. I do not know how total was the German war effort at home, but they certainly failed to harness effectively the economies of the occupied countries.

I returned from leave to find my battery had some Nissen huts on site, so everyone had some protection from the weather. There was little activity; the nights were quiet. It was not an auspicious return. I was met by Bombardier Stan Dungate, (MM and bar) who was quite fearless. He was an original member of the regiment, and had gained his first decorations as a signaller at Alamein, for great coolness under fire in repairing lines to OPs. He grinned cheerfully at me. 'You've had it, chum,' he said, referring to my leave. I had not been back half an hour when there was some desultory shelling and a direct hit on our 'B' Sub. There were casualties; three men were killed, including Dungate. His mocking words and gestures were vividly in my mind, and have long remained so. It was as if his words to me had provoked the Fates, who were quickly exacting retribution. (The gun itself was undamaged.)

Early in November the Canadian Army was given responsibility for the northern sector from the sea to the Reichswald Forest, and the Second Army covered the area from there down to Geilenkirchen, where XXX Corps linked with the newly arrived US Ninth Army. Meanwhile, the US First Army was responsible for the area around Aachen.

We were again caught up in one of those rain-soaked river battles where ground had to be cleared, in this case beyond the Meuse to the Roer. We were diverted to the Geilenkirchen area. The Germans controlled all the Roer dams and could cause inundations at will. There was yet another river, the Würm, which ran through Geilenkirchen to join the Roer. The town had fortifications, being part of the Siegfried Line, and formed a salient between our two armies. The US 84th Division was next door; they were new arrivals. Many of us had Lüger and other captured pistols, and a busy trade developed. Customs examination was non-existent for UK troops going on leave, so there would have been no difficulty in bringing these weapons home. Most of us reflected that there was little point in doing this and so were willing sellers to those many Americans who do not feel properly dressed without a pistol. I sold my specimen to a sergeant in the US 84th Division for £20.

We attacked with the experienced 43rd Division, associated with the 84th Division for whom this was their first action. There was support by the highly specialised 79th Division, which had armoured vehicles for a remarkable number of purposes, and the whole of XXX Corps' artillery. For some reason the Americans were short of ammunition, but we had plenty. The attack was successful in spite of driving rain turning the ground into a morass. I later went into the town which was not itself much damaged, but quite deserted by the inhabitants. It was a strange and elated feeling to be at last standing on German soil. Most of the houses were open but there was little looting. The people had sensibly taken all their most portable and valuable possessions with them. I noticed that nearly all the houses had a stillroom with large quantities of bottled fruit. Those housewives would have been formidable competitors at a Women's Institute show, but then, of course, the Germans always are.

As a result of further reorganisation, the US forces edged further north and XXX Corps was withdrawn and returned to the Nijmegen sector. We were to prepare for yet another watery operation: the clearing of the Reichswald and the area between the Meuse (Maas) and the Lower Rhine, as a preliminary to our crossing of the latter river. Our position was to the south-east of Nijmegen and for the first time in the war, we set up our command post in a house. Normally houses are not to hand, and there was a general reluctance to seek comfortable shelter when the gunners were living rough outside. The house at Postweg, 33 belonged to the Hartmann family and they made us very welcome. I do not think we incommoded them very much, apart from the noise of the guns well to the rear of the house. They had a young daughter, who was very popular with everybody, and an older son we saw occasionally who was an officer in the Resistance. A frequent visitor was a Jesuit priest, with whom I struck up a warm friendship although I am an unbeliever. His English was good, and we discussed a number of subjects, including the shape of post-war Europe. As the only victorious European power, we agreed Britain should, and would, play a dominant role in forming the new Europe, her leadership and moral authority would be beyond question. How wrong we were!

The Reichswald loomed dark and foreboding, and the infantry were finding it a tough proposition. With winter well advanced, it was decided to close down operations for the time being and accept a defensive posture, since breaching the northern section of the Siegfried Line was clearly going to be a formidable operation. As part of this policy, we were withdrawn and sent to s'Hertogenbosch, where the regiment was to spend Christmas in billets. The weather had turned very cold, and the prospect was most inviting. From BBC news bulletins it seemed there was some activity in the Ardennes, but the news was obscure and apparently of no great moment. Our host was a schoolmaster who had a fair command of English but the most atrocious accent. He had obviously learned from books, and seemed to think our pronunciation was as standard as the German. He did not take kindly to correction. The BBC news remained subdued, with an undercurrent of concern, so we were not entirely surprised to receive after only 2 or 3 hours the order to move on Christmas Eve, saying goodbye to the prospect of relative comfort and our Christmas dinner! We were beginning to understand the disadvantage of having a corps commander with dash and intelligence who was much favoured by Monty. His motto seemed to be 'when trouble brews, send for "Jorrocks" and XXX Corps.'

I think we travelled all night and took up a position near Wavre, covering Brussels and Antwerp. I realised we were very near to the Waterloo battlefield and that it was from this area that Blücher had advanced to Wellington's relief. How times had changed! There was no immediate prospect of action, our role was purely precautionary, so I went for a beer in the local pub and found the few Belgians there very depressed at the possibility of again being occupied. I think I cheered them up. I exuded confidence, not from any definite knowledge, but from a certainty that the German offensive would be checked: for one thing the weather was clearing and permitting our air forces to operate. Substance was added to this when we moved next morning and crossed the Meuse at Namur in the wake of our infantry and armour. The penetration of the Ardennes was already under control. Monty commanded the US First and Ninth Armies and had secured a firm shoulder, as had the US forces in the south. Of inestimable value was the besieged 101st Airborne Division at Bastogne, a focal road junction, whose indomitable resistance threw the whole German attack out of gear. (This was the division with which we had linked up in the advance beyond Eindhoven towards Nijmegen.) The situation could be likened to the neck of a bottle, with the Americans on either side and XXX Corps as the cork to be hammered home. I think only one of our brigades was engaged, because we had a precautionary role and casualties were beginning to make Britain scrape the bottom of the manpower barrel. (We still had to cross the Rhine.) The credit for the German repulse therefore belongs to the US divisions who reacted so quickly to the heavy surprise attack on a dangerously lightly held front.

The weather was bitterly cold, with heavy snow, but our aircraft had excellent visibility and were roaming the skies. We were in the area where the enemy had made their deepest penetration towards the Meuse, near Celles and Ciney. We took up position at Hotton, near Marche, and set up the command post in a stout, stone house belonging to the *chef forestier*, the second instance where we had sought such shelter. It was so cold that it would have been difficult to hold a pencil and plot correctly. The gunners did not wear greatcoats; they were too clumsy and hindered movement. Everyone crammed on as much wool as possible under his battledress, with leather jerkins and woollen scarves and balaclavas, for which we gave many thanks to all those devoted lady knitters. Woollen gloves did not find much favour because, after handling shells in the snow, they became soaked. Most country houses in Northern Europe have piles of cut logs for winter, and our crews naturally helped themselves and so had merry fires going. Some of the Belgians took exception to this. Liberation they would accept, but stealing peasant property they thought outrageous! For night firing we issued a rum ration.

It was while we were at Hotton that we saw a most unusual arrangement for civilian bread supply. A baker with a small van carrying a supply of flour and yeast toured the villages near Liège every week, mixing the dough in a great trough and handing the loaves for baking to each household.

We were not heavily in action, but we did all that was expected. The continued American pressure on the flanks of the salient, together with air attacks, sapped the Germans' strength and resolve. There was a persistent risk that their advanced troops would be pinched out. Their attack therefore petered out and the enemy withdrew whence he came.

Before leaving the scene of the Ardennes battle there is one small, sad footnote to be made, illustrating yet again the action of a blind and malignant Fate. One of our men, an artificer, heard that his brother, whom he had not seen for many years, was serving in the area, so permission was given for him to pay a visit. This he did, when the vehicle in which they were travelling overturned on the icy road and the brother was killed. This is the saddest and most poignant reunion of which I have ever heard.

* * * * * * * * * * *

The war was now entering its final, decisive phase, with the Allies aiming to close up to the Rhine on a wide front. The 21st Army Group (with the US Ninth Army under command) was to be responsible for the clearance as far south as Düsseldorf. This would be a formidable operation because it meant taking the area enclosed by the Rhine–Waal and the Meuse, which was intersected by the rivers Roer, Würm, and Niers. This riverine country included the northern section of the Siegfried Line, covered by

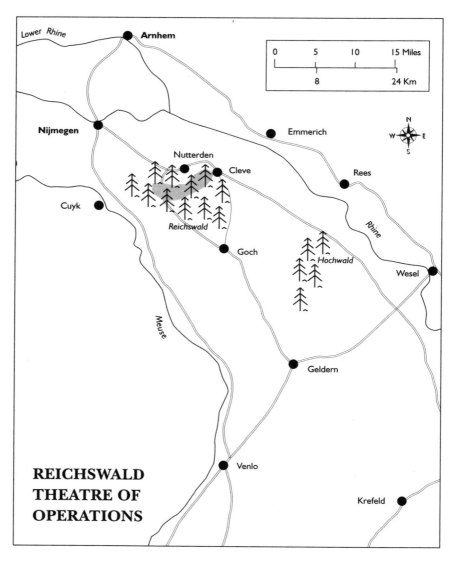

extensive barbed-wire and mines, with anti-tank ditches, concrete emplacements, trenches and fortified towns, as well as concrete pill-boxes and many cellars prepared for defence. In addition, there were many forests, including the Reichswald, to further hinder progress.

XXX Corps was ordered back to the Nijmegen sector to play the key role in the forthcoming battle, attacking south-east, while the Ninth Army came north from the Roer area, so forming a pincer movement. We initially occupied our former gun position with our Dutch friends, the Hartmanns. The pine trees of the Reichswald loomed dark and menacing, and no-one doubted that this would be a fierce and bitterly contested battle. The many inundations would make the ground a quagmire and restrict the use of armour, so the brunt of the fighting would fall on the infantry.

The Germans were expecting an attack, and considerable effort was made to conceal the start concentration areas through a deception plan. The attack began on 8 February, XXX Corps alone being 200,000 strong, a quite exceptional concentration of power. On the right, skirting the Meuse, was the 51st, with the 53rd, 15th, and 2nd Canadian Divisions on their left. The Germans had breached the Rhine dyke walls at numerous places, and beyond the main Nijmegen–Cleve road, the whole polder was flooded for some twenty miles. The extreme left formation (the 3rd Canadian Division) therefore had to operate in amphibious vehicles, mainly 'Buffaloes'. An early thaw had made the going soft, and further rain had made the mud ubiquitous. The thick forest as well as the mines, fortified towns, and concrete pillboxes of the Siegfried Line meant that the infantry had great difficulty in clearing the area. They were helped, however, by units of the 79th Armoured Division, the 'funnies', which, for example, consisted of tanks firing petards at the embrasures of the pill-boxes, or using flamethrowers which incinerated the defenders and were greatly feared. The flail tanks were invaluable in creating paths through the barbed-wire and mines. The opening attack was supported by a barrage by the field artillery, with lifts of 100 yards every four minutes, the end of each lift being signalled by smoke rounds.

The initial frontage of attack was restricted, but then the distance between the Rhine and the Meuse widened, and there was room for the 52nd Division to deploy on the right.

With such formidable obstacles, Horrocks had organised a huge concentration of artillery, reminiscent of the preparations for the battle of Alamein, an impression strengthened by the prominent role of the 4th Survey Regiment, Royal Artillery. The whole area was meticulously surveyed, and every artillery unit was accurately 'fixed', so that massive concentrations were guaranteed. In addition, flash-spotting and sound-ranging, especially of batteries across the Rhine, completed the illusion. But the concentration of firepower was far greater than at Alamein. There we had less than 900 guns, all 25-pounders, except for those of the three medium regiments. Horrocks now had 1,400 guns: each of his infantry divisions contributed 72 field guns; plus independent 25-pounder units; eight medium regiments (predominantly 5.5in, some 'heavies' – 7.2in and 155mm) and batteries of 3.7in anti-aircraft guns in a field role. There was thus full counter-battery potential, with flexible, huge concentrations to give maximum support to our infantry which had to spearhead the attack and deal with numerous and ingenious obstacles. To sustain these operations there were, of course, frequent changes of position. This huge accumulation of firepower was the greatest achieved by the British in the war.

For the infantry it was a hard and painful slog, but with such heavy support, by 18 February the 53rd Division had cleared the farther edge of the Reichswald. The 15th Scottish took the high ground to the north (Nutterden), which was regarded as the hinge of the whole position, and had also breached the Siegfried defences, and, with the 43rd Division (formerly in reserve), captured Cleve. On 9 February the Germans had blown up the Roer dams and a mass of water had surged down the river, preventing the US Ninth Army's convergent attack on the enemy's southern flank. Freed from this threat, the Germans could concentrate on us. Even so, the high ground overlooking Goch was taken by the 43rd Division, and the town itself fell on the 21st to the 51st Highland and 15th Scottish Divisions. (Under a new commander, who was a strict disciplinarian, the Highlanders were now performing with their former courage and skill.)

With the front now wider as we cleared the bottleneck, II Canadian Corps had room to deploy. After heavy fighting they were joined by the 11th and 4th Canadian Armoured and the 43rd Divisions for the last phase: Wesel and the Rhine. Resistance was particularly fierce at Udem, where there was yet another forest, the Hochwald. Udem fell on 26 February, but we could not penetrate beyond the Schlieffen Line, where the Germans had some artillery support, including from across the Rhine. By 4 March, however, the enemy withdrew: the Roer floods had subsided and the US Ninth Army had been able to link up with us at Geldern. To all intents and purposes, the battle to clear the west bank of the Rhine was over by 10 March.

Some days later our artillery was to fire a spectacular concentration over the river. It had a novel feature; we were to use time, not impact, fuses. Time fuses were used for airburst ranging when it was not possible to observe a target closely. They were used very rarely by us, but rather more by the Germans and Italians. I think we had recourse to airburst ranging twice early in the desert, and would wager that the bulk of the artillery, which had only been committed since the Normandy landings, had no knowledge of it at all.

One could guess that the explanation of this spectacular departure from the norm was that someone noticed these unused stocks of time fuses and thought it was a good idea to use them up, since the war was clearly in its closing stages. I had completely forgotten how to set these fuses, since three or four years had elapsed, but I did remember that they had caused a certain amount of confusion and controversy, so I consulted my training manual, which confirmed that the procedure was tricky and it was easy to get it wrong. When we came to set the fuses there was a sharp difference of opinion between the GPO and myself, but eventually I prevailed. When all was ready we went outside to witness the results, since at least the Corps artillery was involved. The effects were quite astonishing. Low down on the horizon, across the Rhine, about ten per cent of the rounds were bursting correctly, but the great bulk of the rounds were bursting at anything up to 50 degrees above the horizon, like some vast and purposeless anti-aircraft barrage. (A few rounds were bursting even higher!) It reminded me of some huge statistical scatter-diagram. Our first reaction was one of shock and shame that the incompetence of our artillery had been demonstrated to the enemy in such a spectacular way. We felt our professionalism had been impugned. Then we thought that the enemy had not drawn this conclusion at all: it was much more likely they thought the display was to impress and intimidate them with the awesome nature of our superiority and so, hopefully, they would be less enthusiastic to continue the war. So we felt comforted. Naturally, nothing was said about this fiasco. It certainly shows the risk of using a procedure which is novel and quite outside the experience of most of those concerned.

For the crossing of the Rhine we reverted to command of the Second Army. Whereas the planning for the Arnhem operation had been hasty and unsound, the result of over-confidence, I believe we now erred too far in the opposite direction, reverting to a cautious approach and meticulous planning. The Germans had suffered heavy casualties in the battles closing up to the Rhine, not only against the British but also the Americans with their abundant manpower. They had also suffered severely as a result of their Ardennes offensive. I believe they were now really 'finished', and were in no position to contest seriously the crossing, which contained a large measure of over-insurance. There was to be a full, showpiece assault crossing on 23 March, with a bombing carpet and an airborne attack by the 6th and US 27th Airborne Divisions along the line of the Ijssel, only a few miles beyond the Rhine. We were not going to repeat the Arnhem mistake with the airborne element outside support range. There was the usual heavy artillery programme. The attack across this massive river obstacle went smoothly and there were few casualties. The 51st Highland Division, now restored to form, was responsible for the XXX Corps crossing at Rees, a few miles downstream from Düsseldorf, which they secured after a sharp engagement.

When our turn came to cross by the Bailey bridge, we halted for a time in Rees and discovered a pipe factory, where I found a very fair imitation of a London briar, which bore the word 'Chancellor' in English, and smoked very well. Steady progress was maintained, our infantry and armour sometimes having sharp engagements with rearguards or in capturing a bridge, as was the case at Lingen on the Dortmund–Ems Canal. So the Ruhr, the industrial heartland, was lost to the Germans.

Towns were deserted, with no sign of the inhabitants. On the Weser near Nienburg we came across a barge which was packed tight with small civilian radio sets of the latest design from Philips of Eindhoven. Unfortunately they all lacked valves (the latest miniature thermionic type) but many of us helped ourselves nevertheless. This was yet another instance of the German failure to exploit the occupied countries for war purposes.

Nienburg surrendered without a struggle. We closed up to the Weser. Those in charge in Bremen were of sterner stuff, and the city was finally cleared by 26 April. To the best of my recollection we were not asked to contribute. Hamburg did not surrender until the general surrender on 5 May. Our forward troops continued their advance cutting off Schleswig–Holstein and Denmark. Still the advance continued to Lübeck and Wismar on the Baltic. During the closing weeks everyone became rather cautious and extra keen on self-preservation. The usual nonchalance disappeared. After having come through so much no-one wanted to get killed so near the end. I had in mind Wilfred Owen (surely the greatest of the 1914–18 British war poets), who tragically was killed within a week of the armistice. On 5 May the Germans in the north formally surrendered unconditionally to Field Marshal Montgomery on Lüneberg Heath, but the war in Europe was not officially over until all German forces surrendered to General Eisenhower, and this became effective on 8 May.

We decided we wanted to go out literally with a bang, not a whimper. At 08.00 hours precisely on 8 May we fired five rounds salvo into the river Weser. It was a strange moment, pregnant with meaning, sharply separating the war from the succeeding peace. I watched the guns clearing for the last time and the muzzle covers being replaced. It was goodbye to our faithful servants and friends, the end of a long love affair. All our long and varied experience, which had made us of such military value, was now worthless. In that moment we lost our function.

We were to live in an uncomfortable limbo for the next few months. Our long and eventful odyssey was nearly over. There was, perversely, almost a sense of regret at the imminent passing of comradeship and professionalism, but, overwhelmingly, relief and thankfulness that the victory for which we, and many others, had fought so hard and long, was at last achieved.

NOTES

1. R. E. Urquhart, *Arnhem*, p. 122.
2. Urquhart, p. 183.

ODYSSEY'S END

The immediate task was to round up the large number of German troops. Because of the proximity of Cuxhaven, Wilhelmshaven and Emden, there was a good proportion of naval personnel. At first we carried rifles, but it soon became apparent these were unnecessary. The prisoners were only too glad the war was over, and accepted a temporary incarceration with resignation. There was nothing more we could do, and we went to the Hanover–Brunswick–Wolfenbüttel area. The destruction in the two larger cities was indescribable, the central areas near the railway stations being nothing but heaps of rubble through which bulldozers had cleared a way. (I believe that during the reconstruction this rubble was used as the core for the embankments of sports stadia, a very sensible solution.)

For a time earlier we had been east of the line agreed with the Russians at Yalta, and so we had had to withdraw. The German civilians told us horrible stories of rape and looting on a wide scale, although this was never confirmed to us. They were terrified and begged us to remain, but we had no option but to withdraw. Our meetings with Russian troops had been reasonably friendly. Their consumer-hunger was vast and insatiable. They wanted anything manufactured; broken fountain pens, defective penknives, old watches. Since their economy has continued to emphasise heavy industry, with consumption as the residual legatee, it is not surprising that consumer-hunger persists.

The invasion had brought a vast Allied army of potential fornicators: with the coming of peace the authorities feared there would be fraternisation with German women, many of whose menfolk were dead or missing. This problem obviously exercised the official mind profoundly. There were printed leaflets discouraging the practice. The extent of it was probably exaggerated, because recent enmity and mutual memories of bombings and so on acted as a natural deterrent, reinforcing policy. There were also other sources of relief for sex-starved troops.

I was put in charge of a transport pool of some twenty of our drivers and vehicles. We were based at Watensstedt, a small unattractive town in the shadow of the great steelworks at Salzgitter, which had been severely bombed. We were billeted in an office block which had had some function related to the steelworks. I had a small office, and along the corridor was a large room which we made into the men's dormitory. Our function was to collect food every morning (usually potatoes) and distribute it to the various POW camps. Our efforts were supplemented by large German lorries with trailers, which, because of the shortage of liquid fuel, operated on bags of gas.

Slave labour had been used in the steelworks, and close by our base were Russian, Italian and Polish displaced persons' camps, while in the adjacent US area was a Yugoslav camp. There were presumably women in the Russian camp, but they were kept well concealed. The Italians had only been enemies of the Germans after the overthrow of Mussolini, and they seemed exclusively men from the north of the country. The women in the Polish camp were only too visible and wandered freely. In a very short time my party had rediscovered the basic economic law: the price of a woman was a tin of corned beef. I soon found the arrangements had been regularised, they formed stable pairs, and the girls spent the night in the dormitory. I was intrigued to know how the affairs of the night were managed, but thought it foolish to enquire. There was nothing I could do to stop these affairs, but I insisted all the women should disappear in the mornings, everyone should parade normally, and our daily duties must not suffer. In practice, my policy was that what consenting adults did in private was none of my business! So the 'non-frat' rule regarding German women had been observed. But there was one exception. One of my drivers was cuckolding the village burgomaster.

This same burgomaster came to see me one day, as the senior British representative! Apparently the Russians had been looting (who can blame them?) and he wanted me to investigate. Foolishly, I agreed, but as soon as we entered the camp I realised it was a blunder to be accompanied by the local official who was certainly a Nazi. The Russians assumed I was on his side, an assumption strengthened by their deep suspicion of their western Allies. I was faced with the 'camp soviet' – a committee of five, clearly party men, who imposed a very tight discipline. They pretended not to understand German, so, sensing a hopeless task, we withdrew.

Shortly afterwards, however, there was a slight thaw. A Ukrainian concert party from the Russian equivalent of ENSA was giving a concert in a nearby town where an early nineteenth-century gilt and red plush theatre had survived the bombing. We were given the job of transporting the Russians to the concert. Compared with the entertainment considered suitable for our troops (incidentally my recollection is that throughout the war ENSA never put on a show for us), what we were offered was 'high culture'. Beside the 'Volga Boatman', the 'Song of the Flea' and so on, there were Neapolitan folk songs and many excerpts from Italian operas. Some of the orchestral music, too, was familiar, e.g. Monti's '*Czardas*'. The standard was high. There was an elderly actor who performed monologues from Russian plays. We could not understand a word, but he held the audience enthralled. Although to our eyes somewhat over-acting, with rolling eyes and striking gestures, we also found him impressive. I was reminded that the USSR is a union of many different nationalities, and I felt the Ukrainians were very 'western'. One could, perhaps, even catch a whiff of irredentism. On our return 'home', one or two of our Russians actually smiled their thanks.

The burgomaster came next with another complaint of looting, this time against the Italians. I did not intend to make my earlier mistake, so went into the camp alone. There were two GIs there, one speaking Italian fluently, the other well over six feet with a pair of mother-of-pearl-handled pistols swinging at his waist. (Not a standard US issue.) With the risk of inter-Allied friction, I decided not to press my enquiry. As far as our Italian-American was concerned, he was chatting to compatriots and was on most friendly terms. But for ex-Eighth Army men, the Italians were recent enemies, and we took a more aloof view. While on the subject of Italians, I should mention Luigi, a remittance man with a good command of English. He was a great 'fixer', and I have no doubt was soon operating profitably in the black market. Within minutes of meeting him he offered me a bottle of 'Spanish fly'! With so much of society disintegrating, it was good to learn that the essentials of civilised life were being preserved!

Some days later I had a visit from one of our regimental officers. He was full of his amorous adventures of the night before. He had been at a party and had laced the drink of a German woman with some of Luigi's elixir. The result much exceeded his expectations. She had become exceptionally passionate and he admitted ruefully that she had lacerated his back with her fingernails. An hour or two later I had a visit from a rather agitated, well-dressed German woman. She wanted to know where she could find Lieutenant X. This was clearly 'the lady with the claws', but I could only say, truthfully, that I did not know. She stalked out in quest of her stupendous British lover! So much for the 'non-frat' policy.

Shortly afterwards, our transport duties terminated as the military government began to establish itself. So we rejoined the regiment. I was billeted in a large house with some other sergeants. The place was full of women and children from the bombed-out cities. They noticed I often had my nose in a book, and called me 'Herr Professor', meaning 'teacher', of course, not a don. This seemed quite appropriate, because I was sent on a course in Brussels on 'British Way and Purpose', a sort of constitutional approach to democracy in the British style. It was while on this course that I met a sergeant from the 7th Armoured Division who told me he was a budding black marketeer, building up a flourishing business in army blankets. He was seriously thinking of settling down in Belgium. Another sergeant was based in the Philips factory at Eindhoven, so I gave him a 'fiver' to send me a set of valves for the radio I had purloined from the barge at Nienburg. This he faithfully did, and the set gave good service for many years.

My battery was in a pleasant, small town, and we set up a sergeants' mess in a house. There was plenty of beer both light and dark, because the army had requisitioned a brewery near Brunswick. We also had our whisky ration. We even acquired a piano. We engaged a German girl as a cook, and it was remarkable what she could concoct out of army rations and sundry local scroungings. We had roast venison several times a month: it seemed plentiful in those parts.

Nothing could disguise the fact that we were bored. No-one imagined for a moment that XXX Corps would be earmarked for the invasion of Japan. We had made up our minds that we had done enough, and that V-E Day meant the end of the war for us. It was just as well that the announced demobilisation plan confirmed our conviction. Age and length of service were the criteria for early release, so most of us would qualify. The nation as a whole was tired after six years of war. Its interest was focused on Europe; Japan was far away. It would have been difficult to secure popular support for getting involved in the invasion of Japan. 'Leave it to the Americans,' would have been a popular cry, leading to some friction with our ally. Fortunately, we were delivered from these looming problems by the atomic bomb. This evil means delivered us from a far greater evil. The invasion of Japan would have been fanatically resisted, and millions of Japanese and Allied casualties would have been the terrible price.

Summer gave way to autumn. A few of the older, long service men had already left. In October the turn came for a number of us. Our goodbyes were curiously muted and nonchalant. We could hardly believe we were leaving the regiment and a way of life, a combination of danger and endeavour, that we had shared for so long. I remember leaving, for ease of travelling, a few personal things in the quartermaster's stores. My reason told me I should never see these things again, yet deep down I felt leaving was unreal and I would be back.

We arrived at the home of the artillery, The Barracks, Woolwich, which we had never seen. Discipline was relaxed, the food in the mess was good. Most of us went home after the midday meal. Parade in the mornings was agreeably late. Then, early in November, my demobilisation came through. I went to Olympia to be kitted out. The tailor (why had he not been called up?) measured me up and called me 'Sir'. It was all over. I went home.

No doubt in Germany the demobilisation proceeded apace. Early in 1946 my regiment would have found that it could no longer justify separate batteries and RHQs. They would be amalgamated. Then, with the haemorrhage continuing, there would not have been enough men to merit a separate regimental existence. The survivors would have gone to an amorphous depot: the regiment would have ceased to exist.

So the wheel had turned full circle. We had been summoned from the void to emerge most inauspiciously as the second-line regiment of a Territorial Army unit, meeting once a week in the local drill hall. We had then been knocked into shape as a run-of-the-mill artillery regiment. Through many vicissitudes, Fate gave us an exceptionally long, active and varied experience. Battle itself is the most instructive mentor. By such strange caprice we had become very professional, with a record as a medium artillery regiment unsurpassed in the whole British army. We had become a crack regiment. Now we were poised for the oblivion from whence we came. At first, not quite forgotten: there was an annual regimental reunion. But as the years passed, the numbers attending dwindled. Some died, and not even this token of our regimental days remains. This book is an attempt to leave some mark of our endeavours.

Yet we are not quite without a memorial. In the collection of the Imperial War Museum[1] is a 4.5in gun, which belonged to the 211th Battery, 64th Medium Regiment, Royal Artillery.

NOTES

1. At Duxford, Cambs.

BIBLIOGRAPHY

Alanbrooke, Field Marshal Lord, *War Diaries 1939–45*. Eds. Danchev and Todman. Weidenfeld and Nicholson. London, 2001

Beevor, A., *Crete – The Battle and the Resistance*. John Murray. London, 1991

Belchem, David, *All in the Day's March*. Collins. London, 1978

Bond, Professor Brian and Taylor, Michael D., (Eds), *The Battle of France and Flanders: Sixty Years On*. Leo Cooper. Barnsley, 2001

Bryant, A., *The Turn of the Tide 1939–43*. Collins. London, 1957

Buckley, C., *Greece and Crete*. HMSO. 1952

Carver, Field Marshal Lord, *El Alamein*. Batsford. London, 1962

—*Dilemmas of the Desert War*. Batsford. London, 1986

Churchill, Winston S., *The Second World War*. 6 vols. Cassell. London, 1948–54

De Guingand, Major-General Sir F. W., *Operation Victory*. London, 1947

Delaforce, P., *The Black Bull*. Alan Sutton. Stroud, 1993

D'Este, Carlo, *Decision in Normandy*. Harper Perennial. London, 1983

Hamilton, *The Making of a General*. Hamish Hamilton. London, 1981

Hamilton, Nigel, *Monty*. Hamish Hamilton. 3 vols. London, 1981, 1983, 1986

Hinsley, F. H., *British Intelligence in the Second World War*, 5 vols. HMSO. London, 1979–90

Horrocks, Lieutenant-General Sir Brian, *A Full Life*. Leo Cooper. London, 1974

—*Corps Commander*. Methuen. London, 1979

North, J., *North-West Europe 1944–45*. HMSO, London, 1977

Richardson, C., *Flashback*. William Kimber, London, 1985

Thomas, D. A., *Crete 1941 – The Battle at Sea*. Andre Deutsch. 1972

Urquhart, Major-General R. E., *Arnhem*. Cassell. London, 1958

Wilmot, C., *The Struggle for Europe*. Collins. 1952

ABBREVIATIONS

AA	Anti-aircraft
AEC	Associated Equipment Company, Southall
AGRA	Army Group Royal Artillery
BC	Battery Commander
BGS	Brigadier General Staff
CBO	Counter-Battery Office, or Organisation
CCRA	Corps Commander Royal Artillery
CGS	Chief of the General Staff
CIGS	Chief of the Imperial General Staff
C-in-C	Commander-in-Chief
CRA	Commander Royal Artillery
DAK	Deutsche Afrika Korps
DMI	Director Military Intelligence
ENSA	Entertainments National Service Association
FDL	Forward Defended Localities
GHQ	General Headquarters
GOC	General Officer Commanding
GPO	Gun Position Officer
GPO Ack.	Gun Position Officer's Assistant
GSO 1	General Staff Officer 1st Grade
HAC	Honourable Artillery Company
HE	High Explosive
HQ	Headquarters
IG	Inspector of Gunnery
LRDG	Long Range Desert Group
LST	Landing Ship, Tanks
MM	Military Medal
MO	Medical Officer
NAAFI	Navy, Army, and Air Force Institutes
NCO	Noncommissioned Officer

OCTU	Officer Cadet Training Unit
OP	Observation Post
OP Ack.	Observation Post Assistant
RA	Royal Artillery
RAF	Royal Air Force
RAOC	Royal Army Ordnance Corps
REME	Royal Electrical and Mechanical Engineers
RHA	Royal Horse Artillery
RHQ	Regimental Headquarters
SP	Self-propelled
TA	Territorial Army
VC	Victoria Cross
WD	War Department

INDEX